Stopwatch
Marketing

PORTFOLIO

Stopwatch Marketing

**TAKE CHARGE OF THE TIME
WHEN YOUR CUSTOMER
DECIDES TO BUY**

John Rosen | AnnaMaria Turano

PORTFOLIO

PORTFOLIO
Published by the Penguin Group
Penguin Group (USA) Inc., 375 Hudson Street,
New York, New York 10014, U.S.A.
Penguin Group (Canada), 90 Eglinton Avenue East, Suite 700, Toronto, Ontario, Canada M4P 2Y3
(a division of Pearson Penguin Canada Inc.)
Penguin Books Ltd, 80 Strand, London WC2R 0RL, England
Penguin Ireland, 25 St. Stephen's Green, Dublin 2, Ireland
(a division of Penguin Books Ltd)
Penguin Books Australia Ltd, 250 Camberwell Road, Camberwell,
Victoria 3124, Australia (a division of Pearson Australia Group Pty Ltd)
Penguin Books India Pvt Ltd, 11 Community Centre, Panchsheel Park,
New Delhi – 110 017, India
Penguin Group (NZ), 67 Apollo Drive, Rosedale, North Shore 0632,
New Zealand (a division of Pearson New Zealand Ltd)
Penguin Books (South Africa) (Pty) Ltd, 24 Sturdee Avenue,
Rosebank, Johannesburg 2196, South Africa

Penguin Books Ltd, Registered Offices: 80 Strand, London WC2R 0RL, England

First published in 2008 by Portfolio, a member of Penguin Group (USA) Inc.

1   3   5   7   9   10   8   6   4   2

Stopwatch Marketing is a service mark of Marketing Consulting Associates, LLC.
Illustrations by Russell Hicks unless otherwise indicated
Figure 3-2: Goodyear Tire & Rubber Company
Figure 7-4: Kathy Bonnist, Bonnist Research

LIBRARY OF CONGRESS CATALOGING-IN-PUBLICATION DATA
Rosen, John.
Stopwatch marketing : take charge of the time when your customer decides to buy /
John Rosen and AnnaMaria Turano.
p.   cm.
Includes bibliographical references and index.
ISBN-13: 978-1-59184-194-4
1. Marketing—Management. 2. Consumer behavior. 3. Consumers' preferences.
4. Product management. I. Turano, AnnaMaria. II. Title.
HF5415.13.R636 2008
658.8—dc22   2007032625

Printed in the United States of America
Set in Meridien and Helvetica Neue
Designed by BTD NYC

This book is dedicated to Pierce, James, and Andreana . . .
for whom our stopwatches will never stop ticking.

"We must use time as a tool, not as a crutch."
—*John F. Kennedy*

"Until we can manage time, we can manage nothing else."
—*Peter F. Drucker*

"Oh! Do not attack me with your watch. A watch is always too fast or too slow.
I cannot be dictated to by a watch."
—*Jane Austen*

Contents

Part One
The Stopwatch

Chapter One

The Problem

 It's about time. All about time.

It's about the time you invested: years, sometimes decades, mastering the skills needed to communicate the virtues of a product or service. It's about the time you committed: months planning the launch on which your continued success depends. The hundreds of hours you spent in focus groups, in littering the floor with dozens of rejected ads. The all-nighters massaging the numbers until they begged for mercy. As the clock ticks down to D-Day, you wonder, for the hundredth time, if you are as prepared as possible. Perhaps you wish for another day; perhaps you cannot wait another minute.

All about time.

In fact, you've entered into a hoped-for bargain, exchanging *your* time, and the time of your colleagues in return for a few minutes—or hours, or days—of someone else's time. The someone else, of course, is your target consumer: the one who holds your future in her hands.

But how can you know whether she is willing to trade her time for yours? How do you know she even has time to listen to your message? How do you know she will take the time to be "sold"? And, most important, *how much time* will she give you to make your pitch?

Understanding the answers to those "how much time?" questions—and understanding how to leverage those answers to increase volume and profit—is the promise of this book.

How, for instance, is Whole Foods Market able to convince consumers to spend hours being "delighted" in their stores on one day of the week while those same consumers just can't wait to get out of a traditional supermarket on the other six days? What is it about the marketing behind the Goodyear Assurance featuring TripleTred Technology tires that captures the consumer's imagination in that very brief moment of opportunity in the local tire store? How has Lexus turned a previously unpleasant haggling activity into an enjoyable experience at the dealership? And how has Microsoft found a way to collapse all the way to zero the time that consumers spend comparing brands?

Put simply, the premise of this book is that purchase or consumption of these products is subject to the ticking of the consumers' internal shopping stopwatches. Slowing down that ticking (Whole Foods) or stopping the ticking immediately (Microsoft) in order to close the sale is the critical challenge faced by marketers.

Imagine, for example, that the sweet spot your strategic research identified is "college educated, dual-income, twenty-eight to forty-four years old, with two to four children under fourteen and incomes in the top two deciles, residing in suburban/exurban zip codes."

Now imagine two houses outside Cleveland. One is blue, the other a kind of pale green, but each has four bedrooms, two and a half baths, a neatly manicured lawn, an attached garage . . . and in each garage is a minivan and slightly sporty coupe. The families living in the two houses are likewise similar: If you randomly lined up the four adults and five children living in the houses, a stranger would find it impossible to sort out who goes with whom. They look similar, dress similarly, and, within limits, act in a similar manner.

Inside each of the houses, one of the adults has drawn the short straw and is in charge of planning a weekend trip to Washington, DC. The components of the trip are air travel (including transportation to and from each family's home airport), accommodations, dinner reservations for the night of arrival, tickets to a show at the Kennedy Center for the Performing Arts . . . the usual.

And, here, the similarity evaporates.

The adult living in the blue house—let's call her Ms. Blue—is traveling to Washington on business. Her shopping expedition for all the travel choices contains nothing of pleasure, and is severely constrained by the fact that she has only twenty-four hours before her departure. On speakerphone, she listens while her corporate travel office details her airline, hotel, rental car, and restaurant reservations and spends so little mental energy on the process that she can simultaneously pack the two mix-and-match outfits that will carry her from client meeting to client entertainment over the next two days.

Meanwhile, in the other house, Mr. Green sits in front of a computer screen, planning a family vacation two months in advance. Travel guides, carefully dog-eared, are piled to his left; the issue of *Consumer Reports* that ranks America's hotel chains is on his right. A quick search on his favored online travel service, Orbitz.com, has yielded a list of thirty-one different hotels that satisfy his criteria. He is weighing the advantages of location (as determined by one of the maps in his three different guidebooks) against a larger fitness center and the availability of a pool. He compares a suite against two doubles easily enough, since an online virtual tour of guest rooms is available for nine of his thirty-one possible choices, and his previous travel experiences have eliminated two of the possibilities, even though he is still a member of the awards program at one of them. His car rental choices are complicated enough that he has set up an Excel spreadsheet to compare the rates for the four-day trip . . . or would it be cheaper to simply rent for the week?

Ms. Blue and the Green family appear to be two fundamentally different consumers, no?

However, both Ms. Blue and the Green family end up in the same Washington, DC, hotel. They rent automobiles from the same company. They don't make dinner reservations at the same place, but only because clients demand a somewhat different ambience than children.

And when, six months later, Ms. Blue is planning *her* family's vacation instead of a business trip, she researches and compares in precisely the same way as Mr. Green.

How do these consumers compare when they're shopping for other types of items? When it came time to buy an expensive consumer durable—his "slightly sporty coupe," something that he would have to live with for four or five years—Mr. Green did all the shopping in two hours, returning with it the same morning. Ms. Blue test-drove five different models, and waited six months before the right combination of color and options was available.

The hypothetical Blue and Green families are models of contemporary consumer behavior, but the models are pretty erratic ones. Multiply the number of behavioral models exhibited by Ms. Blue and Mr. Green by the one hundred million or so American households, and you will confront the marketing challenge faced by every commercial enterprise in the country. The model that matters most today is not measured by income statistics, educational attainment, or political affiliation. It is measured by the clock.

For despite thousands of technological developments, from UPC codes, to telemarketing and direct mail, to 500-channel cable TV, to broadband Internet access, every one of which was supposed to "change everything about the way business is done," the most important constant in marketing hasn't changed since the discovery of fire allowed humans to stay awake past sunset. The number of hours that a human being *could* theoretically spend in the path of commerce hasn't changed significantly since then, and the hours that they *do* spend there, shopping and buying, has increased only marginally since the introduction of television. What *has* changed, of course, is the number of messages competing for those hours . . . and the way in which those hours are now controlled. Consumers don't spend any more time standing in line to examine your product than their grandparents did, but they have a *lot* more lines to choose from. So if one line isn't moving at the speed they like, they move to another one.

Marketers who want to succeed today have to give their customers more than the traditional four *P*s (Price, Product, Promotion, and Place); they have to reduce the length of the queue waiting to enter the consciousness of a potential customer. If they want to convince Mr. Green to make a reservation in their hotel, they need to start pitching weeks, months—sometimes years—before he is decision-ready. If they want to rent Ms. Blue a car, they can't waste a second of her time. If they want to succeed in *any* marketing effort, they have to cut in line at the same place, and at the same moment, that their customers do. They have to make sure that they can deliver what their customers want before those customers glance at their metaphorical watches, and decide either not to buy, or—even worse—leave for another, competing, line. They have to time their selling messages to be no longer than the amount of time that buyers have allocated for hearing them.

Stopping that consumer at precisely the right time requires a set of disciplines that we call stopwatch marketing.

A Promise

A thousand marketing gurus, most prominently Philip Kotler, have reminded us that a brand is, at its heart, a promise. So, we believe, is a book. The promise of the book you hold in your hand is that it will show how to analyze, evaluate, and exploit the time that represents every shopper's most important resource . . . to understand how to measure the length of time your customer will spend searching for your product or service . . . and how to make absolutely certain that your product or service is close to the front of your customer's queue: that lineup of shopping options that gets longer for consumers every year.

No one doubts that the power of brands is in severe decline. The proportion of the buying audience who try to stick to well-known brand names dropped by nearly a quarter between 1975 and 2000.[1] The sort of consumer who spends a lifetime driving Chevrolet sedans, buying Sony TVs, drinking Dr Pepper, and wearing Levi's jeans is thinner on the ground every day.

The likeliest reason for this decline in brand power is the combination of the increasing number of consumer options and the increasing amount of information about those choices. The hours of shopping time available to choose among them has, of course, remained fixed. And, we're not just talking about choosing between Skippy and Jif. The average American supermarket now contains more than 30,000 separate products; a single Barnes & Noble Superstore can carry up to 90,000 titles and the bn.com website carries more than a million.*

Shoppers need a lot of help in sifting through such an unprecedented number of choices, and advertisers have been leaping to their aid; in 1985, the typical consumer received something like 650 marketing messages every twenty-four hours; today, that figure is estimated to be greater than 3,000.[2] The consequence of this glut of messages was predictable: fragmentation of attention. In 1980, a single thirty-second, off-peak television advertisement could reach nearly 80 percent of the audience targeted by that ad; with the average cable subscriber now divided among ten times the number of channels, it can now take hundreds of prime-time spots to reach the same audience . . . if it can be reached at all.[3]

We are utterly convinced that the overwhelming number of consumer choices available to the twenty-first-century American has complicated the marketing task, particularly because the daily hours available for making those choices have only decreased since the days when the Sears,

---

* As part of the research for his book *The Long Tail*, journalist Chris Anderson reported a survey of 1.2 million titles in print . . . of which more than three-quarters sold fewer than a hundred copies in a given year.

Roebuck and Montgomery Ward catalogs represented the state-of-the-art in shopping.

Academics have debated—from Adam Smith in the eighteenth century to Theodore Levitt in the twenty-first century—about whether the priority in marketing rests with the product or the buyer. It is our belief, however, that (a) consumers behave differently depending on the product and the occasion for which they are searching; and (b) every product and/or occasion has buyers whose patterns of behavior—whose stopwatches—occupy every different point along a continuum.

Because of a perversity of the Internet age, information is so ubiquitous that leveraging it to create a loyal customer is becoming more expensive every day. Never before in the history of business has ownership of a shopper's time been so valuable, nor has surrendering it ever been so dangerous.

This wasn't how it was supposed to happen. Basic supply-and-demand economics teaches us that as the supply of any commodity increases, its price declines. Even not-so-basic economics teaches that while the demand for some commodities is more elastic than others, *nothing* is supposed to become more costly as it becomes easier to acquire and more widely available. Over the last twenty years, information about any product's price, features, and availability has not only exploded, but its acquisition has become easier than ever before. Any American with an Internet connection[4]— and that's 147 million American adults, nearly 85 million with broadband access—can find the price and features of violins, sofa beds, children's toys, kitchen appliances, and a thousand other items with a dozen keystrokes. They can find (relatively) unbiased evaluations, price comparisons, shipping information . . . even evaluations of companies selling the items, with comments from satisfied and unsatisfied customers. They can read reviews of new automobiles, get blue-book prices for used ones, and study U.S. government crash test results and mileage calculations for both. In an hour, a woman in San Diego can find a replacement shift knob for a 1964 MG for sale in Duluth; she can buy it in a minute; and have it delivered in a day. No consumers in all of human history have ever had so much information with which to make a buying decision.

Human assumptions about trends tend to be linear: If some is good, more must be better, and a graph plotting information availability and information cost should, naturally, be a straight line, as shown in Figure 1-1.

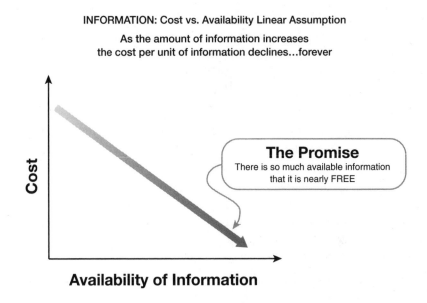

Figure 1-1

It is, in fact, hyperbolic—U-shaped, as in Figure 1-2.

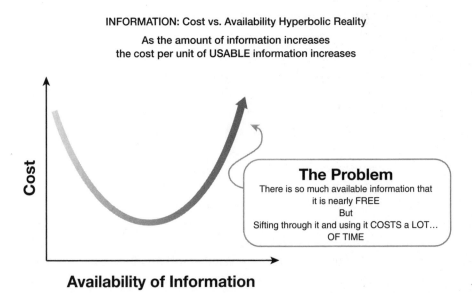

Figure 1-2

As more information becomes easy to find, its cost does decline . . . for a while. At some point, however, the sheer number of data points that need to be plotted becomes overwhelming. Since, in an online world, the largest cost of acquiring information is time, and since more information means more time sifting, the cost of information rises. To keep the cost under control, consumers of *your* product or *your* service (cars, insurance, hotel rooms, mystery novels, and tuna fish) apply rules (the fancy word is *algorithms*). Sometimes, as with the well-known dictum that cautions diners about eating oysters in months containing the letter *R*, these rules are simply discovered; other times, consumers (or their chosen influencers) invent them: Robert Parker's famous 100-point rating system for wines, for example. And sometimes they are created by sellers, as with the ratings attached to movies by the Motion Picture Association of America.

Such rules are very handy. Indeed, they are often referred to as time savers. Now, consider: What if *use* of the rule—use of the time saver— were itself actually an enjoyable experience?

In 1961, a future Nobel Prize–winning economist at the University of Chicago named George Stigler wrote an article in which he drew a famous distinction between two sorts of consumers: searchers and non-searchers—those who try to find the best seller (or buyer) and those who don't. In Stigler's words, "The cost of search, for a consumer, may be taken as approximately proportional to the number of sellers approached, for the chief cost is time . . . The assimilation of information is not an easy or pleasant task for most people, and *they may well be willing to pay more for the information when supplied in an enjoyable form*"[5] (emphasis added).

Obvious in retrospect, powerful in application, Stigler's article founded an academic cottage industry that has spent decades calculating the importance of searching behavior. The justly celebrated success of the online search engine known as Google is only the latest gloss on Stigler's perception: By linking relevant advertising to search terms, Google not only supplies a value to its users in the form of saved shopping time, and charges advertisers based on the number of times the ad is seen (nothing new here; magazines were publishing per-inquiry rates for bind-in cards thirty years ago) but has actually created a market in the keywords themselves, for which advertisers actively bid.

Everyone, it seems, places a different value on the search for information prior to buying . . . what ordinary people call shopping. Some people like to shop all the time; everybody likes shopping some of the time. Sometimes shopping—searching for information—takes minutes, but is still too long; sometimes shopping takes months, and the shopper is sad to see it end.

In more than twenty-five years of helping clients persuade consumers to purchase everything from imported all-natural Asian fruit and vegetable juice to mutual funds to auto parts, we have learned to apply the insights of Stigler and the dozens of marketing gurus who have followed in his path.

The Cost of Time

Twenty years ago, the management theorist Michael Porter described the phenomenon more elegantly by observing that one of the two ways that firms create value for buyers is by lowering buyer cost[6] . . . and one of those costs is *always* the amount of time invested in shopping. Providing the most persuasion in the least amount of time—effective signals of product value (brands, design features, textures, etc.) such as the Sub-Zero plaque on a $10,000 refrigerator—is so important that, as Porter puts it, "A firm that delivers only modest value but signals it more effectively may actually command a higher price than a firm that delivers higher value but signals it poorly."[7]

Armen Alchian and William Allen proposed that as consumers absorb higher fixed costs, they are more willing to choose pricier goods. The original example, which came to be known as the Alchian and Allen Proposition, supposed that, since it costs the same to ship both choice and standard grapes from California to New York, the price differential of 100 percent would narrow to the point that relatively more choice grapes would be purchased in New York than in California, even though the absolute price is higher. Research consistently demonstrates that this is so. *Cost,* as in manufacturing cost, is only a part of *price,* or the total cost of delivery. The impact of proximity, frequency of purchase, familiarity, exclusiveness, and, we believe, most important, time, must be factored in by marketers . . . since they are most certainly factored in by consumers.

As reinforcement for the basic proposition of stopwatch marketing—that perceived time spent shopping is the key variable driving sales volume *and* profit margins—it is important to remember that the general proposition works in reverse. Travelers who fly to Orlando from Seattle, for example, consistently show less price resistance to the goodies available at Disney World than do otherwise similar travelers who depart from Miami or Atlanta. Spending more time lowers the resistance to higher-priced goods . . . and shifting marketing resources from an area where consumers spend less time shopping to one where they are likely to spend more can have a huge impact on profit margins.

What we have learned, and will be sharing in the pages and the chapters that follow, is that time isn't money; it's *much* more important than that.

Chapter Two

The Solution

 The recent best-seller *Blink,* Malcolm Gladwell's "intellectual adventure story" about rapid cognition, reveals the enormous range of decision making that occurs in a tiny increment of time . . . in Gladwell's viewpoint, two seconds. Many of his examples deal with purchase decisions, and it is unarguably true not only that many commercial transactions *are* made on a few seconds' worth of information collection, but that they *should be.*

Both the research cited in *Blink* and our own experience demonstrate that buyers frequently experience no greater satisfaction with their purchases whether they spend more or less time considering them. Frequently, but not always. What is *always* true is that consumer decision making is time-dependent, and that time is always measured by the consumer, either implicitly or explicitly. Time is the constant. As is the instrument that measures it.

Imagine a stopwatch. Better yet, imagine a hundred stopwatches, or a thousand. Imagine that every one is held by a potential customer. Some are ticking very fast, some glacially slow. Some, in fact, aren't ticking at all.

All stopwatches measure time, but the shopping stopwatch measures a very specific sort of time. The slower it ticks, the more time and energy a consumer is willing to spend shopping for a particular purchase, and the more opportunity a marketer has to influence and ultimately capture a purchase decision.

Whether they do so explicitly or implicitly, all successful marketers are aware of the shopping stopwatch, the image we use to describe not only the willingness to spend time on any purchase decision, but the ability of businesses to use the elements of the marketing mix to influence that decision. We have found the image to be a powerful one, able to display the dynamic path of any buying decision, since every one of our shopping stopwatches can be speeded up or slowed down in dozens of different ways that direct the flow of consumer attention throughout the time available to influence it. These accelerators and brakes, of course, are the touchpoints so beloved of marketing professionals, who define them as every point of interaction a potential customer has with a product. By themselves, however, interactions are only modestly valuable; parking next to a Toyota Sienna counts as a touchpoint, but doesn't really sell huge numbers of the minivans. In order to change consumer behavior, touchpoints need to channel demand into an area—call it a catchpoint— where the shopper can turn into a customer. Every time an advertising media buyer buys a week-long flight of local radio spots, she is calculating the ticking speed of her target's shopping stopwatch; whenever a retailer announces a price increase, or a marketing manager launches a brand extension, they are placing touchpoints and catchpoints inside the workings of the watch.

Even though they don't use the term, researchers have long distinguished among consumers based on their shopping stopwatches . . . differentiating between hedonistic and utilitarian shoppers, for example— those who derive value from *shopping* and those who derive value from *owning*. This would be a useful model, but for two things: First, our own experience has demonstrated that consumers are too ornery to stay in one place on any scale—remember Ms. Blue and Mr. Green?—which is why labeling *consumers,* rather than *consumption,* is the sort of simplifying assumption that frankly does not apply to real situations.

On any given day, at any given life stage, in any given economic environment, individual consumers—about which we as marketers think we know so much—will behave differently than a backward-looking model would suggest. The same consumer utilizes different stopwatches for different purchases on different days and in different states of mind, often without knowing it and certainly without calling it out. The chronic complaints of contemporary marketers—fragmented media, time poverty, and gnatlike attention spans—are really just other ways of asking *"Why won't they just stay put?!"* It's the predictable result of addressing consumers, instead of consumption.

The other reason we don't find the hedonist-utilitarian model very useful is this: We are marketers rather than social psychologists. Our interest is in helping sellers to maximize profit, rather than helping buyers to understand their motivations. The stopwatch marketing model contrasts high-margin and low-margin selling with high-time-value and low-time-value buying. Businesses are constrained by the number of touchpoints and catchpoints they can afford as well as the diameter and speed of the shopping stopwatch. To apply Stigler's insight to a *particular business,* rather than to an entire economy, more than two flavors of consumer are needed. The most powerful model we use, in fact, has four quadrants.

Welcome to the matrix.

Clustering customers into groups with distinct patterns of behavior is nothing new; familiar behavioral clusters include Basic shoppers (seekers after essentials and convenience, in that order), Apathetic shoppers (those who lack interest in virtually every aspect of shopping), Destination shoppers (for whom the mall, or supermarket, or mass merchant is reason enough for shopping, even absent convenience or brand-name merchandise not associated with the merchant), and Enthusiast shoppers (the mirror image of Destination shoppers, consumers who will spend days shopping for the same handbag at a dozen stores).[1]

American marketers have invested tens of millions of dollars in data analysis hoping to find a magic formula that reveals the secret to consumer decision making. Such typing systems, whether based on psychometric exam results (such as SRI's Fulfilleds) or zip codes (like Claritas's Gold Coasters), are a logical outgrowth of a powerful, but fundamentally flawed theory: that consumers fit, more or less comfortably, into categories. The power of such systems has been too well documented to bear repeating; not so their flaws. Typing consumers is not the same as typing consumption.

At MCAworks, we have designed a model that measures consumption— *not* consumers—along two axes: the disposition to spend time shopping for a particular product or service; and the net margin of that product or service. (Since marketing resources, over time, must be a fraction of any business's gross margin, they will determine the quantity and quality of the touchpoints and catchpoints—the resources available for marketing the product or service). This model segments shopping style into understandable groupings, so that marketers can align their marketing strategies to those segments . . . what we call their marketing styles. In this model, transactions tend to fall somewhere within one of the four quadrants that comprise the matrix: In one, we match low-margin products or services with consumers who have a low willingness to spend time shopping; others match low-margin with high willingness; high-margin/low willingness; and high-margin/high willingness. Of course, since we're marketers who understand the importance of packaging, we actually give the quadrants slightly less imposing names:

Few touchpoints + lower margin/Fast stopwatch = Reluctant shopping
Many touchpoints + higher margin/Fast stopwatch = Impatient shopping
Few touchpoints + lower margin/Slow stopwatch = Recreational shopping
Many touchpoints + higher margin/Slow stopwatch = Painstaking shopping

These are shown in Figure 2-1, with some easily identified examples of products and services illustrating the typical consumption behavior often observed in that quadrant.

THE MATRIX: Example Products and Services

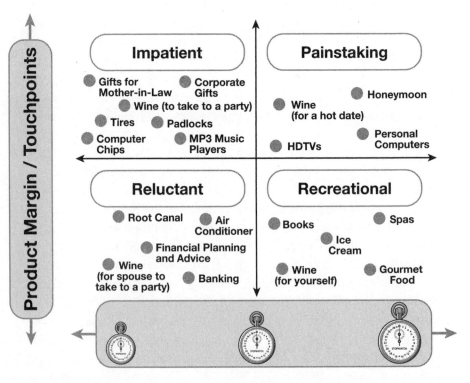

Figure 2-1

To read the matrix in Figure 2-1, think about, for example, air-conditioning in the reluctant quadrant. Purchase of a new air conditioner, especially a central-air unit, is nearly always done by a reluctant consumer. The consumer is not an expert, is usually in a hurry (she has a quickly ticking stopwatch), and the reason for the purchase is likely an unplanned event (it's August and the darn thing just broke!). Moreover, there are few touchpoints: Almost certainly, there are more conveniently located, well-lighted, and comfortable Starbucks than central-air-conditioning showrooms in her neighborhood.

Understanding the real estate your customers occupy on this map—their shopping style—is the single most important thing you need to know in order to succeed in selling your product or service to them. The relevant customers for some products occupy only a small section of a single quadrant of the matrix; others cover large sections of the map, with customers appearing in more than one quadrant, such as the Green and Blue families. In general, most businesses will find the behavior of their most important customers congregating around a single shopping quadrant . . . though, of course, we never forget that even the most reluctant shopping experience is a joy to some small fraction of shoppers. This highlights an important consideration for marketers in understanding and using this matrix construct—a consumer's or customer's placement in a quadrant is situational (it's August and it broke!), behavioral (I'm not the type to comparison shop), and emotional (I'm just getting too old to be uncomfortable in my own house). Later on, we describe some market research techniques for uncovering both; for now, we simply illustrate this in Figure 2-2.

The theme of this book, then, can be phrased as "How to synchronize your marketing strategy with your customers' shopping styles," or, as the subtitle states, "Take Charge of the Time When Your Customer Decides to Buy." The axes on this matrix track the two dynamics noted in that subtitle. The horizontal axis tracks the shopper's willingness to spend time and effort in the process of gathering information about a particular product or service . . . their shopping styles. The vertical axis illustrates the resources available to turn those shoppers into customers . . . the profit margins that provide the money to establish touchpoints—ways and methods of communicating with consumers, of affecting their purchase decisions.

Identifying the quadrant that best describes the purchasing dynamic

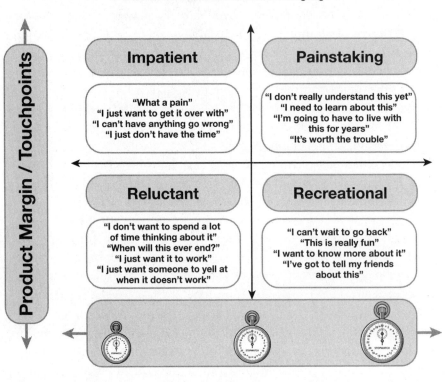

Figure 2-2

for a product or service is the number one priority for any business. But measuring the ticks on the stopwatch is only the beginning of the process. A successful marketer uses that metric to apply available marketing resources—the advertisements, in-store promotions, sponsorships, even customer service feedback, which are collectively her touchpoints and catchpoints—during the time that the customer clicks the stopwatch, when a purchasing decision is made. In many cases, marketers use the touchpoints as shortcuts: ways to truncate the journey from unformed demand to purchase.

Really successful marketers don't stop there. Some of them, as we shall see, change the ticking speed and/or the diameter of the shopping stopwatch itself. In the chapters that follow, you'll encounter:

1. The launch of Goodyear's Assurance TripleTred tires, a billion-dollar success story built on a shopping cycle that generally takes less than an hour;

2. How controlling the fifty-second-long search pattern of the typical user of the Yellow Pages made Roto-Rooter the only legitimate national brand in its category;

3. Whole Foods Market's reinvention of the supermarket shopping experience by turning it from slow-moving drudgery into theater;

4. The embrace, extend, and extinguish strategy used by Microsoft to exploit shoppers' reluctance to spend time researching alternatives to the Office suite of computer software applications;

5. The touchpoints planted by Toyota's premium brand, Lexus, up to a year before a customer places a foot inside a dealer showroom.

You'll also encounter studies of the cellular telephone, hardware, and retail banking industries . . . even the careful, sometimes years-long, shopping behavior exhibited by high school seniors (and their parents) applying to college.

And, because of our belief that the principles of stopwatch marketing are equally applicable to businesses of all sizes, you'll see how the proprietors of a wine shop with a single location in New York City were able to use the same measurement and execution strategies as our Fortune 500 clients.

In a much-reprinted 1996 article, the paleontologist and sports fan Stephen Jay Gould applied his keen intelligence to a subject of seemingly marginal relevance to his own academic specialty (to say nothing of the practice of marketing): the demise of baseball's .400 hitter. Though never precisely common, the threshold of finishing a baseball season with four hits in every ten at-bats had been reached twenty-four times between 1894 and 1925, but only once since (and that more than sixty years ago). Applying the logic of Darwinian natural selection to the evolution of baseball skill, Gould argued that as the expertise of the game's players grew, so too did the distance separating its most accomplished from its least. Thus, not only did the .400 hitter vanish, but so did the .180 hitter, as both, in the language of statistics, reverted to the mean. While enough differences in talent survive that complete evolutionary perfection—an entire league of .260 hitters—so far remains elusive, the deviation from that mean has narrowed. Once upon a time, some players could parlay unique and distinctive advantages to a huge disparity in accomplishment, but no more. Information about hitting technique, particularly, is too widely available for the .400 hitter to retain a monopoly position.

As it happens, there may be fewer .400 hitters in the business world, as well. Everyone has figured out where to cut costs, to eliminate unnecessary links in the supply chain, to focus on competitive advantages. They have outsourced, re-engineered, and reinvented themselves. The easy fixes are gone. Even executives at Microsoft and Wal-Mart live in a state of chronic anxiety about market leadership, precisely because they know how hard it is to maintain it. Like Lewis Carroll's Red Queen, they must run as fast as possible just to stay where they are.

In order to run faster, of course, it is necessary to measure one's pace. That is what stopwatches are for.

Tools of the Trade

Galileo, in possession of the world's first working telescope, couldn't point it anywhere in the sky without discovering something new. It has been easy to believe that the tools of stopwatch marketing are something like that telescope: Every time we aim it at a business or industry, it seems to bring that business's successes and failures into focus.

Aside from the grandiosity of comparing ourselves to Galileo (all new toys have some of the properties of a telescope, after all, but no one expects them to change the world), this is a bit of a trap. Just as the possession of a hammer tends to make all problems look like nails, so too does ownership of a lens suggest that the most important objects in the world are the ones that appear clearest. Knowing when to use a magnifying glass instead of binoculars remains a matter of fine judgment.

Some of the world's best-known and most successful companies are using the insights that drive the shopping stopwatch every day to achieve spectacular growth in both margin and market share, and their stories will be included. But the book you are holding in your hand is intended to be far more than a collection of case studies; our hope is that you will find it a highly useful guide to applying such judgment in *any* business, using time-tested and empirically verifiable techniques. It is a description of the unique challenges of twenty-first-century commerce, and a prescription for overcoming them.

Part Two
The Matrix

Chapter Three

Impatient Shopping

No one knows for certain whom to credit with the baseball adage "Wait, wait, then quick, quick." Popular candidates include Hall of Fame outfielders Ted Williams and Tony Gwynn—and with lifetime batting averages of .344 and .338, respectively, both are worth listening to, on the subject of hitting, anyway. The slightly elliptical advice is, of course, a shorthand for the idea that hitting a pitch on the outside corner of the plate depends on exhibiting enough patience to wait for the fraction of a second in which the eye sees whether a pitch can be hit . . . and then using that fraction to move two pounds of wood through the arc that intersects the path of a ball from pitcher's hand to home plate. A perfect swing is wasted unless it is timed to meet the ball, which is disobligingly traveling at upward of ninety miles an hour, and often spinning in a way that makes it appear to curve.

Makes selling tires sound easy.

Succeeding in the impatient shopping quadrant requires absolute mastery of "wait, wait, then quick, quick" strategies. Impatient shopping applies largely to products or services that are urgently needed, but rarely purchased in advance of that need. Impatient shopping differs from reluctant shopping—the subject of chapter 5—in that consumers don't avoid shopping for products in the impatient quadrant; they simply, and correctly, calculate that the advantages of buying before the product is needed are small, while the costs are high. A rational person might keep bottled water or batteries around in case of an emergency, but is unlikely to keep half a dozen extra tanks of propane in the garage against the possibility that the gas grill runs out of fuel.

Our work with clients competing in this category has revealed that impatient shopping is characterized by two dynamics: emotions and speed.

1. Emotions: Most of the time products and services competing in the impatient quadrant are, almost by definition, unimportant,

uninteresting, uninvolved categories ("wait, wait . . ."). However, when the tire is flat, when the freshly scrubbed middle-schooler has forgotten until 11 P.M. the night before the first day of school to ask his parents for a padlock for his locker, when the guest toilet backs up the day of a dinner party, or the fan breaks in mid-July . . . suddenly the need to solve the problem is overwhelming. The consumer's determination to get the problem solved *right now* and, more important, get it done right, so right that the spouse or child can have no reason to complain, can lead, literally, to a rapidly increased heartbeat, cold sweats, family arguments, and so on. Precisely because these are generally low-interest categories, the opportunity to make a visible mistake is large, and the shopper knows that.

2. Quick trigger on the stopwatch: Whether or not the consumer brings a lot of internal emotional baggage to the shopping experience, she is still confronted by external phenomena. Even those time-starved parents who want to spend their Saturday afternoons sitting around a tire store, discussing the intricacies of fibers, composite materials, and steel belts (they don't; the word they typically use to describe such time is *wasted*), still have to calculate their time value as compared to missing their kids' soccer games or piano recitals. This, after all, is the basic definition of the impatient quadrant.

To summarize, impatient purchases are emotional because the opportunity to make a mistake is very high. They are also quick-trigger because the consumer almost certainly would prefer to be doing something else: Drivers don't want to dawdle longer than necessary on the way to work to learn about tires when they are already late for their first meeting due to the blown-out tire.

Products and services competing for customers in the impatient quadrant are, truly, the offensive linemen of the American economy: noticed only when they fail. Thus, while the demand for them may be great, the fundamental characteristic of the quadrant—the small time window for consumer decision making—means that impatient shopping almost inevitably occurs in an environment where many competitors try to crowd into that window. The result can often be a loss of pricing power, and therefore margin. In fact, the key competitive weapons are generally not price, but such features as convenience, sales training, durability/ extended warranties, branding, and mnemonic visual cues.

Hundreds of companies, even entire industries, cope with the challenges of the impatient quadrant daily, but relatively few solve the problem of their customers' short attention span—their quickly ticking stopwatches—in ways that expand both market share *and* operating margins. One such is a classic old economy behemoth: the Goodyear Tire & Rubber Company.

Advantage, Goodyear

On January 30, 2005, guard Richard Hamilton took the floor for the Detroit Pistons in a home game against the New York Knicks at The Palace of Auburn Hills. Hamilton, the leading scorer for the Pistons during their championship season that had ended seven months previously, was by far the most recognizable of the fairly anonymous Pistons, largely because of the transparent mask he wore to protect his face from damage. On this night, however, his appearance was distinctive for another reason: carved into his hair was the pattern of a tire tread.

Not, of course, a generic pattern. The haircut—for which Hamilton had been paid a large but undisclosed sum[1]—was the latest episode in a marketing campaign by The Goodyear Tire & Rubber Company that is a near-perfect application of stopwatch marketing principles within the impatient-shopping quadrant.

To understand why, it is instructive to examine both the fundamentals of Goodyear's industry, and the specific circumstances that preceded the introduction of the Assurance tire.

By the end of the twentieth century, one of the signature American industries had been almost entirely acquired by foreigners. Firestone, General Tire, and B. F. Goodrich had become subsidiaries, respectively, of Japan's Bridgestone, Germany's Continental AG, and France's Michelin. And, they had all removed their headquarters' operations out of the city of Akron, Ohio, the original home of the giant corporations that began as manufacturers of pneumatic tires for bicycles. In one of globalization's longer-gestating perversities, the American industry to first establish itself internationally (in order to ensure access to their primary input, U.S. tire manufacturers started acquiring Southeast Asian rubber plantations as early as 1910) had only one major representative that remained American-owned and Akron-based: The Goodyear Tire & Rubber Company.

Founded in 1898 by the industrialist Frank Seiberling (the company took the name of Charles Goodyear, who had invented vulcanized rubber fifty years previously), Goodyear was a multibillion-dollar behemoth as it entered its second century, the world's largest tire manufacturer, with sales exceeding $14 billion. It was, in the summer of 2000, ideally positioned to take advantage of one of the greatest opportunities to take market share from a competitor in the history of American business.

For three months that summer, no American could get very far away from the story of how Firestone tires had led to a series of accidents involving the Ford Explorer. After dozens of recalls, hundreds of lawsuits, and probably thousands of press conferences, Firestone's future was trading at a huge discount, and that of its prime competitors looked rosy indeed.

Not, however, for long. Firestone's parent company, the Japanese giant Bridgestone, reacted quickly to preserve its share of the U.S. market, even if that meant writing off the now-toxic Firestone brand name. Within weeks, they had shifted ad dollars from Firestone to Bridgestone—a *lot* of ad dollars; from 2000 to 2001, the corporation increased advertising for the Bridgestone name from $400,000 to $12 million, and decreased spending on Firestone from $8 million to $1.3 million.[2] In any event, they were able to shift consumers to the Bridgestone brand, and held erosion of their U.S. market share to a mere two points.[3]

The demonstration was not lost on Goodyear's new CEO, Robert Keegan, who had joined the company in October of 2000. The battle over the consumer replacement tire market—200 million units per year, with Goodyear selling more than 35 percent of them—could not be won by a reliance on brand loyalty. The introduction of belted radials so dramatically extended tire life that they have, perversely, eliminated the historical reasons for brand loyalty. The danger, of course, is that when consumers no longer believe one brand is superior to another, cost becomes the only consumer driver. In the words of industry analyst Henry Millis, "It's [like] the airline industry now," with the consequent damage to a manufacturer's profitability.[4] Not coincidentally, one of the pressures on profitability comes—as always—from the Wal-Mart effect. This is true even though no one knows for certain Wal-Mart's share of the roughly 200 million replacement tires sold in the United States annually; estimates range from 18 to 32 million. The Tire Industry Association estimates around 22 million, which means around 10 percent of the national total.

However, this is one business in which Wal-Mart's advantages are not quite as terrifying as they are to retailers of paper towels or inexpensive apparel. The Wal-Mart model, so effective in most categories, causes the company to deliberately restrict their SKUs to the most popular sizes, and to make a policy of offering only minimal service on the cars themselves, which both reduces their opportunity to channel service customers into tire sales, and lowers consumer confidence in this confusing category.[5]

As a result, under pressure from its own retailers, and from the fundamental characteristics of the impatient quadrant, Goodyear had fallen into a marketing scheme that depended on periodic price promotions and escalating warranties.

The answer, as Keegan saw, was the regular introduction of new products—an area in which Goodyear had not exactly burned brightest in recent years. In fact, it had not launched a significant new product since the highly successful Aquatred in 1991. When we were invited, in 2003, to work with Goodyear's North American Tire division on its revitalization through new product introductions, the company had already started to change that. In fact, the company had invested heavily in engineering and R&D. Truly electrifying product, material, and tread designs were coming out of that process, resulting in a plethora of new product ideas searching for a filtering mechanism to prioritize and position them for consumers.

All companies give at least lip service to the need for change, but Goodyear meant it. It was determined to take its existing market share advantage in the midsize and economy automobile classes into the premium/luxury and the high-performance segments. This, in turn, meant confronting the company that was the 800-pound gorilla in both of the latter classes: Michelin. The French company's brilliant and consistent advertising (has there ever been an image that conjured the idea of safety more effectively than the baby protected by Michelin tires?) and its ability to deliver very high-quality products were bad enough. But Michelin's huge advantage in supplying original equipment to premium-car manufacturers was like starting a marathon with a five-mile lead; no category of tire buyers is likelier to replace their existing tires with the same brand.

Nonetheless, and in response to a revitalized marketing department pursuing the strategic vision of both Keegan and Jon Rich, then Goodyear's president of North American operations, we began the work of adding to Goodyear's existing understanding of the perceived needs and desires of consumers for replacement tires and mapping those needs against Goodyear's ability to deliver profitable solutions.

Any decent map describes its territory; a really useful one also shows the best route across it. Our goal was a map that would show the best path for Goodyear to follow in launching a series of technologically innovative products. The company had spent considerable time, effort, and money developing an understanding of the market that rested on a very sophisticated consumer segmentation scheme . . . far more sophisticated—and useful—than traditional *product* segmentation.

We knew that the high-end and middle-level consumers that Goodyear had targeted were buying based on a combination of the promise of safety and performance. By early 2003, the situation could be summarized as follows. Goodyear was:

1. Almost desperate for a new product success;
2. Focused on the higher-margin, higher-priced segments;
3. Armed with significant technology that, in theory, anyway, could be applied to a wide range of perceived consumer needs.

So, our first priority was to use market research to define, in the consumer's own words, the most important benefits that these high-end consumers look for—more precisely, the benefits that they *believe* they look for—when buying tires: things such as responsiveness, reliability, or durability (which, together, appeared as the first choice of nearly 40 percent of tire buyers). High-margin consumers want tires that hold the road well. That handle well in emergencies. That have a comfortable ride, a short braking distance, possess environmentally-friendly features, and can be recycled.

Consumers told us about their overall needs regarding tires, which we summarized with the (not very original) phrase "peace of mind." In short, high-end consumers' definition of having it all in replacement tires was: safety and performance under any and all conditions—all weather, all performance, and all durable. And Goodyear's engineers were prepared to produce a tire that would deliver on all of them. All their marketers had to do was to deliver the message to consumers. And do it before their watches stop.

Their stopwatches.

One of the most difficult challenges in marketing replacement tires is changing the consumers' shopping time horizon. Quite simply, tires are replaced when they need replacing, because of either wear or—less frequently—damage. Both are so influenced by climate that a prediction of good weather in Europe for the coming year can reduce Goodyear's anticipated earnings by enough to move the stock price.[6] In 2003, Goodyear Canada built its marketing around a newspaper advertisement showing a faux weather map with the worst imaginable winter weather . . . in the fall. Changing the demand timing for replacement tire sales is about as easy as reversing global warming.

In any event, the driver's awareness of need occurs when his or her peace of mind gets interrupted. This can happen for any one of a number of reasons, such as discovering that the current tires are worn or damaged, actually having a flat, failing to get the expected mileage, lack of time available to go buy new tires, and discomfort with the actual buying process for the replacement tires.

At this point, consumers have been driving around with plenty of peace of mind not thinking about tires for, quite literally, years. Then, suddenly, they have a problem they want solved *right now*. Their stopwatch is ticking and it isn't going to tick for very long. Moreover, their tires have not only blown out, but their peace of mind has been blown up. Bad things are the only things that can happen now: high price, early wear out, wasted time shopping for and buying tires, and so forth. Consumers are no longer in control or confident. Now, for the few hours or, at most, few days that this purchase is at the top of mind, there is a lot of risk—risk of paying too much; failing to get the best deal; failing to get the best tire for your driving style, car, weather conditions; and so on. And, this top-of-mind problem—replacing tires—comes as an unpleasant surprise: the process itself is taking time away from something else the consumer had planned to do with his or her time this day. The consumer becomes increasingly impatient to get it over with. For this brief period—this quickly ticking stopwatch—replacing tires has become very emotional.

The flip side of this emotional reaction is also quite interesting. Consumers nearly always return to a solid peace-of-mind state once the transaction is completed and they are driving around on new tires. New tires—no matter the brand, the type, the tread design, and so on—almost always means better tires. That is, new tires equal better tires equal safer tires equal peace of mind.

For almost everyone, buying replacement tires is right in the middle of the impatient-shopping quadrant: a transaction that no one seeks in advance of need, but can't put off once the need appears.

Goodyear's executives knew they could not affect primary demand, which meant that targeting the buyers of high-margin tires also meant taking them away from a competitor, mostly Michelin. But the time available to influence the buying decision for a new tire is measured in days, if not hours; when a mechanic tells a customer that her tires are worn out, he doesn't say, "Drive them for a few weeks while you think about which model to buy."

That mechanic also doesn't want to hand the potential buyer a sheet of technical specifications that illustrates the breaking strength of the tire's fibers, or Impulse of Force equations like $\Delta p = F_{net}t$. Engineers can be seduced with equations, but civilians need images.

Defining the consumer's needs, then, must be done in their language. They will often initially use terms that imply empirical or technological solutions such as safety, control, traction, handling, and so forth. However, when pressed via skilled researchers as to the deeper, unstated, derived needs, the consumer will phrase things in their own words with comments like, "I won't be alone at night with a flat tire or an accident," "I won't spin out, no matter what the weather," and "I don't have to be vigilant."

Important to note is that consumers are truly impatient with the technological details and respond instead to visual cues, tread design, branding, product names, and recommendations from the dealer. This helps explain the great success of Aquatred a generation earlier—a solid brand (Goodyear), a good name that communicated the product's essence (Aquatred), and clear, reinforcing visual cues (aqua channels that move water out of the way). So, in determining which of the various tire concepts coming out of the labs to fully develop and launch, Goodyear was faced with the need to develop:

1. A useful visual depiction of the tread—that's the primary cue that consumers look at and understand—as well as a good visual on the sidewall, which consumers look at, salespeople point to, and often contains nothing but the mother brand and a bunch of indecipherable numbers;

2. A product name that would both communicate benefits and point to the visual cues in much the same manner as Aquatred had in the 1990s;

3. A family name that would resonate and provide an umbrella for future offerings;

4. An overall solution that added to the strength of the Goodyear brand while commanding a price premium. That is, when any of the various concepts were tied on measures of purchase intent, Goodyear then looked at (a) price expectations and (b) positive impact on the Goodyear brand (remember all the dying old-line American Akron, Ohio–based Rust Belt company stuff at the outset of the chapter).

The full set of challenges could be graphically depicted in the flowchart in Figure 3-1.

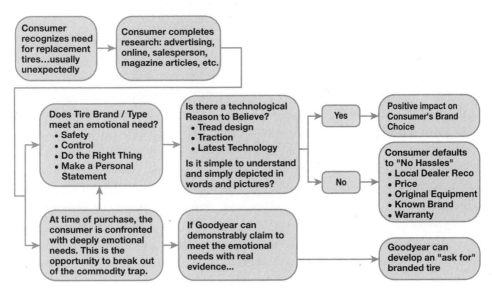

Figure 3-1

Note that there aren't very many touchpoints in this impatient process where Goodyear can influence a decision. There are, of course, advertising and brand-building generally. When the "lost peace of mind" moment occurs, however, the stopwatch starts ticking very quickly. A consumer might check around in some newspaper ads for prices and availability, but is likely to simply head to the no-hassles option—the dealer nearest home or work. Most of the critical touchpoints occur relative to the dealer—visibility and location, in-store collateral material, salesperson interaction, and quick in and out of the dealership. A good dealer network represents the perfect swing mentioned in our discussion of Tony Gwynn and Ted Williams at the outset of this chapter. We noted that even a perfect swing must be combined with good timing. That timing came together when Goodyear was able to bring to the market the right product, with the right features, right visual cues, and right marketing for the moment.

Steve Jobs used to tell employees—literally scream at them—"Design isn't what a product looks like. It's what a product *does.*" Enter TripleTred, officially named "Goodyear Assurance Featuring TripleTred Technology." The three-way design of what was to become Goodyear's flagship product was created to offer a simultaneous improvement while driving on dry pavement, on snow and ice, and through water. And it does all three superbly well. Fortunately, the technology involved three visually distinct sections of the tire with observably different tread designs, allowing a clear linkage among the benefit (safety and performance under three different weather conditions), the most important visual cue (the tread), and the product name (TripleTred). Making the tread the centerpiece of marketing the Assurance tire, however, was stopwatch marketing to its core. The Assurance was explicitly designed to be bought and sold in an environment where five steps in the classic purchasing dynamic—Awareness, Consideration, Trial, Purchase, and Use—are often separated by minutes.

The launch of the Assurance, in February of 2004, was one of the most significant in the history of American business, much less Goodyear. The company's inability to exploit Firestone's 2000 disaster presaged what were three of the company's worst years since the Depression, ending 2002 with a $1.2 billion loss, and a drop in the value of Goodyear's stock from more than $62 per share in 1997 to less than $8. Bob Keegan and Jon Rich needed a hit. And they were prepared to back their play with a $50 million advertising plan featuring the voice of Patrick Stewart and the most extensive dealer training and incentive program in the history of the tire industry.[7]

In addition to the usual suspects of male-oriented advertising placement like sporting events, Goodyear specifically went after less traditional media. For example, the TripleTred launch advertising was placed in an extensive buy in movie theaters to appear before the feature film. This was obviously intended to build awareness and predisposition . . . no one got up from the movie and went to the tire store before finding out what became of the Prisoner of Azkaban or whether Shrek would finally be accepted by his beloved's family. That is, in our terms, the heavy advertising was an attempt to lengthen the stopwatch by generating greater awareness in advance of the catalyzing lost peace-of-mind moment.

But by all accounts, the key moment in the success of the Assurance with TripleTred, and its sister tire, the Assurance with ComforTred, occurred when buyers were able to see the tire itself: what the company called its "long, sculpted, sensual shapes that draw the consumer's attention . . . [an] aggressive appearance that helps the dealer explain the tire's benefits and technology to consumers, which simplifies the purchasing decision of consumers who place safety as a priority." The icon on the tire's sidewall—a sun, three raindrops, and a snowflake—only underlined the tire's unique appeal.

The family name, Goodyear Assurance, not only worked in research, it attacked directly the consumer need for peace of mind and the Michelin safety baby positioning. Moreover, the name Assurance (now the company's ongoing designation for virtually all car and minivan tires) provides an umbrella for the sister premium-priced product, Assurance Featuring ComforTred Technology. The sidewall visual cue for ComforTred is a feather.

Finally, the company invested heavily in dealer promotion and training for the Assurance launch to be certain of their support. This was critical: the dealers were, and are, in a position of power because they operate in the impatient quadrant. Consumers come in, hoping to get this over with quickly and are generally—and admittedly—subject to a sales pitch.

But even more so, the sale of replacement tires has a special character that reinforces the importance of the last-minute interaction between consumer and dealer. In the words of Andy Traicoff, Goodyear's Director of Customer Development, "Tires are nearly unique in the automobile aftermarket, as it is one of the few branded products visible to the owner. More important, the buyer is paying not only for the product, but for its mounting and installation. Even the 'do it yourself' car owner rarely owns the equipment required to mount a tire on a wheel. This makes dealers a critical link in the value chain: critical to buyers, and to Goodyear." As a result, Goodyear focused, laserlike, on its dealers' need for training and education not only on the technology, features, and benefits but also, as important, on their (the dealers') ability to earn a nice margin on the product. In that very short time when the consumer is in the dealership, ready to buy TripleTred, Goodyear had to be certain no salesperson was saying, "I've got something just as good for $15 less from Toyo, or Yokohama, or Gislaved." Even among buyers of ultra-high-performance tires, often costing $200 or more apiece (and, more properly, part of the painstaking segment) only 33 percent even had a specific brand in mind when they entered the dealership.[8] Even the most particular shopper is likely to be flabbergasted by the almost willfully obscure code—P205/60R15, with additional codes designating maximum load, speed rating, and so on.

Given the critical importance of the Assurance launch, Goodyear could not depend on the visuals of the TripleTred design alone, powerful as those visuals might be. The marketing effort placed dozens of touchpoints along the "wait, wait . . ." phase of the tire customer's path. These included such tactics as the $50 million advertising campaign that heralded the Assurance's arrival and the $60 rebates offered by the company during the first three months Assurance was on sale. Perhaps most important, in recognition of the fact that the dealer network would be the final (often, the only) touchpoint for potential buyers, Goodyear committed to thirteen huge dog-and-pony shows—known as Goodyear's State of Assurance Ride-and-Drives—which represented its largest dealer communications, training, and incentive program ever.[9]

Figure 3-2 contains two key pages from the Goodyear website highlighting TripleTred and ComforTred.

And it worked. As Andy Traicoff recalls, "We knew we had a winner the first time a consumer told us, 'It *looks* like it does what you *say* it does.'" And how. The Assurance was the most successful launch in Goodyear's history, with demand more than three times the company's most aggressive estimates. Because it was priced at a premium—average retail price greater than $95—the volume translated into even higher profits. The success of Assurance with TripleTred depended, in the end, on dozens of different touchpoints, from print advertising to consumer rebates to dealer incentives to, yes, Richard Hamilton's haircut. But the last word (or, at least, the last tick of the stopwatch) goes to the heart of the most

GOODYEAR ASSURANCE WEBSITE: Example Pages

Figure 3-2

important instant in the most impatient of shopping decisions: "The guys in the store are telling us it sold itself," said Ron Meredith, Executive Vice President of Lamb's Tire & Automotive Centers in Austin, Texas.[10]

Locked and Loaded

The lesson of Goodyear's turnaround might be simply stated this way: When marketing in the impatient quadrant, the most powerful touch-point may be the way in which the product's appearance communicates its competitive advantage. Everything about TripleTred, from its name to its "long, sculpted lines" to the icons appearing on its sidewall, reinforces the unique benefit of the brand. In the highly compressed time during which an impatient shopping decision is made, nothing works better than a gestalt—a depiction in which an entire picture, rich in information content, is seen at once, rather than as a series of parts. The TripleTred may be one of the great marketing gestalts in history.

A test of the value of the product-that-sells-itself-visually theory would, therefore, be stronger for a product that placed even more of its marketing resources behind the buying decisions made at the point of sale. A product like, for example, a padlock.

Like so many of America's industrial titans, Master Lock is understandable only in historical context. As with Goodyear, its founding is a story of the development and exploitation of a technological innovation—vulcanized rubber for Goodyear; laminated steel for Master Lock. Unlike Goodyear, however, Master Lock was able to assert patent protection for its competitive advantage, which granted it an almost biblical seventy years of prosperity . . . but also left the Milwaukee-based manufacturer handicapped when its basic patents expired.

The handicap is a familiar one to anyone who studies corporate organizations. For decades, Master Lock's culture remained true to the engineering brilliance of its founder, Harry Soref. The company so insulated itself from consumer perception that it was convinced that people bought padlocks because of their engineering and manufacturing excellence. Master Lock loved its products, and thought its buyers did as well. Thus, they were caught by surprise when, upon expiration of its patents in 1994, its retailers were deluged with locks from overseas that were just as heavy (and, presumably, as strong) as Master Locks, and a whole lot cheaper. By the time John Heppner became COO in 2001, the company was heading toward the precipice reserved for manufacturers unable to cope with a global economy.

Under pressure not only from foreign competition but, indirectly, from its own largest retailers, including Wal-Mart and Home Depot, Master Lock had to change. Though Master Lock retained *some* pricing power, the heritage of seven decades of producing a first-rate product, it was severely limited. In the words of Randall Larrimore, Heppner's predecessor, "Everyone was willing to pay more for a Master Lock. But how much more?"[11]

Translating Master Lock's brand equity into an acceptable profit margin was an even greater challenge because of the category's shopping environment. As with tires, locks are overwhelmingly purchased either as replacements for other locks or to secure something that was recently purchased. This seems a trivial observation, but was central to Master Lock's turnaround. For the first time in its history, Master Lock had asked its customers why they bought their products, and had learned the humbling truth that people didn't really focus on locks at all, but on security for the possessions that locks protect. Consumers spend time shopping for backpacks, or bicycles, or garden sheds; they don't want to spend additional time shopping for locks, and will therefore almost always decide between competing brands at the point of sale in a matter of minutes if not seconds.

The implications, for Master Lock, were the same as for Goodyear, but the lock company lacked one weapon available to the tire manufacturer: A dealer training and incentive program that was affordable for a set of $100 tires was clearly excessive for a $9 padlock. This put even more pressure on the product's visual appeal . . . on making it, perhaps even more than Assurance, sell itself.

The very small number of ticks on the customer's shopping stopwatch could also be turned into a competitive advantage. Armed with the knowledge that they were selling security rather than laminated steel padlocks, Master Lock was able to carve up its product line into category-specific locks—locks designed with nonconventional colors and nontraditional shapes to appeal to different segments.[12] In 2001, the company introduced a new boat trailer lock that might have been a template for stopwatch marketing:

1. It was designed to be perceived *immediately* as offering extremely high security, with bulky and heavy components that scream, "Your (very

expensive) boat will be safe with me." No need to read a spec sheet for this lock. Touchpoints made: one. Number of ticks on the shopping stopwatch: one.

2. It was produced so that a single size would fit all the major hitch sizes, thus eliminating the lost sale while the customer tries to remember the diameter of his trailer hitch . . . and, not coincidentally, saves retailer space by offering only a single SKU.[13] Touchpoints made: one. Number of ticks on the shopping stopwatch: two . . . maybe.

3. Finally, this lock wasn't displayed in the hardware department; it was displayed in the automotive department—the department stocking whatever product the consumer wanted to ultimately lock up. This saves still more ticks on the shopping stopwatch, eliminating the need to wander from aisle to aisle. In John Heppner's own words, "When a customer goes to Wal-Mart, he expects to find the lock in the automotive section."[14]

Heppner is justifiably proud. After decades during which the traditional Master Lock padlock was the company's best-selling product at Wal-Mart, in 2002, the former champion was dethroned by the company's new trailer lock, which is not only one of Wal-Mart's number one aftermarket automobile accessories, but has permitted Master Lock to open accounts with specialty retailers like Pep Boys and Auto Zone.

The principle that impatient shopping rewards products whose design sells itself now permeates Master Lock. The company now changes its designs as frequently as an apparel manufacturer, with colorful—and pricey—category leaders like the Fusion ($8), Sphero ($7), and Titanium ($12+) padlocks and the $60 Force 5 bicycle lock. The once-dowdy manufacturer is now so in love with design as a selling advantage that it has turned the award-winning Design Continuum into its virtual in-house art department, and has entered into a long-term relationship with the Milwaukee Institute of Art and Design.

Master Lock maintains its long-standing, overall brand image with the marksman ad, which ran during twenty-one consecutive Super Bowls. Information-heavy point-of-purchase material located *where the consumer wants and expects it,* combined with visual cues in the product's design, allow Master Lock to leverage the brand. Master Lock retains its hold on the category, selling three locks every two seconds.

Or, alternatively, every two ticks on their impatient customers' shopping stopwatches.

Plumber as Helper

Over and over, examination of the impatient-shopping quadrant reveals success stories of manufacturers who are prospering by incorporating visual cues to their products' competitive advantage into the product itself. From the cord-retaining pigtail on Black & Decker's electric hedge trimmer to the vortex airflow on the Vornado fan, customers who are unwilling to spend hours shopping are being captured by a single picture . . . one that communicates a persuasive marketing message quickly and accurately to even the most impatient shopper.

But what about impatient shopping for services? Well, what could be more impatient than someone with a backed-up sink?

No one has yet demonstrated whether toilets and sinks actually break down more frequently on weekends, or just seem to. The likeliest explanation (for those unpersuaded by the conspiracy theory that plumbers actually design them that way, in order to take advantage of higher evening and weekend rates) is that more family members using the facilities place more, ahem, stress on the system during weekends. And, of course, more family members are available on weekends to notice. And notice they do. With the possible exception of electric power, no modern convenience is more truly convenient than running water. And while batteries and flashlights can substitute, in a pinch, for a loss of electricity, the alternatives to the flush toilet are downright primitive. So when the complicated system of pipes and valves that carry the ejecta of modern life into either a septic tank or sewer system stops working, phones start ringing. Impatiently.

But, since modern plumbing is both complicated and highly reliable, most users don't have much experience with the men and women trained to repair them; most people buy cars more often than they call a plumber. Recall that the defining characteristic of impatient-shopping phenomena is that, like an All-Pro tackle, they are mentioned only in connection with penalties, and you may be able to appreciate just how remarkable it is that one of the best-known corporate names in America got its name when Lettie Blanc took a look at the gizmo her husband, Sam, had cobbled together from a washing machine motor, a pair of roller-skate wheels, rotating knives, and a hunk of three-eighths-inch cable. She called it a "roto-rooter."

In 1933, when Lettie Blanc christened the first machine that could cut through pipe clogs without digging, the market for consumer plumbing services (as distinguished from steam fitting, pipe laying, and other more industrial aspects of the trade) was highly atomized and exclusively local. With the exception of Roto-Rooter Inc., now a part of Cincinnati-based Chemed Corp., it remains so today. It is also a business whose practitioners struggle daily with the realities of the impatient quadrant; the marketing plans promoted by specialty firms to plumbing contractors are thick with methods to break out of I'll-call-the-plumber-when-the-water-heater-breaks-and-not-before behavior. Typical strategies include letters timed to arrive just prior to the expiration of manufacturer warranties; flat-rate service contracts that effectively extend such warranties; discounts and rebates . . . in short, everything that trapped Goodyear into the lower-margin section of the impatient quadrant prior to the introduction of the Assurance.

And plumbing contractors are scarcely able to attract attention to their services with multimillion-dollar ad campaigns. Their combination of a tiny marketing budget and a local customer base would normally suggest a combination of radio and newspaper advertising, but these are luxuries when the time separating need awareness from action is measured in hours. Plumbers typically spend at least half their marketing dollars in the ultimate impatient advertising medium: the phone book.

Ever since the 1880s, when Reuben Donnelly founded what would become the largest printing corporation in the world by organizing local businesses into an alphabetical directory that charged those businesses for inclusion, the Yellow Pages (the legend is that the pages were printed in yellow for the simple reason that an earlier version ran out of white paper) have occupied ground zero for impatient shopping. And that means plumbers are quite rational in their dependence on the medium; in 2003, plumbing contractors were the Yellow Pages' ninth most popular search category . . . and, with 91 percent of those searches resulting in a purchase, plumbers were surpassed in their closing rate only by restaurants delivering pizza[15]—another archetypal impatient purchase.

Over the years, millions have been spent in researching the use and efficacy of the Yellow Pages. And while phone company deregulation—

what once was a local monopoly is now a free-for-all with as many as nine different editions competing for the larger local markets—and the rise of the Internet have changed the way in which consumers rely on the ubiquitous directories, that research remains instructive. It may not matter any longer to repeat the commonplace finding that four times as many people recall a quarter-page Yellow Pages advertisement as a regular listing, or that adding color to such an ad increases recall even more. However, two bits of data about use of the Yellow Pages, data that have remained consistent over time, are these:

1. Consumers using the Yellow Pages spend less than fifty seconds in a typical search.
2. They spend 6.4 seconds on the ad they act upon.[16]

Few people can recite the Pledge of Allegiance in seven seconds, much less absorb the information needed to make a decision that will cost hundreds of dollars. Planting an actionable idea that can bloom in less than seven seconds is a lot easier when it is sown on prepared ground. Roto-Rooter's preparation included the television advertising financed by its status as the only national competitor in its category, and the jingle familiar to every reader over the age of forty: "Call Roto-Rooter, that's the name, and away go troubles down the drain." But both ad and song depend on the same sort of corporate asset used to such great effect by Goodyear and Master Lock: the distinctive rotating blades that have featured in every Roto-Rooter ad ever made, a memorable, visible, and iconic claim on the attention of millions of impatient shoppers for more than fifty years.

• • •

If, after mapping your own customers onto the shopping matrix (see chapter 7), you find a large swath of them occupying space in the impatient quadrant, as in Figure 3-3, then the lessons of such impatient success stories as the Goodyear Assurance with TripleTred and Master Lock's Titanium locks should be stenciled on the insides of your eyelids:

1. If your customers can't understand what makes your product superior just by looking at it—at *it*, not at an advertisement, or a

IMPATIENT QUADRANT

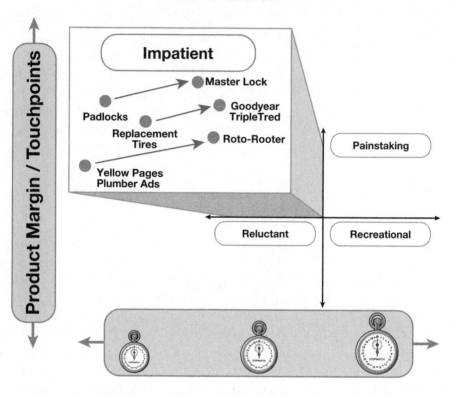

Figure 3-3

point-of-sale display, or a press release—you have an opportunity going unmet.

2. It doesn't matter how visually obvious you make your competitive advantage if your customer spends an extra minute in finding it. More than anywhere else on the shopping matrix, the impatient quadrant punishes products that demand search time.

3. On the other hand, the impatient quadrant rewards those marketers who can slow the ticking productively and ever so slightly in their favor—for example, by getting their prospective customers to look closely for a minute or two at the sidewall of the Goodyear Assurance with TripleTred. In stopwatch marketing terms, this represents a critical shift in customer behavior—moving them east (slowing the ticking on the stopwatch) and north (one more touchpoint and a few dollars more in margin!). For a

summary of the vision in this chapter—capitalizing on the quickly ticking stopwatch of impatient customers while finding ways to drive them to be a little more painstaking (and profitable)—see the illustration in Figure 3-3.

If this sounds familiar—if this describes what you know to be true of your own marketing challenges—then help is at hand. And you can skip ahead to Part Three of *Stopwatch Marketing*, and find out how to put stopwatch principles to work in your own business.

Chapter Four

Recreational Shopping

 Shopping as recreation, shopping as entertainment, shopping as theater . . . recreational shopping is frequently caricatured as the hobby of desperate housewives with too many hours to fill and too many credit cards to fill them with. So common is this cartoon version that recreational shopping seems, at first glance, to be an artifact of late capitalist affluence. It is, in fact, the oldest of all documented commercial behaviors. From the Athenian agora to Constantinople's Mese to Bronze Age market days, men *and* women have occupied themselves with shopping whose point is less the acquisition of a highly valued purchase (for that, see chapter 6, "Painstaking Shopping") but the shopping experience itself.

The recreational shopper cliché is no myth—if it were, parking on Rodeo Drive would be a *lot* easier. But we've learned that the most instructive success stories in the recreational quadrant are to be found not at Neiman Marcus or Bergdorf Goodman, but at businesses with relatively low margins, whose buyers are quite willing to spend time shopping. Great *potential* willingness, that is; the businesses that can teach the most about recreational shopping strategies are those that have entered the quadrant from somewhere else, usually, because they saw an opportunity to improve their margins relative to their competitors. They do this, generally, by improving the quality of their customers' shopping experience, because when consumers perceive shopping not as a cost, but as a *pleasure,* their stopwatches slow; sometimes, they even seem to stop entirely.

An encouragingly wide range of businesses are using stopwatch principles (whether or not they actually refer to them as such) to great effect within the recreational quadrant, from Charles Schwab to Apple Computer. But nowhere is the recreational shopping stopwatch on better display than in a three-year-old supermarket located in the Time Warner Center on the west side of New York City's Columbus Circle.

From Drudgery to Delight

Consider the shopping experience in a traditional supermarket. Decades of research make the case that buying groceries, with its combination of high time value and low margins, is firmly planted in the quadrant we call reluctant shopping. In our own work with consumers regarding their everyday shopping and usage habits, we have been astonished at the language they use to describe their time in a traditional supermarket. Words such as *time-consuming, avoid, dread, stupid,* and, much more worrisome (if you're running a supermarket chain), *disgust* and *hate* come up all the time. Consumers relate to typical supermarket shopping in much the same way they relate to other such favorite activities as filling out a loan application, completing a dental insurance claim form, and paying taxes. In a traditional supermarket, consumers are convinced that they won't find what they want, and, if they do, they won't find it in the right shape/size/pack configuration, and if it is, it will be priced too high—if, indeed, they can figure out what the price *is,* given the annoyance of comparing, for example, two jars of olives, one of which is priced by the pound, the other by the ounce. If they decide to pay for it anyway, they will wait in an unacceptably long line at the end of which they will be treated badly by a surly cashier with a room temperature IQ, whose linguistic fluency is limited to "credit or debit" and who will expect them to bag their own groceries. One of our consulting partners summarized it for a retailer client quite succinctly: "Most consumers come away from a supermarket retail experience feeling deflated and defeated." Avoiding this—customer deflation—is the first rule of the business.

In discussing Whole Foods Market, *supermarket* may not be the most accurate descriptor. With a "surprise" gourmet sampler or demonstration around every corner, an aisle in which customers can grind their own flour, and a 248-seat café, the store resides comfortably on the edge of retailing's innovation envelope. We're describing one of the flagships of the 190-store Whole Foods Market chain, of course. The chain is so unusual and customer experience so central, that many branches even house something called a "Chocolate Enrobing Station" where customers are invited to have anything in the store covered in you-know-what. No one has yet enrobed Whole Foods Market's wild-caught Alaska salmon, or its antibiotic-free beef tenderloin in the organically-grown-and-fair-traded cocoa mixture, but it can only be a matter of time. Ten blocks south, two tickets to a Broadway show will set a pair of theatergoers back any-where from $200 to $400. The same amount will—just about—fill one of Whole Foods's shopping carts, and it's a hard call which experience is more theatrical.

One thing that Whole Foods doesn't do is speed up the supermarket shopping experience. So why is it appearing in a book called *Stopwatch Marketing*?

To understand both the brilliance and the limitations of the Whole Foods recipe for success, it's necessary to spend a few moments thinking about the supermarket business . . . or, at least, what the supermarket business looked like, BWF (Before Whole Foods).

Though both Piggly Wiggly and A&P started replacing their traditional over-the-counter model with self-service groceries in the 1920s, the country's first true supermarket was the King Kullen that Michael Cullen opened in Jamaica, Queens, in 1930. Like all truly great inventions, it had its problems getting traction. In fact, it took the nation's explosive post–World War II growth—in pent-up demand after fifteen years of depression and war; in automobile ownership and travel; and in suburban construction—before the supermarket became as familiar a part of America's landscape as billboards. And for the same reason: As the number of automobile-owning households skyrocketed, so did the time efficiencies of one-stop shopping in places with large parking lots. As an alternative to separate visits to butcher, baker, greengrocer, and pharmacy, the super-market was the ultimate 1950s time-saver, at a moment when the supply of Americans' shopping time was starting its decades-long decline.

One of the reasons for the immediate and unchanged appeal of one-stop supermarkets is that grocery shopping, historically, has been as re-petitive as working on an assembly line . . . and nearly as much fun. Supermarkets were the answer to a classic reluctant purchase that none-theless needs to be made every week, and for fifty years, the corporations that owned them took it for granted that, travel distance being equal, the key to successfully luring the reluctant shopper was pricing strategy. The two competing strategies, which the academics who study them—more than you might think—long ago christened EDLP and HILO. Whether we realize it or not, all of us are the strategic objectives in the battle between the *Every Day Low Price* stores and their competitors, whose habit of using loss leaders and promotional offers to *Lower* the price on selected goods forces them to raise the prices on everything else even *Higher* . . . a battle that continues to this day.

It is a military (and marketing) truism that the battlefield determines the tactics. In this case, the battlefield—the customers—tends to fall into one of two types, each preferring one pricing model over the other. Those who like to cherry pick, buying only what's on sale, favor the HILO stores; those who don't want to cherry pick, shop EDLP. By extension, the appeal of one sort of pricing model increases in direct proportion to the size of the typical basket of goods with which our hypothetical shopper leaves the store: the bigger the basket, the better for Every Day Low Pricers.

However, a trap lurks at the end of that path. EDLP supermarkets (the most recent and successful models of which are the warehouse clubs like Costco, BJ's, and Sam's Club) can't afford to be too successful in luring customers away from their HILO competitors, since turning those shoppers into the big-basket variety forces the EDLP store to lower its prices to the level that approaches the price that the HILO store offers as a deal. Even Costco can afford to convince only so many Kroger customers to visit their markets before they find themselves selling milk below cost in order to compete. Long term, the pressure on margins is one reason that supermarkets net less than two cents on every sales dollar.

Except, that is, for Whole Foods Market.

The key ingredient in the success of Whole Foods can be found in a single line appearing in each of their last five annual reports: Whole Foods' corporate mission is to "satisfy *and delight* our customers" (emphasis added).

Delight? Large-basket or small-basket, one word that America's shoppers consistently fail to use in describing supermarket shopping is *delight. Drudgery?* Yes. *Work?* Certainly. Something to be done either as infrequently (large-basket) or quickly (small-basket) as possible? Absolutely. Whether supermarket shoppers are using an EDLP shortcut ("I can depend on the fact that my overall basket will cost less, and I don't have to price shop") or a HILO shortcut ("I'll come back when the ketchup is on sale"), the time costs of traditional supermarket shopping are high. The loyalty of supermarket shoppers is low, and their willingness to pay a premium is even lower.

But what if you could change the rules?

The brilliance of Whole Foods' current strategy is its recognition that the time cost of putting food in the refrigerator is not fixed, but subjective: that a significant number of customers would rather spend one hour roaming the aisles of a delightful supermarket than ten minutes pushing a cart through one that isn't. The movement of millions of American households from one quadrant to another—the slowing of their stop-watches—is one of the biggest stories in the history of retailing.

When it was founded in 1980, Whole Foods Market likely did not an-ticipate the phenomenon that has taken them to more than $5 billion in annual sales (with expectations of doubling that in the next ten years). John Mackey's first store, the ancestor of the Whole Foods empire, was, after all, called Safer Way Natural Foods, which strongly suggests that the original appeal was less delight than it was security: a fear of additives, corporate food manufacturing, and decidedly un-natural ingredients. It was a model with real appeal whose limits were frequently defined by the reach of college radio stations (Whole Foods started in the university town of Austin). As Harvey Hartman, a recognized expert in natural-food marketing, puts it, "Their original proxy for store locations was high edu-cation, therefore their connection to college towns." This college town strategy was quickly expanded to acquisitions, including Wellspring Gro-cery of Durham, North Carolina; Bread & Circus of Brookline, Cambridge, and Wellesley, Massachusetts; Mrs. Gooch's of Westwood, California; Al-legro Coffee of Boulder, Colorado. The communities surrounding Duke, Harvard, UCLA, and the University of Colorado were an ideal laboratory for Mackey's experiment. And, as is often the case, the experiment pro-duced unexpected results. Many of the company's customers proved will-ing to pay a premium for the Whole Foods Seal of Approval—the explicit promise that "if we put it on our shelves, you can put it in your body." This is a pretty important advantage all by itself, given the time required to parse the health claims of sixty different breakfast cereals, for example. But even more significant, in the long run, was the discovery that far more people than anyone thought were ready to take the road to healthy living if the route were as much fun as going to the mall. They wouldn't even notice if the route took longer, or cost more.

Delightful.

After twenty-five years of building gorgeous pyramids of organically grown melons, of hiring restaurant-quality chefs to produce free-range chicken dijonnaise, and fifteen separate acquisitions later, Whole Foods

Market's transformation into a supermarket-as-theater is complete.* With more than two-thirds of its revenue coming from high-margin perishables (the typical number for a traditional supermarket is less than half) and by far the highest prices for packaged and prepared foods in the business, it's little wonder that Whole Foods is showing both rapid growth and profit margins that are nearly twice that of the category's average. The announcement, in February 2007, of the planned acquisition of the 110 outlets owned by Wild Oats—a retailer whose strategic positioning was far closer to the health food roots of the category—simply confirmed what had become impossible to ignore: Whole Foods' mastery of the recreational quadrant.

Were Whole Foods Market the only player in this migration of supermarket purchases from reluctant to recreational quadrants, you might be forgiven for wondering at its significance. After all, though Whole Foods' annual sales certainly add up to a respectable piece of change ($6 billion), it's not much more than a rounding error to the more than $500 billion that Americans spend on groceries every year. While a single Whole Foods Market store can turn an impressive weekly nut—the store average is $593,000—that number can be produced by stealing fewer than two thousand households from the competition.

There is, however, another chain that has made a traditionally reluctant shopping experience much more fulfilling, even enjoyable: Wal-Mart. Or, more precisely, Wal-Mart Supercenters.

As of this writing, the 2,326 Wal-Mart Supercenters, astonishingly, account for more than 20 percent of U.S. grocery sales.† And, though their presentation is wildly different from Whole Foods, they share the most important characteristic: Both, in the words of grocery store analyst Peter Murane, "are fast becoming destination attractions for consumers." Cus-

---

* The company has not entirely forgotten its countercultural roots. The 2005 Whole Foods Market, Inc. Annual Report reproduces—in a section on its employees—Abraham Maslow's hierarchy of values, with an urge that all the company's stakeholders ascend to the nirvana of self-actualization. The accompanying caption reads "Creative love by awakened humans will transform and heal our world."

† While Wal-Mart-level dominance seems a creation of the modern world, in the 1920s and 1930s, A&P was, in percentage terms, even larger: five times more stores and 80 percent of the supermarket business (Charles Fishman, "The Wal-Mart You Don't Know," *Fast Company,* December 2003).

tomers of Wal-Mart Supercenters can't grind their own flour, or enrobe strawberries in artisanal chocolate . . . but they can eat at an in-store McDonald's, browse sporting goods, get manicures, and have their eyes examined. They don't think of a trip to Wal-Mart as drudgery any more than do Whole Foods shoppers.

The reasons are not hard to figure out: Though that annual grocery bill of $500 billion+ is an all-time high in absolute terms, it's an all-time *low* when measured as a percentage of Americans' annual income. A family growing up in the 1950s was spending more than 17 percent of its income on food; the number today is 6 percent, and dropping. As price decisions become a less and less important component of food-buying decisions, consumers are, more and more, deciding where to shop on other grounds. They're deciding to shop where the perceived time cost—*not* the actual time cost—is lowest. They're going where their stopwatches are slowest. They're shopping recreationally.

Wal-Mart continues to grow, prosper, and, indeed, frighten its competitors. This comes up in nearly every conversation we have with clients. When we ask clients what's really on their minds and what's keeping them up at night, every client of our firm who deals in consumer products and services has the same answer: "What do I do about Wal-Mart?" If the client is a manufacturer of consumer products, then Wal-Mart now accounts for at least 20 percent of their business, a degree of manufacturer dependency and retailer leverage that they find, literally, frightening. If the client is a retailer, well, the concern is much more visceral: "How do I keep Wal-Mart from beating my brains out?"

The actions of local community groups, municipalities, and even chambers of commerce in attempting to block the entry of Wal-Mart into their communities have been well documented and publicized. As consultants who celebrate effective marketing and business models, well aware of the shortcomings of traditional supermarkets mentioned above, we have always been puzzled by this attempt by local communities to preserve their traditional (deflating and defeating!) local retailers. A little research and inspection makes the answer quite clear: Wal-Mart has cracked the nut on a very difficult challenge, achieving two triumphs simultaneously—they are the ultimate EDLP retailer who *also* provides a pleasant shopping experience. There are, literally, hundreds of thousands of pages of consumer research detailing the fact that consumers' immediate word associations with Wal-Mart are *low price* and *discount*.

Meanwhile, the low cost structure allows Wal-Mart to generate the funds to hire and train greeters to meet consumers as they enter the store. Wal-Mart's most loyal customers, free of the knowledge that shopping at Wal-Mart was an aesthetically impoverishing experience, consistently fail to describe it as unpleasant.

It gives pleasure. Maybe even delight.

This, of course is the key to understanding Wal-Mart's impressive awareness of its customers' willingness to let their respective stopwatches run. Though it sometimes seems that Wal-Marts are as ubiquitous as gas stations, there are really only 2,326 in a country with more than 34,000 other supermarkets (and more than 100,000 stores selling groceries of some kind). This means that Wal-Mart shoppers are, on average, closer to at least a dozen competitors . . . and they still choose Wal-Mart.

The challenge of convincing customers to drive an additional ten miles in order to shop locally is even more acute for the 190+ Whole Foods Markets. Most midsize cities (defined as big enough to attract a baseball team, but too small to bid for the Olympics; examples include Kansas City, Pittsburgh, and Minneapolis) have only one or two Whole Foods, often located near the major university. On the other hand, these cities have hundreds of traditional supermarkets. This means that a significant number of Whole Foods shoppers are, quite literally, driving past *fifty* supermarkets or more for their once-a-month uplifting experience.

Now *that's* a slowly ticking stopwatch.

And it's full of touchpoints and catchpoints for those manufacturers lucky enough to be represented on Whole Foods' shelves. One of the most highly valued features that Whole Foods provides to its consumers is the implied endorsement of everything on the shelf: Consumers believe—quite correctly—that Whole Foods wouldn't think of putting anything in that is not natural or organic, or that is pumped full of chemicals or preservatives, or that is the result of highly industrialized, pesticide- and chemicals-driven agriculture and food processing, from Third World dictatorships where the workers of the world are terribly exploited. Whole Foods shoppers can engage not only in pleasurable shopping, but shopping that is *completely guilt-free.* This is nontrivial: Much research over the years has indicated that consumers give tremendous lip service to this need to avoid guilt but, in the rush, complexity, and hassles of their everyday lives, are unwilling to act on it. Convenience (the traditional supermarket's original advantage) trumped the otherwise huge investment of time in traveling across town to a small health food co-op where the most visible fresh produce was spotted organic bananas and the packaged goods were uniformly unfamiliar. This is why the so-called health food store industry was for so long quite tiny and consisted more of vitamin supplements than food.

Whole Foods changed all that by making the old-fashioned health food store not only trustworthy—the store's explicit message is that "we [Whole Foods] have already done the research and guarantee this stuff is natural, good for you, and good for the earth"—but familiar: It does, after all, look just like a traditional supermarket, with wide aisles, clean checkout counters, and uniformed employees.

Morphing health food stores into big supermarket-like natural-foods markets was necessary to achieve the volume, profitability, and economies of scale while legitimizing a traditionally mom-and-pop industry. It was, however, insufficient. To achieve their current level of success, Whole Foods had to also deliver a retail experience that borders on the addictive. Our research on Whole Foods customers shows that they view the store rather differently than traditional supermarkets: terms such as *love, delight,* and *can't wait* come up all the time. Digging deeper, we found that these real emotions did not spring from the big beautiful stores; in marketing jargon, the excitement of a new Whole Foods store opening only buys trial: Consumers would have tried Whole Foods once, but they would never have come back if the only retail therapy they got was a big pretty store. This is the twenty-first century, after all, and consumers have lots of options for big beautiful stores and other sensory delights beyond a pyramid of organic vegetables.

What we found was that what so many frequent Whole Foods shoppers find so exciting about the store is that they feel they will constantly find something new, different, exciting, and fun. What they find, in short, is theater. And it looks to be quite a while before Whole Foods runs out of consumers willing to invest both drive time and shopping and knowingly pay a premium price for the theatrical experience. Harvey Hartman summarizes all this by pointing out that "discovery is a compelling experience in a customer's journey [along with] sharing that experience with like-minded friends in the customer's social network. In addition, [Whole Foods'] halo is not necessarily 'good for you,' it can be very indulgent. So it's a community where natural and indulgent coexist under a 'high quality food experience.'"

The implications are scary indeed for traditional grocery stores that run the risk of becoming huge 7-Elevens, used only for small-basket, last-minute items. The dangers of being neither fish nor fowl in the new Wal-Mart + Whole Foods universe are real. But so is the danger of assuming that adding layer upon layer of theatrical experience to a commercial transaction is a can't-miss strategy to transform a low-margin reluctant shopping experience into a high-margin recreational one. It's not so long ago that Internet-based retailers like Boo.com, Value America, eToys, Pets.com, and Kozmo.com burned through hundreds of billions of venture capital dollars trying to build stickiness into their websites, offering the unwary web surfer everything from music to games to interactive tests, all in an attempt to keep potential buyers online long enough to type a credit card number. Almost all of them, from Kozmo to Excite, misunderstood both the attractions of web-based entertainment, and the willingness of significant numbers of buyers to migrate their *consumption* to the recreational quadrant as delivered on the web. Consumers migrated to the websites, all right; they just didn't buy much once they got there, not because the sites failed to be entertaining enough, but because the products themselves, whether pet food or board games, were no different from those available elsewhere.

That can scarcely be said of Apple Computer . . . or, more accurately, Apple's iTunes Music Store, which launched on April 28, 2003, almost precisely three years after the Internet bubble exploded, taking with it nearly two trillion dollars in delusional stock market value. It may seem that the worlds of Whole Foods' organic produce and Apple's Internet commerce are separated by distances best measured in light years, but in fact success for both companies depended on overcoming the same challenge: persuading a mass audience to behave like hobbyists.

As marketers, we often use terms like *hobbyists, loyalists, fanatics,* and *addicts* interchangeably. Whatever the specific or most useful moniker chosen, we have found the most useful definition to be this: Hobbyists are a subspecies of recreational shoppers. Every product or service has *some* consumers who love it so much that they wallow in its every aspect, and thoroughly enjoy every minute spent shopping for it. Most of Goodyear's tires are purchased impatiently, but there really are some people who can't drive past a tire store without checking out the new merchandise. The great insight of John Mackey was that the demographic cohort who had spent decades making fun of their neighbors' obsession with varieties of spelt and rennetless cheese had become old enough to start worrying about their health, and affluent enough to pay a premium for the foods that might preserve it. By eliminating the barriers that deterred them from traditional organic groceries, Mackey turned off or slowed down their recreational stopwatches. And got very rich.

iWorld

Steve Jobs was already rich in January of 2001 when he announced that Apple's new strategy was to make the Macintosh the digital hub for its owners' lifestyles. At the time, the hub contained spokes labeled photos, calendar, and movies but the only one that really counted was called music. Jobs's use of the word *lifestyles* was quite accurate: in our work with clients we often refer to Apple as a technology lifestyle brand, comparing it, for instance, to Ralph Lauren. We get a lot of head-nodding from our clients and, very often, a request like, "How can we do that?"

Ever since the days of the Apple II, the company had retained a powerful appeal among some buyers, and by the time Jobs returned to the company he had founded, as many as 78 percent of new buyers in the segment of self-described creative computer users were buying Macintosh computers.[1] Though that segment then represented a market share for Mac of less than 3 percent (down from more than 10 percent ten years earlier), the experience serving the demands of creatives was an underappreciated source of value. Better than any of its competitors in the computer hardware business, Apple had mastered what observers call "churn,"[2] which means managing the product cycle introduction so that it remains fast enough to generate new profits, but not so fast that potential buyers opt out (the best-known violators are Sony and Palm). Staying aware of new product developments in the Apple world was one of the ways that Macintosh owners, far more than the users of Windows-based PCs, defined themselves. It takes a lot of time to keep up-to-date on the latest Apple product lines, but what is time when you're having fun?

It's recreational shopping, that's what it is.

Those recreational shoppers—those hobbyists—were, like the Marines, both few and proud. The first practical step in changing the behavior of the non-Macintosh world was the announcement, ten months after Jobs's digital hub speech at the biennial Macworld convention in San

Francisco*, of the first iPod, a $399 digital music player designed in less than a year by Apple's chief hardware engineer, Jon Rubenstein.

Many, if not most, analysts trying to explain the iPod's appeal give priority to the machine's design, which is pretty spectacular. But the sales curve of products that depend on novel design typically slopes seriously downward five years after introduction, and nearly seven-eighths of all the 100 million (as of this writing) iPods ever sold have been purchased in the last twenty-four months. Which is why the *really* important date in the history of Apple's recreational shopping triumph is April 28, 2003, the date the iTunes Music Store opened for business. In the store's first eighteen hours, 275,000 songs, at $.99 apiece, were sold; 1 million in its first week. By February 23, 2006, 1 billion songs and 15 million videos had been downloaded from the iTunes store. In a bit more than a thousand days, the number of iTunes downloads has doubled just about every month. Perhaps accidentally, the world's most celebrated boomer billionaire had figured out something about the music-buying habits of his birth cohort that turned out to apply to everyone else. Traditionally, the *enjoyment* of music (a slowly ticking stopwatch exercise) was differentiated entirely from the *purchase* of music (a quickly ticking get-me-in-and-out-of-the-store-fast experience). But, what Apple has now demonstrated is that if the price is low enough, and the process is simple enough, consumers will *buy* billions of songs, essentially at the same time that they are *enjoying* the songs.

For at least two decades before that April 2003 launch of the iTunes Music Store, "real" music sales had been in decline, a decline masked by the replacement of millions of LPs and cassettes with compact discs. The primary reason for the decline was the historical fact that the recreational shopping for recorded music is profoundly age-linked. As the generation that had bought Smokey Robinson and Bruce Springsteen got older, they stopped shopping for music recreationally, and one reason was their discomfort with the shopping environment; the hostility of the clerks in the movie *High Fidelity* is an only slightly exaggerated version of the real thing.

But the hobbyist audience hadn't vanished. It just got older. iTunes'

---

* The notion of a computer company as cult is a strange one, indeed. But anyone who doubts the avidity of Apple's hobbyist appeal is invited to attend one of these biennial extravaganzas.

phenomenal success was driven partly by technology—a confluence of broadband Internet availability with a music industry panicked by the peer-to-peer sharing of music—and partly by demographics.

Observers were initially mixed on the value of Jobs's digital hub. Because the current gross margin on iPod sales was estimated to be 22 percent,[3] and the company's overall margin is about 29 percent—still a healthy lead over the much larger Dell Computer's 18 percent—the iPod's runaway success, in the minds of some analysts, actually weakened Apple's margins. However, while Apple's revenue has increased 29 percent (2005–2006 quarter-to-quarter), gross margins, as of January 2007, have reached 31 percent, up from 27 percent during the previous year's comparable performance.

The reasons are simple algebra: Apple retains 35 percent on music sales (iTunes downloads). At 5 million songs a day,[4] downloads account for several hundred million dollars in gross margin annually.

For a company like Apple, this is not immaterial to its total financial health, but it may not matter. Steve Jobs has been quoted as saying, "We would like to break even [or] make a little bit of money [on the iTunes Music Store] but it's not a money maker." What *is* making money for the company is its sale of iPods, which represent nearly a quarter of the company's revenues, and whose sales track almost precisely with the growth of iTunes. As a case in point, 14 million iPods were sold in the first quarter of 2006; as iTunes increased from 800 million downloads to more than a billion, iPod sales—with gross margins nearly four times higher than the sale of music—increased, quarter-to-quarter, to 22 million. Those sales are a direct outgrowth of the time that users are spending at the iTunes store; Apple estimates that one third of all song purchases are preceded by a thirty-second sampling, with a sampling-to-purchase ratio of approximately four-to-one. This adds up to more than 2,000 *years* of listening time, not counting podcasts, television shows, and who knows what. That's a lot of very slow-moving stopwatches. To repeat, Apple has found a way to turn *enjoyment* (slow ticking) into continued opportunities to *purchase*, whether the purchase is a $.99 download or a $100 iPod.

Naturally, this strategy delivers a lot of profit. For the first quarter of 2007, Apple reported earnings of $1 billion on revenues of $7.1 billion (after reporting earnings of $565 million, then the highest in company history, only a year previously).

Another, perhaps even more successful, investment in recreational shopping has already paid off for Apple. By May of 2006, the company's retail stores—the first two of which were inaugurated in May of 2001— had grown to 147, with forty more opening every year. The stores, with free help provided by noncommissioned salespeople and free Internet access, have become recreational destinations for millions of customers who use the stores to check e-mail, surf the web, and write the Great American Novel or Screenplay. As a result, the stores are producing nearly $4,000 of revenue per square foot.[5] That number is probably heading nowhere but up with the July 2007 introduction of the most eagerly awaited product in the history of consumer electronics: the iPhone.

As of this writing, it remains too soon to evaluate the long-term success of Apple's web-surfing, music-playing, photograph-storing smartphone, though the short-term numbers are startling: more than 750,000 units sold in the first two days on sale, with gross margins (estimated from the cost of components) somewhere north of 55 percent on the $600 unit. It is also not yet time for a verdict on whether Apple has changed forever the relationship between cell phone manufacturers and service providers (for more about the cell phone industry—a classic reluctant shopping experience—see page 76). It is not too early, however, to observe that such success can be best understood as an economy-size dose of recreational marketing. The iPhone's irresistible interface, even when demonstrated on the company's website, has already turned the smartphone-plus-PDA from a hobbyist's toy (or, more accurately, addiction; they don't call them "crackberrys" for nothing) into the most lusted-after piece of consumer electronics since . . . well, since the iPod.

Apple's successful retail stores represent another venue for consumers to enjoy and sample the latest from Apple's labs. When consumers are hanging out at the Apple Store, their stopwatches have clearly slowed. By comparison, when consumers go on a competitor's website, they are likely to be short of time (quickly ticking) and they are certainly not enjoying a breakthrough tourist destination retail experience. Hence, as noted above, Apple's gross margins are as much as ten percentage points higher than those of Dell.

• • •

Both the iTunes Music Store and Whole Foods Market—and, perhaps especially, Wal-Mart Supercenters—are examples of what journalist and business writer Christopher Anderson called, in a 2004 article in *Wired* magazine, "long-tail commerce." The long tail is a popularized and memorable term for the sort of statistical distribution in which the aggregate of low-frequency events outnumbers the aggregate of high-frequency events. One of the best-known examples of what economists call a Pareto distribution is the frequency of appearance of words in a typical book. Most frequent English words are conjunctions like *the, but,* and so on . . . but low-frequency words (like *frequency*) will, *in the aggregate,* take up far more of the total text even though no one of them is nearly as popular as the simple conjunctions and articles.* In a supermarket, milk may be the most popular item . . . but the anchovies, garbage bags, deodorant, frozen pizzas, and imported preserves will, in the aggregate, generate more revenue. And, on iTunes (and Amazon, and Netflix, and many others) far more revenue is generated by the books, songs, and movies ranked 51–999 than those occupying places 1–50.

The importance of the long tail to the recreational shopping quadrant is, upon reflection, obvious.

The long tail (also the title for Anderson's excellent book, published in July 2006) is mostly supply-driven: because they are able to maintain effectively unlimited inventories, Amazon and Netflix can carry many more SKUs than the largest bricks-and-mortar competitor. But this misses the importance of demand. An unlimited inventory of anything is useless, from a commercial standpoint, unless a buyer can find something to buy. That, in turn, is a function of time: How much will she spend browsing your infinitely large inventory?

The key to making the long tail wag profitably is keeping the buyer's attention until demand can be translated to transaction. The most important stopwatch principle in the recreational quadrant is this: The longer a potential buyer spends shopping, the greater likelihood of finding even a low-frequency item. Note that the time must be spent *shopping,* not simply being entertained.

Both Whole Foods and Apple's iTunes/iPod have succeeded (whether opportunistically or strategically) by identifying a niche that offered tremendous potential within the long tail of potential purchases, but that was ripe for expansion because existing competitors with the same supply

---

* This is sometimes known as Zipf's Law, after the linguist George Zipf who first noted it.

profile were unable or unwilling to migrate into that niche. The challenge met by both Whole Foods and Apple was simultaneously to expand a hobbyist market, and to change the behavior of nonhobbyists so that it mimics that of hobbyists.

In even simpler terms, the route to recreational shopping success taken by John Mackey's Whole Foods and Steve Jobs's Apple lay in attracting impatient consumers (in the case of Whole Foods and iPod) and painstaking ones (in the case of Apple Computer). As it happens, another opportunity—perhaps the richest of all—lay in attracting consumers from a business that had almost never left the reluctant quadrant: investing.

Talk to Chuck

Though people have been investing in commodities for at least five millennia—some of the earliest examples of the written word are Mesopotamian cuneiform tablets recording the transfer of ownership of grain shipments, the Sumerian equivalent of the paper slips that cover the floor of Chicago's Mercantile Exchange—the first true buying and selling of stocks in commercial enterprises dates from only 1602, when the Dutch East Indian Company issued its first shares on what would become the Amsterdam Stock Exchange.

For most of the next 400 years, stock market investing was almost exclusively an activity reserved for the wealthiest members of the world's richest communities. As late as 1952, a mere 4 percent of the U.S. population owned shares of stock. Even after more than twenty years of almost nonstop economic expansion, that number was only a bit over 15 percent when the SEC, in 1975, put an end to the fixed brokerage commissions that had enriched generations of traditional stockbrokers.

Almost simultaneously, one of those traditional brokers, based in San Francisco, started offering discounted, commission-free stock trading. Its thirty-eight-year-old head was a Stanford MBA named Charles R. Schwab.

The explosion in stock ownership ignited by the SEC's deregulation, and the concomitant growth of Schwab—the world's largest discount brokerage, now managing more than $800 billion in 7.5 million accounts—is best explained by attending to the actual product being bought and sold by what now adds up to nearly half the adult population of the United States. It isn't stocks, or bonds, or commodities futures; it's information.

Economic historians have long understood this, of course. And so have the stockbrokers who have been persuading investors to turn one form of wealth into another since the days of the Dutch East India Company. A broker's stock in trade is information . . . some datum or other about a potential investment that will convince a potential investor—a shopper—to buy.

For centuries, those shoppers have been entrenched in the reluctant quadrant . . . as any traditional retail broker who remembers making cold calls will testify. With a business challenge only slightly less difficult than selling life insurance, stockbrokers must overcome the classic avoidance behaviors of reluctant shopping: the awareness that a wrong decision is far more dangerous than a correct decision is beneficial; the fear of being ripped off. Everyone knows that they really *should* reallocate investments, save for college, plan for retirement, and so forth. They are also completely reluctant to spend sufficient time on shopping for the right approach because, well, it's just so tedious. As with all businesses that depend on reluctant shoppers, from men's apparel to aluminum siding, the most important element in the marketing mix is what used to be called "old-fashioned selling" . . . the touchpoint, usually no more than a few minutes long, between salesperson and customer. Quite properly, then, the largest marketing expense is usually the commission paid to salespeople.

The opportunity for stockbrokers presented by the elimination of fixed brokerage commissions thirty years ago was really a chance to cut a marketing expense that was unneeded and unvalued by a significant niche. That niche consists of those investors who had no use for advice, largely because of another innovation of the mid-1970s: mutual funds indexed to the larger stock market. The first such fund, the First Index Investment Trust, was launched in 1976; its success—it is now known as the Vanguard 500 Index Fund, and is one of the world's largest, managing more than $100 billion—was a testament to the belief that no one possessed information valuable enough to warrant the paying of large commissions. The economist's name for this belief is the Efficient Markets Hypothesis.

First articulated in an article titled "Efficient Capital Markets," published in the *Journal of Finance* in 1970 and written by a University of Chicago economist named Eugene Fama, the Efficient Markets Hypothesis, or EMH, argues that information is so rapidly aggregated that it shows up almost immediately in the price of any traded stock, and as a consequence all fluctuations in stock market shares are fundamentally random.

Though this simplifies his original theory immensely, it is generally true that, if EMH was correct, no package of individual stocks, however cleverly selected, can outperform the overall market in which they are traded over time. Put simply, no one beats the market over time, but in America, the market does pretty well over time. The best portfolio is one that, quite literally, matches the overall market.

The implications for investors are enormous: one needn't spend a lot of time researching investments, studying balance sheets, timing buys and sells, and so on. *You no longer need information; you just need an index fund.* Consequently, for nearly two decades, large index funds and other no-brainer investment vehicles, fueled by the tax advantages of 401(k)s and IRAs, grew at a frightening clip. By 2000, nearly 50 percent of American households owned stocks, generally through mutual funds.

And a huge percentage of those households also owned something else: a connection to the Internet. In 1997, 3 million individuals were actively investing online; two years later, that number had doubled.

However, this notion that you don't really have to do anything or even know anything (just buy an index fund) is highly counterintuitive to a large segment of the investing public: "You can't make money investing on the basis of very expensively acquired information???" So, that large segment of investors continues to seek information. They generally refer to this information as "hot tips." And this means that while you can't make money investing on the basis of information, you can (if you have a broker's license) make money selling the information, indirectly, by using it to prompt transactions.

While the Efficient Markets Hypothesis is a purely rational theory, there exists a contrarian point of view known as Behavioral Finance, articulated by the economists Daniel Kahneman (of Princeton) and Amos Tversky (of Stanford). Their work demonstrated that actual behavior can't depend on the collection and comparison of all relevant data. Instead, investors—all shoppers, really—use *heuristics,* the kind of simplifying patterns that depend on finding a small piece of information that can stand in for all the other information that can't efficiently be discovered in real time.

Without heuristics, getting through the day would be virtually impossible. Heuristics tell an urban pedestrian to be more wary of six twenty-year-old men carrying baseball bats than six nuns; they might be on their way to a softball game, but the pattern is disquieting. In the same way, people are more likely to avoid a car whose previous model gave them trouble, than to evaluate the entire body of data available from *Consumer Reports* and the EPA. Heuristics are great time-savers. When they're right. When they're wrong, as they frequently are, they waste more than time.

Investors are notorious practitioners—and victims—of the frequent fallacies inherent in heuristics. Investors often act on the most personal or recent—not the most relevant—information. For example, what Kahneman and Tversky called the Law of Small Numbers, explains the predilection on the part of most people to overstate the importance of findings taken from unreasonably small samples. Your Camry might have been a lemon, but it was only 1 of more than 400,000 sold that year. A government report announcing change in employment statistics, or housing starts, or the Consumer Price Index frequently triggers major buying and selling in the stock and bond markets. The "availability bias" overvalues the importance of recent events, while the "representativeness bias" exploits the tendency of humans to assume that superficial similarities mean more than they should; a harmless Scarlet King snake is virtually identical to the deadly coral snake.

In combination, these biases explain the otherwise unaccountable attraction exerted on investors by the hottest funds, stocks, and advisers. If investors actually acted on a belief in efficient markets, they would know that anything that *overperforms* in Year 1 is far more likely to *underperform* in Year 2. Regression to the mean is no match for the availability bias.

For Schwab, the conceptual journey from a belief in EMH to Behavioral Finance was more than an intellectual exercise. EMH reduced brokers, including Schwab, to mere processors of monthly contributions to 401(k)s containing index funds. Behavioral Finance got them back in the game of providing—and profiting from—information. By the late 1990s, Schwab had finally absorbed the lesson of their competitors in traditional brokerages: while customers may claim to dislike spending time listening to a broker's pitch, they tend to make fewer trades without one; fewer touchpoints mean lower commissions. The Internet promised brokers they could add touchpoints—add *time*—back into the investing experience while finessing both the cost of traditional brokers and the resistance of new investors. With the launch of Schwab.com, the brokerage that had prospered by offering no advice—an implicit endorsement of the Efficient Markets Hypothesis—departed from its roots in dramatic fashion, though they had done so at what seems, in retrospect, a dangerous time. Between

1998 and 2000, more than 140 online investment companies registered with the regulatory bodies charged with representing them; by 2001, only 6 were still in business.[6] Schwab.com, which integrated the company's heavily advice-driven Mutual Fund OneSource program into it, was one of them.

One of the reasons is that Schwab, unlike the hundred failed online investing ventures of the bubble years, applied stopwatch marketing principles (presumably without calling them that) to their business, which meant building around consumer behavior, rather than supplier costs. In this, they are unusual; we've learned over and over again that the advantages of online investing are understood differently by suppliers than their consumers. When asked about their online investing sites, representatives of companies like Merrill Lynch, Vanguard, and Marketrade.com cite "higher levels of efficiency." They mention "lower costs." Sometimes the telling point is the "no fixed costs of maintaining bricks-and-mortar locations."

But the most frequent reason given by investors for selecting a particular broker is not expense, but rather "ease of access *at any time*" (emphasis added).[7] This is not because they are impatient, or reluctant, or even painstaking. The typical online investor spends hours weekly on sites like Schwab.com for reasons that can only be called recreational. They behave less like fortune hunters than the folks whose idea of a perfect Sunday afternoon is a trip to an outlet mall. The "access at any time," so highly valued by online investors, places them squarely in the world of shoppers going online for everything from sporting goods to high-end electronics. Numerous investigators have discovered that online research (i.e., shopping) peaks at different times of the day than transactions (i.e., buying), whether the commodity is a digital video recorder or shares in General Electric; a study that separated click-through rates and conversion rates by sites selling merchandise and investment advice found the latter peaking between the hours of 9 A.M. and 8 P.M. and the former peaking between 8 P.M. and 2 A.M.[8] One might as well call them the hours on a recreational stopwatch.

A typical visitor to Schwab.com enters the investing world's most popular recreational quadrant. Those visitors consistently report spending their evenings riveted to their computer screens on Schwab's Market Insight, reading articles on everything from commodities prices in emerging markets to the impact of presidential election cycles on the stock market (many written by Chief Investment Strategist Liz Ann Sonders, tellingly a former regular on *Wall $treet Week With Louis Rukeyser,* which spent thirty-five years entertaining investors on television). They occupy themselves with the investment equivalent of interactive video gaming, massaging hypothetical portfolios until they match a particular risk profile. Like fairy tale misers hiding in their cellars counting gold, Schwab.com visitors can watch their fortunes rise and fall, and even count down the days until a retirement target is reached.

And they can talk to Chuck.

The final piece of Schwab's recreational strategy integrates the brand's old-media advertising with its new-media shopping experience. The "Talk to Chuck" television campaign that went national in early 2006 features animated characters expressing general dissatisfaction with traditional stockbrokers. One wonders, thinking about all the conversations with his former broker that resulted in a trade—and therefore commissions— "Were we discussing my children's future? Or his?" Another asks for a "dog-meter" to evaluate poor performers. In concert with a print campaign with provocative epigraphs like "Waiting for the market to come back? It isn't waiting for you" and "'My house is worth a million' is not a retirement plan" the campaign drives invites visitors to the Schwab.com website, where they can, if not talk to Chuck, listen to him, as the star of seven separate video presentations.

The campaign, and the stopwatch marketing principles it embodies, is the brainchild of EVP/Chief Marketing Officer Becky Saeger and Ben Stuart, VP of Brand Strategy and Advertising, but its inspiration is clearly Charles Schwab himself, who returned in 2004 to the company he founded, and quickly restored its original mission, which might be best understood as "the more time they spend with us, the more money they spend with us." The advertising campaign has achieved what ad campaigns are supposed to achieve; it has done precisely what it was designed to do:

1. Find investors who are unhappy—Schwab calls them "money in motion"[9]—with the time they spend with their existing brokers.
2. Attract them to the website, where they can spend their evening hours (and more) finding dozens of highly appealing touchpoints, including— of course—the videos of Chuck himself.
3. Send them, during the daylight hours (when the markets, not at all

coincidentally, are open), to Schwab Portfolio Solutions, where they can invest in equities like the mutual funds managed by Schwab, using their own proprietary ratings system; like Schwab's index funds, which they call MarketTrack Portfolios; or Schwab Target Funds, an age-based fund that automatically redeploys investments based on a particular target date, with a progressively lower risk profile as the target date, typically retirement, approaches.

Since the return of Charles Schwab, and the creation of the investing world's most recreational strategy, the company's performance has been outstanding. By the end of 2005, Schwab had posted its biggest quarterly profit ever: $207 million.

· · ·

Opportunities for success in the recreational quadrant, then, are available to a wide range of businesses. It includes retailers like Whole Foods, but also more obvious recreational shopping triumphs like Barnes & Noble and Starbucks; it is a rule of thumb that any commercial establishment with couches in it is occupying space in the recreational quadrant. It also, less intuitively, rewards manufacturers like Apple and service providers like Charles Schwab. When it comes to recreational shopping, we see stopwatch marketing principles at their most basic: More time equals more money.

A more nuanced view of these disparate success stories reveals even more. Each of the recreational quadrant opportunities illustrated in Figure 4-1 originally presented themselves as migrations from other quadrants.

Whole Foods turned impatient grocery shoppers into indulgent the-atergoers; Apple gave impatient music buyers back their youth; Charles Schwab persuaded reluctant investors that their evenings would be well spent reading about fixed annuities; and Wal-Mart became the ultimate EDLP retailer that *also* provides a pleasant shopping experience. Each of them succeeded by convincing huge numbers of plain-vanilla consumers to behave like hobbyists.

When we meet with clients, we frequently remind them that every business has hobbyists, those consumers who shop recreationally often for the most unlikely stuff. For manufacturers and retailers outside the

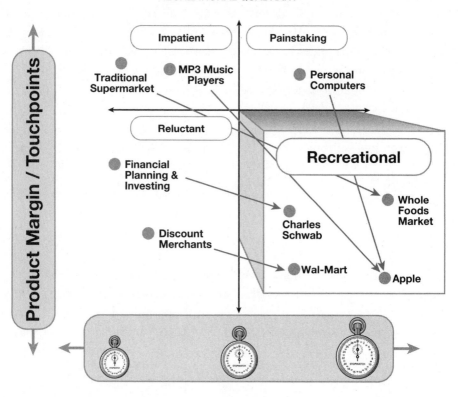

Figure 4-1

core hobbyist areas like sporting goods and books, this audience tends to remain peripheral.

But sometimes, consumers can be lured from periphery to core. John Mackey's most valuable insight was seeing consumers wearing Earth Shoes or Birkenstocks spending hours in the aisles of old-style health food shops and imagining them transformed into more fashionable—and prosperous—Betsey Johnsons, or even Pradas. It's the sort of revelation on which fortunes can be made. There is no systematic way to pull recreational gold out of the ocean of commercial possibilities, but we've worked with enough clients, and seen enough examples, to suggest where some of the best fishing can be found.

Some of it is overseas. Over and over, we've seen other regions of the world, usually Europe, serve as test markets for this particular stopwatch phenomenon . . . the mass-ification of recreational behavior. Victoria's Secret is a classic import of European recreational behavior, specifically the French obsession with the lingerie produced by companies like Groupe Chantelle. The margins on a bra purchased after half an hour of shopping—and experiencing the boutique environment at Victoria's Secret—are significantly higher than one purchased after two minutes at the local discount store on the way home from work. The idea of luxe lingerie is actually the most important example in another book, *Trading Up*, which focuses on the power—and payback—of convincing a large number of middle-class Americans to pursue new luxury goods.

Sometimes the opportunities are closer to home. Dozens of times, we see companies (clients and nonclients) whose industry is largely defined by impatient, or reluctant, or painstaking stopwatches, but with a small segment of recreational buyers who are frequently the category's most devoted customers. When a company recognizes the ways in which demographics, increasing affluence, and some corollary effects (such as, for example, the dramatic increase in European travel by Americans occasioned by lower fares) combine to make the stopwatches of an entire retail category run at recreational speeds, it can grow into something that looks a lot like Williams-Sonoma. For more about the ways in which you can apply recreational stopwatch marketing principles in your own business, see chapter 10.

But before we depart the recreational quadrant, a word of caution about the undeniable attractions that it presents. The formula for success is not simply offering entertainment to customers while shopping, but making the shopping itself the entertainment. Never forget that any time that recreation can be separated from commerce, it will be. Taverns hire bands to play free music to patrons, knowing that the more time spent at the bar, the more beer sold. Providing free music without tying it to a potential sale is not recreational marketing: it's public charity.

Chapter Five

Reluctant Shopping

It's a lot easier to put off the call than to complete it . . . assuming that you *can* complete it in the first place. No matter how lousy your service gets, dialing your cell phone provider to cancel remains an especially intimidating action. Even with the statutory right to retain an existing cell phone number—a right most users don't believe they will be able to secure—comparison shopping for cellular service is a task requiring the patience of a stalking tiger, combined with the interpretive skills of a legal scholar. A powerful spreadsheet is a must, as is a magnifying glass, in order to read the 4-point type in which the penalties for early cancellation are listed ("the net value of either your first car, or second home, whichever is greater . . .").

Nonetheless, you make the call. You have to, external events having forced your hand. Your daughter has turned twelve, and you are informed that she will be the only seventh grader east of the Mississippi without her own cell phone. Moreover, you have endured two years' worth of dropped calls, incomprehensible statements, and progressively more obsolete equipment, and are now free of those aforementioned penalties. You've also survived six months of family complaints, dating back to when your daughter was the only *sixth* grader east of the Mississippi, and so on. Fear of a mutinous family exceeds fear of phone company, so you sit down at the computer and Google "cellular phone plans."

You are a reluctant shopper.

Reluctant shoppers use the same fast-ticking stopwatch as the impatient shoppers we met in chapter 3; once either one starts shopping, neither can wait for it to be over. What distinguishes the two is the amount of time that separates the moment of recognizing a particular need from the action taken to satisfy it; shopping for tires or plumbers may be distasteful, but it is seldom delayed. The same cannot be said for automobile insurance, computer operating systems, or bank accounts, all of which are seldom acquired under conditions of urgency. And reluctant shoppers differ from the painstaking shoppers described in the next chapter by the way they measure the downside of a particular consumer choice: painstaking shopping is characterized by fear of making the *wrong* decision; reluctant shopping by fear of making *any* decision, or of changing any decision once made.

For that reason, the opportunities to take advantage of reluctant-shopping behavior are richest wherever consumers have an ongoing relationship with a business. This is not, as with recreational shoppers, because they enjoy shopping there. It is a direct consequence of the fact that, once having embraced a cell phone provider, or bank, or electric utility, or insurance company, the costs of leaving it are just too high.

Switching costs, as both economists and marketers call them, are central to reluctant stopwatch strategies. The categories where the reluctant stopwatch looms largest, therefore, are those where large numbers of consumers can be persuaded to spend significant money for a product they regard the way Winston Churchill described democracy: the worst of all possible choices, except for all the others.

Such as, for example, a computer operating system.

Embrace and Extend

According to our calculations, no company in the last ten years has extracted more profit from the reluctant quadrant than the behemoth of Redmond, Washington: the Microsoft Corporation, which extracted tens of billions of dollars from consumers' reluctance even to try competing products. Even now, three decades after its founding by Harvard dropout Bill Gates and his onetime prep school classmate Paul Allen as the Micro-Soft Corporation of Albuquerque—neither the hyphen nor the New Mexico address lasted very long—Microsoft's numbers still possess the power to amaze. Over the ten years ending in June of 2005, Microsoft had generated a cumulative operating income of $90 billion, on revenue of only $263 billion . . . an operating margin of more than 34 percent. So productive, indeed, had Microsoft been over that decade that by the end of 2004 it was sitting on the largest cash reserve in the history of American business: more than $60 billion.

Even more impressive is the fact that more than 85 percent of Microsoft's income comes from just two products: Windows and Microsoft Office.*

Those two products make Microsoft the ultimate laboratory for reluctant stopwatch strategies, partly because of their astonishing success, but also because, unusually, exhaustive detail for these strategies—their origins, implementation, and effects—are available for public scrutiny, thanks to the Antitrust Division of the U.S. Department of Justice. By the time the "antitrust case of the century" was settled in July of 2004, hundreds of thousands of pages of investigation, deposition, and expert testimony had been accumulated, all in service of the accusation that Microsoft was the most predatory American company since John Rockefeller's old Standard Oil. The foundation, however, of a case like *United States v. Microsoft Civil Action No. 98-1232* is the notion that also lies at the heart of much reluctant shopping: the power of network effects.

A shopper in the reluctant space, almost by definition, feels forced into the specific brand, product, or service purchased. Since the companies that excel in the reluctant arena often become big, powerful, and profitable from their leverage—or dominance—of the network, consumer advocates and governments are often on the lookout for a chance to prove that the company (Microsoft, IBM, ExxonMobil, AT&T) got that big and rich through some nefarious activity. The reality may more likely be that the company understood the reluctant nature of its customer base and the power of the network in which the company operated, setting out, therefore, to leverage that network so effectively that the reluctant shopper does, indeed, feel he or she simply has no other choice.

The "network effect" (the term has achieved the same cliché status as its cousin, the "first-mover advantage") is a term that economists use when the number of existing users of a product is directly related to the product's appeal . . . the "fifty million Frenchmen can't be wrong" argument. Under this theory, consumers will even buy a second-rate product because of their belief that it's no fun to own the last Betamax player in America.

----

* Microsoft actually breaks out its financials into seven segments, with the somewhat opaque designations "Server and Tools," "Microsoft Business Solutions," "Mobile and Embedded Devices," and so on. The largest, "Client" segment, consists almost entirely of the Windows operating system; the "Information Worker" segment, likewise, is a proxy for the production and sale of the Microsoft Office suite of computer applications.

From the perspective of economists, some network effects are natural, even unavoidable. For example, a brand new HDTV is only as good as the network to which it is connected. If the U.S. TV and cable networks provide less bandwidth than their analogues in Japan, well, then U.S. viewers will simply have to settle for inferior TVs, even though better TVs clearly exist and are in use in Japan. The computer software equivalent are the arbitrary tasks whose mastery enhances any repetitive task like word processing or Internet browsing. Clearly, once computer users have invested time in learning to navigate through Windows or Office menus, they have increased the switching costs of changing to any other system. Powerful though these effects are, Microsoft wasn't satisfied with them. They had another stopwatch strategy to play. And they weren't shy about telling everyone about it.

On February 23, 1996, a Microsoft employee named Dean Ballard posted a set of motivational lyrics on one of the company's newsgroups. Titled *The Battle Hymn of the Reorg,* it read in part:

> Oh, our eyes have seen the glory of the coming of the Net,
> We are ramping up our market share, objectives will be met.
> Soon our browser will be everywhere, you ain't seen nothin' yet,
> We embrace and we extend!

The phrase "embrace and extend" was an abbreviation for a widely used internal mantra that read, in full: "Embrace, extend, and extinguish" (sometimes "exterminate"). And every one of Microsoft's 60,000 employees understood the meaning of the three axioms:

1. Embrace: Develop a product compatible with either a public standard, or one compatible with a leading competitor's offering.
2. Extend: Add features that are *not* part of the competition, or publicly available.
3. Extinguish: The proprietary extensions become the new standard, and competitors die on the vine.

The central axiom of reluctant stopwatch marketing is this: To capture the dollars of consumers who are inherently unwilling to spend time in shopping for alternatives, *even though they know that their reluctance is costly,* you must lower switching costs *in* while raising switching costs *out.*

Microsoft understood this to the tips of their programmers' fingers. Far more valuable than the skills acquired in mastering Word, or Outlook, or Internet Explorer are the tens, perhaps hundreds, of billions of dollars in assets stored on hard disks in formats readable only by Microsoft Office programs: spreadsheets, word processing files, contracts, correspondence, and, of course, the manuscript for this book.

This is the fundamental difference between the two pillars of Microsoft's dominance: The value to consumers of applications software is measured in the time they have spent mastering its intricacies *plus* the work they have saved using those applications. The value to consumers of an operating system isn't really measured at all.

An operating system is a utility, a *must-have*.

As a result, the time spent shopping for a computer operating system, for the overwhelming majority of people, is effectively zero. The same consumer who will spend hours, or even days, shopping for computer hardware (which delivers a 5 percent gross margin to its manufacturer) will, nine times in ten, have it running the latest version of the Windows operating system (on which Microsoft earns a gross margin of 84 percent . . . which is one reason that the computer manufacturer earns only 5 percent; license fees to Microsoft can easily be greater than the net profit on the sale of a low-end computer system). Microsoft currently owns an estimated 90 percent share of the desktop/personal computing market, and, because the company's browser software, Internet Explorer, comes preinstalled on the operating system, an equally enviable position in the browser category. When, in November 2004, the market share for Internet Explorer dropped to only 92.9 percent, it was front-page news in the computer industry trade publications.

But since Windows isn't truly shopped for, the greater triumph of reluctant stopwatch marketing is Microsoft Office. Despite Windows' category dominance and startling contribution to Microsoft's bottom line—in 2005, the program generated $12.2 billion in revenue . . . and $9.4 billion in operating income (OI)*—most of that contribution is in the form of license fees paid by computer manufacturers who install the program on

---

* Microsoft calculates revenue and OI by division, but carries a huge amount of corporate overhead that does not appear in those divisional breakouts. In the last fiscal year, this overhead exceeded $5 billion.

new machines. People buy those machines, however, not to run an operating system, but to produce documents, calculate, communicate, and create presentations. This has been true ever since files were stored on eight-inch floppy disks and printed on daisy wheel printers. Or, more specifically, since the *annus mirabilis* for personal computer applications software, 1978, when both WordStar and VisiCalc, the first commercial word processing and spreadsheet programs, were launched.

The transformative power of these product launches, only months apart, can hardly be overstated. In stopwatch marketing terms, a business that had been more or less evenly divided between the recreational (read: hobbyist) and painstaking (read: IT professionals . . . even though the term hadn't yet been invented) quadrants added millions of potential consumers, almost all of them inherently reluctant. They were never more reluctant than they were during those early years, when retailers of computer software were required to stock SKUs for half a dozen different hardware configurations and operating systems in order to accommodate all the available hardware configurations—remember the Commodore 64? Only the tiny size of the original market, and its consequently rapid growth, was able to overcome that reluctance, by guaranteeing that huge numbers of new consumers joined the game each year with no investment in a particular format. Switching in costs, for these new consumers, were zero, and even so their behavior remained highly reluctant; millions of potential buyers of computer hardware and software were regularly convinced that the computer/software system they bought today would be twice as fast and half the cost a year later, which made them more than a little anxious about buying.

And they were right to be anxious. A dizzying number of applications packages succeeded one another over more than a decade, as WordStar gave way to WordPerfect and VisiCalc to Lotus 1-2-3, and their success finally tempted Microsoft to get into the applications software game. And to master marketing to reluctant shoppers.

Because 1-2-3, the category leader, didn't run on Windows, the strategic objective for Microsoft's newest spreadsheet program, Excel, was to assure the popularity of its operating system. Soon enough, Windows was returning the favor: Windows 3.0, launched in 1990, sold more than 5 million copies in its first six months on sale, relegating its competitors (buffs will recall the euphonious names CP/M, OS/2, and MS-DOS) to historical footnotes. The decision to integrate its applications software with its operating system gave Microsoft a huge natural advantage, even though the divisions developing each were barred from direct communication because of what would turn out to be a fruitless attempt to defang any future antitrust complaints.

An even larger advantage for Microsoft, in the long run, was that both Word and Excel—and, after 1989, when they were combined in the suite of programs known as Microsoft Office—permitted users to import files from WordPerfect and Lotus 1-2-3 in a completely clean manner. But when the process was reversed, the design of Word and Excel practically guaranteed that features—underlining, displays, and calculations—would be lost.[1] In a programming version of the once-upon-a-time pest control traps known as the Roach Motel, consumers can check into Microsoft Office . . . but they can't afford to check out. So successful has the strategy been that typical consumers spend the entirety of their shopping time deciding whether to buy Word, or Excel, à la carte, or as part of Microsoft Office. The result was a textbook example of "embrace, expand, and you-know-what."

The motivational song turned around to bite Microsoft, when the Justice Department actually cited it in their antitrust claim. The specific allegations were fairly technical; among other things, Microsoft was accused of using a technique known as Object Linking and Embedding (OLE) architecture in order to degrade the performance, relative to Microsoft's Internet Explorer, of the search engine Netscape Navigator. The decision, however, was fairly sweeping: Microsoft was required to permit rivals producing applications software to be folded into the Windows operating system.

At the time, libertarian critics of the government position tended to argue that artificially imposed switching costs are almost always temporary, and so a poor choice for legal action. Whatever the rightness of that argument, it is one that Microsoft itself shared. For just as the company had used the power of the reluctant stopwatch to become one of the world's most profitable companies, that same stopwatch was proving an obstacle to Microsoft's future.

Even Microsoft, it turns out, is subject to the same axioms of reluctant shopping as anyone else, and the company is therefore starting to look vulnerable to the same "embrace and expand" strategies that permitted it to become so successful in the first place. The folks in Redmond aren't the only ones trying to lower switching costs in, and the company's fear of open-source (read: free for the asking) programs, and of free Internet browsers like Firefox, which are even quicker than Internet Explorer, was predictable. It is also now part of the public record, via the leak of some rather embarrassing internal memos.* In the words of analyst Rob Enderle, being "outmarketed by people with no marketing budget"[2] can't be much fun.

It is bad enough that others are lowering the costs of switching from Microsoft. Even more troubling to the company is a turbocharged case of the "good enough" problem: it's getting harder and harder to convince anyone to spend hundreds of dollars for a new edition of Microsoft Office, when the biggest improvement on offer is thirty new typefaces. A proposition in economics argues that, for a true durable good (one that never truly wears out or needs to be replaced) even a monopolist is forced to lower prices closer and closer to marginal cost in order to attract new customers. High-demand types, goes the theory, buy early; but with low marginal costs and zero deterioration, the low-demand types can be attracted as well. This notion, called the Coase Conjecture (for its creator, Ronald Coase, the Nobel Prize–winning economist), isn't universally, or even widely, accepted . . . but it is giving Microsoft (whose founder famously called software the "ultimate durable good"[3]) a bad case of the shakes. Fearful of losing its pricing power, the company, which now launches very few new consumer products—sometimes years go by without a new version of either Office or Windows and Xbox games are still not much more than a rounding error for the company—has rejiggered its entire marketing organization. The new organization, known as Marketing@Microsoft, is charged with developing a capacity for establishing ongoing relationships with consumers . . . for turning the world's

―――――――――

* These documents, christened "The Halloween Memos," make pretty enlightening reading. Among other things, they state that "OSS [Open Source Software] is long-term credible if FUD tactics cannot be used to combat it." The first citation for the acronym FUD—for "fear, uncertainty, and doubt"—dates back to the 1970s, when Gene Amdahl, founder of the Amdahl corporation, referred to it as the strategy used by the IBM sales force as the original high-tech reluctant stopwatch. The objective, in the words of Eric Raymond, author of *The New Hacker's Dictionary*, was "to persuade buyers to go with safe IBM gear rather than with competitors' equipment. This implicit coercion was traditionally accomplished by promising that good things would happen to people who stuck with IBM, but Dark Shadows loomed over the future of competitors' equipment or software."

greatest reluctant shopping experience into one with tentacles into the recreational and painstaking quadrants. It seems to us, however, that this decision is less a criticism of the reluctant stopwatch than an example of its success: When you have no dollars left in one quadrant, it's time to start working another.

Few categories, and even fewer companies, have such high-class problems. Microsoft enjoys market shares as high as 90 percent in most of its businesses, largely as a result of its recognition of the naturally high switching costs for consumers of computer software. Sometimes, high switching costs aren't a fundamental characteristic of a product, but can nonetheless be exploited as a way of profiting from the reluctant shopping quadrant. A familiar example is the world's newest multibillion-dollar industry . . . the same one that opened this chapter: cellular telephone service.

Coverage

Given the ubiquity of cell phones, younger readers may be forgiven for thinking that they have been around forever. The most notable thing about cellular service, though, is not how common it is, but how young. Though mobile telephone service was developed by the 1970s—and was authorized by the Federal Communications Commission in 1982—it was not until 1997 that it started to resemble the business we know today. Before April of that year, when the FCC conducted an auction of the frequencies of the radio spectrum slated for use by wireless communication, cellular telephone service was dominated by startups like McCaw Cellular or Voicestream, now parts of AT&T and T-Mobile, respectively. The first cellular—named for the cells that divided the service area into bite-size units—telephone service was launched in Chicago in 1983.

As recently as 1990, however, the industry was still small. That year, Microsoft sold 5 million copies of Windows 3.0 in less than six months while fewer than one and a half million Americans had cell phones. After 1997, however, with the entry of local and long-distance phone companies (some of them, slightly ironically, onetime parts of the Bell System, which held most of the basic patents that drive cellular technology) the game changed forever . . . and not always in predictable fashion. Though companies like AT&T, Sprint, and Verizon were almost unimaginably wealthy in both financial and intellectual capital, they were also relatively impoverished when it came to experience in consumer marketing. The top executives at virtually all of the new cellular giants had grown up in regulated monopoly businesses, and entered the brave new competitive world of cellular service with, perhaps, more guts than sense.

Luckily, their product was the proverbial better mousetrap. In 1987, cellular companies had fewer than a million customers; five years later, that number had grown to 11 million, and five years after *that,* when the FCC auctioned off the mobile phone frequencies, to 55 million.[4] And, despite an industry-wide panic that the penetration of cell phone service would top out at only 50 percent, an additional 150 million subscribers were found by the end of 2005.

It seems counterintuitive to locate an industry with this sort of growth curve in the reluctant-shopping quadrant. Nonetheless, that's where it belongs, even if cellular's reluctant stopwatch was set for reasons other than consumer marketing appeal. The cellular industry turned its customers into reluctant shoppers not because they wanted to, but because they had to.

When Andrew Sukawaty joined Sprint in 1996, they had just completed the first rollout of the PCS, or Personal Computer Services network. PCS, which operates in the 1.9-gigahertz band of the radio spectrum, offered the potential for selling customers a huge range of digital services in addition to voice communication, including text messaging, picture transfer, even, with the addition of yet another technical improvement called EV-DO, television and radio. However, all such services depended on widespread use of telephones that were both modern enough and standardized enough to handle them. Letting people choose inexpensive phones to access that system made as much sense as running a pufferbelly locomotive on a track built for the bullet train.

Getting people to pay for their own bullet trains, however, was a daunting prospect; one of the most reliable truths of high-tech marketing is that consumers *never* know what they want in a new technology before they already have it. Faced with the gap between what his customers needed, and what they were willing to pay for, Sukawaty decided that Sprint needed to take possession of the phone, subsidizing it in order to guarantee the future value of Sprint's network.

These subsidies weren't small, sometimes running into hundreds of dollars per customer, and the only way to justify them was to amortize them over a long period of time. Thus was the two-year contract born, and with it, the migration of cell phone shopping into the reluctant quadrant.

It should be underlined that there was nothing inevitable about long-term contracts; the European model (an attractive one, given Europe's even greater level of market penetration) is diametrically opposite. There, the manufacturers of handsets are at least equal partners with providers of cell phone service. The United States is different: 41 percent of cell phone buyers get a new handset only when also signing up for a new cellular service plan; 29 percent buy only to repair or replace a broken or lost phone. Competing for the remaining 30 percent as a stand-alone handset manufacturer—that is, one independent of a cellular service pro-vider—is virtually impossible in the United States, where Verizon alone spends three times as much on advertising as all handset manufacturers combined. All by itself, this fact explains why Nokia, the world's largest cell phone manufacturer, has stubbed its toe in America, where its 16 percent market share is less than half what the Finnish giant enjoys in Europe.

Rather than simplifying the task for consumers, however, the decision by Sprint and its competitors to combine cellular service with heavily subsidized handsets complicated it. With the days of easy acquisition of new subscribers behind them—by 2006, nearly 80 percent of potential cell phone users had been turned into actual customers—the cellular in-dustry began using a new calculus of success, one based on margin, rather than growth . . . or, in the acronym-happy world of cellular, ARPU, for Average Revenue Per User.

Average revenue was an objective only peripherally associated with the key drivers of consumer choice in the cellular category. Our ex-perience in this category has shown us that consumers shop along four separate dimensions, simultaneously evaluating the handset, the cover-age area of the cellular carrier, the price per call, and the availability of additional features such as text messaging and customized ringtones; and only the last dimension offers potential improvement in ARPU for the provider.

In any case, the closer you approach these four dimensions, the more their ability to help a shopper make a buying decision recedes. Own-ing the sexiest new handset may be the objective of some consumers, but their chance of finding it at their chosen cellular provider is not high. We informally asked a group of high-income, highly educated cell phone users to evaluate the phones available from the cellular providers Verizon, T-Mobile, and Sprint PCS on price, features, and style, and soon discovered that:

1. Out of more than eighty phones, nearly fifty of which were on sale for $49.99 or less, only a single model was available from more than one provider (and that one, the Motorola RAZR, was available in a different color set from those providers).
2. It took our group more than an hour to work up a decent comparison chart, even though we had done the work of listing all the phones and prices beforehand.

An hour. Just to *start* shopping. And, at the end, to discover that, if you had your heart set on the Nokia 8801, you had better like T-Mobile, because neither Sprint nor Verizon offer it. If you are one of those shoppers, handsets are the decisive component in the choice of cellular provider. You are also, based on most market estimates, rare indeed: Fewer than one in fifty cellular users chose service based on a desire to own a particular phone.

The component that matters most to shoppers—coverage—is also the most problematic, because it is also often the most difficult claim to quantify. Cingular can boast of fewest dropped calls, or Verizon of being the most reliable national network, but consumers are, quite logically, skeptical of such claims. Even though both assertions are objectively true, they mean very little to a typical user; Verizon may have coverage along 95 percent of the 200-mile-long corridor that leads from Washington, DC, to New York . . . but this means that a Verizon subscriber riding an Amtrak train can start a call somewhere outside Baltimore and have an even chance of a dropped call every thirty minutes. Dead zones persist even in zones with full coverage. Roaming charge alerts can appear as users move from one aisle of a supermarket to another.

One can, of course, download a coverage map from a cellular provider's website, and attempt to find your typical commuting path within the amoeba-like shapes that describe the provider's service area. You can even compare them with one another . . . if, that is, you have another hour to spend after evaluating five dozen different phones.

Features *do* matter, though the generic ones are scarcely a reason to select one carrier over another, since everyone offers plans with text messaging and call forwarding, and phones with built-in cameras, PDAs, and music downloads.* More promising, because it is creating exclusivity, is the family of brands offered as premium add-ons by Sprint/Nextel, including the National Football League, Disney, and ESPN, which offer both the benefits of distinctive programming and the same powerful affinity that prompts the acquisition of branded credit cards.

Which leaves price.

Because of its intrinsic clarity, pricing is the most effective way to short-circuit the intimidation that is the defining characteristic of reluctant shopping behavior. To anyone lacking the knowledge needed to compare choices in a high-tech category, a simple measure like price looks like a life raft to a drowning man. You don't have to know whether CDMA is superior to GSM, or if your Nokia 3120 is compatible with your AT&T SIM card, or whether you have the right OBEX profile for your phone's Bluetooth capability (and just what *is* Bluetooth, anyway?). You just have to compare dollars and cents.

Not so fast. The correct pricing decision for most customers would be to select the plan offering the lowest monthly cost, but calculating that future expense is, if anything, more daunting than comparing phones, or drawing coverage maps. *Some* combination of free minutes, low-cost (or free) calls to family members, and monthly subscription fees is the best one, but unless the customer has been obsessive about keeping records of her family's cell phone habits for months, and knows how to analyze all the permutations on an Excel spreadsheet, she's out of luck. As a result, she typically picks the simplest flat rate plan available, even when a more complicated pay-per-use plan would be significantly cheaper.

Even though two-thirds of them lose money doing so, U.S. households generally prefer flat rates not only for cellular service, but for utilities, power, gas, water, even health clubs. This is because of something called "flat rate bias." Economics teaches us to look for four different potential sources of this bias in favor of flat rates. First is the "taxi meter effect," which argues that consumers find transactions more enjoyable when payment and use aren't simultaneously in view. The "insurance

---

* As of this writing, that is. We are well aware that, by the time you are reading this, chances are good that a "generic" phone will be opening garage doors, activating ATMs, replacing credit card "swipes," and managing video teleconferencing.

effect" is sought by risk-averse customers to avoid unanticipated variation in their expenses.* There is also a "convenience effect," in which search costs represent too much time needed to identify alternative costs—the hours needed to draw those coverage maps, compare those features, and do a sensitivity analysis on those free minutes. But the most significant flat-rate bias in the cellular phone business is the "overestimation effect"; a decade of research has consistently shown that consumers overestimate their own demand. Cellular users who estimate that they use 800 minutes monthly actually use, on average, only 220.[5]

The reluctant-shopping stopwatch works best when it runs at different speeds for different customers: fast for existing customers, slow for prospective ones. By design and accident, cellular phone providers have speeded up the stopwatch so much for their existing customers that it stops long before most of them can calculate the benefits of a new provider . . . long before most even make that phone call with which this chapter began. In the event that such a call is made, however, the typical cellular service provider has another arrow in its quiver. Though the industry is too young to have much experience with segmenting *potential* customers, it collects a staggering amount of information about its *existing* customers. Whenever one of those existing customers shows that her stopwatch, at least, will keep running long enough to shop for another provider, her existing provider can, in real time, not only see what future plan would best match her calling patterns—thus saving her money—but her payment history. Together with the cancellation call itself, the cellular company can calculate:

1. The customer's time value;
2. Her potential use of the company's service;
3. Her credit worthiness—which, all by itself, is of considerable value in a business whose bad debt annually reduces its profit by nearly 6 percent.

These three metrics can permit the cellular provider to compete for its own customer . . . and to know, with a very high degree of precision, just

---

* In 1999, Tversky and Hahneman, our Nobel Prize–winning friends from recreational shopping, showed that shoppers weigh small monetary losses twice as much as gains of the same magnitude.

how much to spend on keeping her. It is at this precise moment that cellular companies exhibit mastery of the most critical touchpoint in the reluctant quadrant: the moment when an existing (and profitable) customer tries to become an ex-customer. Despite what economist Tim Harford calls "confusion pricing," virtually every cellular service provider will, when asked, clear up any confusion about the best plan for any particular customer, quickly suggesting money-saving alternatives.[6]

Note the clause "when asked." Though Sprint/Nextel and its competitors have invested in both the software and the training needed to quickly assess the calling history and optimal rate plan for any customer, none of them offer such a service *unless* asked. Both Harford and Eugenio Miravete, who have studied bargain seeking among customers of cell phone companies, suggest that their choice to reserve this asset—their most powerful touchpoint—for customers who are, by definition, unsatisfied, is a form of price discrimination: segmentation by willingness to pay.[7] Those customers unwilling to spend five minutes shopping for a better deal (one might as well just call them reluctant) pay more; others less. As the Cingulars, Sprints, T-Mobiles, and Verizons enter their second decade, achieving their target, increased Average Revenue Per User, will probably demand more actively focused segmentation for their satisfied customers than they already exhibit with those who are ready to leave. The criteria for such segmentation schemes are likely to include calling behavior, credit history, and stopwatch speed. Thus far, their existing model has proved profitable enough that the key touchpoint in marketing their service will stay where it is—focused on price.

It may seem surprising to argue that an industry that has grown from 50 million to 200 million subscribers in less than a decade has been better at the sort of reluctant strategies that keep customers from leaving, than at those that acquire them in the first place. The plain fact, however, is that the stunning growth of the cellular industry has been built less on its marketing savvy than on the appeal of completely portable telephone communication. This is to take nothing away from the cellular achievement; growth is growth, even if it is in an industry that started from a baseline of zero. The same cannot be said about the final example of success in the application of reluctant strategies, in an industry that has been around since the time of Babylonia.

America's Friendliest Bank

The North American Industrial Classification System (NAICS), a joint effort of the U.S. Census Bureau, the Bureau of Labor Statistics, and the
Bureau of Economic Analysis, attaches six digit codes to every conceiv-
able commercial organization. The closer one classification number is to
another, the more similar the businesses. Thus, magazine publishers
(511120) are closer to book publishers (511130) than to motion picture
theaters (512131) though all three can be found in the Information sector
(51). Using the same logic, the NAICS directory divides banks into codes
52110 and 52120 . . . nowhere near sectors 44 and 45, Retail Trade, which
contains everything from shoe stores to supermarkets to gas stations.

The NAICS has obviously never heard of Commerce Bank.

Founded in 1973 by Vernon W. Hill II, at the time (and still today) a
successful owner of forty-one Burger King franchises in eastern Pennsylvania's Montgomery and Bucks Counties, Commerce Bank has grown
into a regional financial power—over the last five years, as the bank
established itself in the mid-Atlantic from Virginia to Connecticut to
Florida, its assets have grown, on average 36 percent, and its net income
31 percent—by changing the dynamic of that most reluctant of businesses, retail banking.

Though there is no record of either the Knights Templar or the Roth-
schilds heading off-site to debate their strategic futures, banks have been
confronting the realities of the retail marketplace ever since they first set
up their benches—in Italian, *banca*—in public squares as a place to accept
deposits and grant loans. Today, those realities are daunting indeed: Not-
withstanding the tens of millions of dollars spent on one branding campaign after another, banking is largely perceived as a commodity; since
most banks sell the same products and provide mediocre service, one
bank is just like another. Moreover, despite the availability of phone and
Internet banking, banks are still maintaining, at much higher costs per
transaction, branch networks . . . and have performed poorly at using
those branches to deliver high-quality experiences to their customers.[*]

---

[*] In recent comprehensive Six Sigma–based mystery assessments of banks' in-person branch
sales experiences across the United States by Novantas, LLC, the *best* banks barely achieve
an overall "Average" rating of their branch sales experience, for example, a 4 on a 7-point
scale, with huge geographical variations. And they have many branches that are rated a 1

Deposits are retail banking's primary profit driver . . . but the highest profit segment, small-business households, are typically underserved, partly because of the lack of tools needed to predict, with any degree of useful accuracy, lifetime customer profitability. Given that difficulty in estimating profitability, it is scarcely surprising that few banks have exhibited much competence at growing profits by moving existing customers from low- to high-profit tiers.

Challenged by customers who view them as indistinguishable from their competitors, saddled with costly yet ineffective customer-facing branches, unable to meaningfully segment customers, it is hardly surprising that the usual tactics of Consumer Retail Marketing (CRM) have proved disappointing.

Of all these challenges facing Hill's new venture thirty years ago, the one he, accurately, perceived to have the greatest leverage was the branch banking experience. At precisely the historical moment when other banks started seeing their branch systems as cost centers ripe for trimming, Commerce saw theirs as a differentiating asset. By improving the customer's experience within the branch, Hill reasoned, he could simultaneously increase the propensity of other banks' customers to change, and increase the reluctance of Commerce's customers to leave. Or, to put it another way, he would use the same asset, Commerce's retail branches, to lower switching costs in, while raising switching costs out.

His first innovation, appropriately enough for a master of stopwatch marketing, targeted the customers' perception of their own time value. Other banks could keep banker's hours; Commerce would not. "You don't have to think about when a Home Depot, a McDonald's, or a Starbucks is open. They're open. You just go. My theory was, if you advertise that you're open on Sunday, the consumer will automatically believe you're open all the time. That message is more important than the savings. It says, 'We're always there for you.' "[8] And they are: all of Commerce's branches are open seven days a week, typically from 8:30 A.M. to 5 P.M. on weekdays (with two nights open late) and half days on Saturday and Sunday.

---

or 2 (Poor). Many banks are rated "Below Average" overall. Not surprisingly, since higher sales experience ratings typically result in higher sales growth and customer satisfaction, improving key components of the sales experience is critical.

For the customer, the advantages of Commerce's extended hours were many, but for the bank itself, only one mattered. Like Microsoft offering all the same features as Lotus 1-2-3 or WordPerfect, Commerce offered the same basic banking services as First Union or Citibank. But they offered them for twenty more hours a week. And Commerce greatly simplified the buying process by focusing almost singlemindedly on free checking rather than trying to sell all things to all people.

Additional hours and a simplified buying process combined to entice potential new customers, who found it far easier to make time to open an account at Commerce than any of its competitors. But it was only the beginning. A determination to succeed in the reluctant quadrant by imitating the strategies of recreational success stories like Wal-Mart and Apple meant more than just staying open late. It meant treating depositors, in the words stenciled inside the eyelids of every Commerce employee, as *fans*. It meant embracing a philosophy that the function of each branch was to "Wow! the Customer" every time he or she passed through the front doors.

It meant, in short, defining itself not as a bank at all, but as a power retailer.

When we present stopwatch marketing principles to clients, we frequently refer to what we call the "Ten Commandments of Power Retailing":

Thou shalt know thy customer.

Thou shalt develop precise definitions of thy target, emphasizing heavy users.

Thou shalt develop a brand promise that establishes an emotional connection.

Thou shalt not waver in demonstrating unswerving commitment to your brand.

Thou shalt ensure a consistent brand experience.

Thou shalt create a retail environment that thy consumers appreciate.

Thou shalt continuously innovate products and services.

Thou shalt expand profitability into new markets and channels.

Thou shalt not centralize the day-to-day execution (but thou *shalt* centralize brand image).

Thou shalt obsessively measure the brand and business operations.

The Commandments are more than just an easy-to-remember Power-Point slide; while they work as guides to an overall marketing philosophy, they are also intended to be mapped to specific marketing touchpoints . . . and, as we never tire of repeating, every touchpoint is associated with a particular tick on a particular customer's stopwatch. In the case of retail banking, the very first tick can be critical. Our research indicates that families become at least passive shoppers for banking services whenever they change residences, for example; evidently the need to order new checks prompts many consumers to reconsider their existing banking relationships.

Most banks define their heavy users as their business customers . . . the sort who needs the widest range of banking services. But when Commerce does so, they define them in a very different way: low-cost core deposits with long lives.[9] This means customers who are willing to accept lower-than-market rates on their deposits . . . but whose willingness is not because of an inability to get banking services elsewhere because of bad credit histories or other problems. It means simplified checking; offering free transactions at non-Commerce ATMs; issuing debit/credit cards to new depositors minutes after they open accounts; even clearing deposits the same day they arrive. What it doesn't mean is following the time-honored banking tradition of charging more fees to the customers who use retail functions that produce only 20 percent of typical banking revenue. The insight of Vernon Hill—the once and future fast-food franchisee—was that, even though soft drinks and fries were much more profitable than burgers, Burger King doesn't make customers who only want a Whopper wait in a longer line. "The truth is, bankers aren't very smart. The ones that have followed the 80/20 rule have had the worst results."[10] Hill understood that customers choose Burger King or McDonald's not because of the price, but because of the consistent brand experience.

The McDonald's model is a pervasive one for any business seeking to apply the Commandments of Power Retailing. Not only does Commerce open branches the way the fast-food giant opens new franchises—with weeks of preopening advertising, compelling direct-mail offers, opening-day parades, balloons, gifts for kids—but they train their customer-facing staff the same way. The Cherry Hill, New Jersey–based Commerce University, a direct copy of McDonald's Hamburger University, is a full-bore indoctrination into the customer service culture of Commerce Bank, run by a onetime McDonald's employee. Every year, the graduates of Commerce University—representatives from the bank's 400+ branches—assemble at the Commerce Bank "Wow!" Awards, a combination of frat party, motivational sales meeting, and incentive awards banquet, where the company's "Best Full-Time Teller" and "Best Retail Support" staff are given statuettes shaped like the company's signature "C."[11]

Grand store openings, friendly and welcoming staff, staying open late and on weekends, and traditional advertising (built around Commerce's motto and Unique Selling Proposition . . . one that speaks directly to the heart of the reluctant shopper: "America's Most Convenient Bank") are all touchpoints whose place on the stopwatch dial occur early in the shopping process. In the reluctant quadrant, however, the stopwatch never really stops ticking; the real measure of success is not just *acquiring* customers, but *keeping* them. Reluctant shoppers may take months or years before they accumulate enough energy to change software operating systems, or cellular providers, but a company whose profit model is derived from finding customers willing to forgo higher deposit rates in favor of better customer service can lose that shopper—that depositor—with a single bad customer interaction. The in-branch experience has to be as consistent as a fast-food cheeseburger.

This is why Commerce Bank, uniquely in the banking industry, spends so much on mystery shopping: visits by paid investigators, who submit reports on the shopping experience to Commerce's home office. The bank currently funds some eighty thousand mystery shops annually, which means nearly two hundred visits per bank per year. Along with the other traditional measure of retail success—comparing same-store sales year to year—Commerce uses the mystery shops to model the legendary service taught at Commerce University . . . and, not incidentally, to make those shoppers reluctant only to leave Commerce. As Les Dinkin, a managing director at the leading financial services consultancy, Novantas, puts it, "Among retail banks, Commerce was one of the few who figured out and, more importantly, consistently executed what retailers in other industries have understood for generations: If you create an environment and sales experience that your customers enjoy, instead of just tolerate, they are much more likely to not only do more business with you, they stick with you, and also take the initiative to recommend you to their friends and co-workers."

Successful? Reducing the reluctance of new customers to open accounts (and increasing the reluctance of existing customers to close out those accounts) allows Commerce to not only pay lower interest on deposits,[12] but to increase the profitability of its loan portfolio by forgoing subprime, indirect, or third-party loans.[13] The bank appears less vulnerable to the subprime meltdown afflicting the financial services sector. Presumably because of its dependence on its distinctively motivated employee base, Commerce has, thus far, avoided acquisition of other banks (though they did acquire, in early 2006, the online service eMoney Advisor). Internally, however, they are still growing at a dramatic pace, expanding into Florida, New York, and, very probably, the rest of the nation.

Such ambitions are part of the patrimony that Vernon Hill has bequeathed Commerce Bank, along with its extraordinary profitability and future prospects. His other legacies proved less happy: in June of 2007, after a series of revelations about Hill's casual attitude toward corporate governance—for years, his company leased real estate in which Hill had a personal interest—Commerce Bank's CEO resigned. Companies that are identified with single charismatic leaders sometimes fail to survive their departures (see Chrysler and Iacocca); sometimes they achieve even greater success (see McDonald's and Kroc). And sometimes they even try to recapture the magic by bringing the same guy back (Michael Dell, Steve Jobs). It will be interesting, over the next few years, to see whether the consumer-focused, "let's-make-banking-fun" recreational approach so effectively institutionalized by Vern has become a part of Commerce's DNA. If Commerce stays independent—by no means a certainty as of this writing—will it continue to be an innovator, or will it revert to type? Will it continue to strive to be "America's favorite bank" or become as hated as most of their competition? Will transactions at Commerce continue to be recreational, or slide back into reluctance and impatience?

• • •

Mapping these reluctant shopping case studies to the stopwatch marketing matrix results in something that looks like Figure 5-1.

The lessons of the cell phone, consumer banking, and computer software industries are, we believe, ones that apply to any enterprise that derives significant revenue from customers who are putting off a decision that they *know* they ought to make, and doing so because the amount of

RELUCTANT / RECREATIONAL QUADRANTS

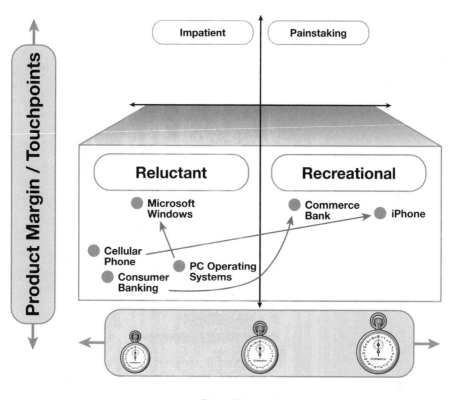

Figure 5-1

effort seems disproportionate to the reward. Most, though not all, such businesses are engaged in an ongoing relationship with their customers . . . which is simultaneously an advantage for the status quo (regular communication with customers, in the form of invoices, statements, online communication) and a disadvantage for a new competitor attempting to disrupt that status quo. Distilling the experiences of successful software manufacturers, cellular telephone services, and banks, and applying them to the reluctant shopper, we submit that the key elements of marketing in this quadrant are:

1. Recognize the percentage of revenue coming from the reluctant quadrant (for more on this, see chapter 7).
2. Identify the *first* tick on the reluctant shopping stopwatch . . . one that is

frequently driven by external events. The openness to a new banking relationship among recently relocated families is a clear example.

3. Identify the *decisive* tick . . . the moment when a transaction can occur. This can be when a potential customer first takes a step—a reluctant step—into a branch office, or when she dials an 800# asking for pricing information.

4. At that decisive tick, offer *everything* that a competitor provides . . . and at least one thing more.

And finally,

5. Manage the customer through the *critical* ticks on the stopwatch during which an existing customer is at risk of becoming an ex-customer.

Successful marketers in the reluctant quadrant, having temporarily reduced customer reluctance (and closed the initial sale), immediately thereafter do everything imaginable to increase it. From a practical standpoint, this means building a system that guarantees regular—at least monthly—customer exposure to a touchpoint that reinforces the unique advantages of your business.

Reluctant shoppers, as we have seen, can be a profit machine for companies that attend to these rules: companies that place touchpoints to overcome the reluctant shopper's anxiety about changing anything that is probably "good enough" already. In the next chapter, we'll see a very different set of strategies for shoppers whose biggest concern is achieving not "good enough" . . . but "perfect."

Chapter Six

Painstaking Shopping

It's a typical American wedding . . . which is to say, pretty luxurious, with nearly $30,000 of flowers, food, monogrammed napkins, photographers, musicians, color-coordinated bridesmaid outfits—to say nothing of the bride's dress, train, veil, and shoes—on display for the guests. Unseen, but easily assumed, is the amount of time all of this represents: months, even years, of comparison shopping for all of the dozens of purchases needed to turn a young woman, in the words of a recent book,[1] into a "celebrity for a day."

More important, when the shopper in question regards choosing one limousine over another not as the difference between good and better, but between perfect and disastrous, it makes sense—we use the term cautiously—to take infinite pains in checking out every car service in town. It makes sense for the consumption of such a service to be, in short, painstaking.

The painstaking shopping experience need not be painful, but it is inevitably long, consuming days, months . . . even years. Because of this characteristic of the painstaking quadrant, including the amount of time spent in both active and passive shopping behaviors, successful companies working here tend to think of their customers' stopwatches in a different manner from companies targeting reluctant, recreational, or impatient shoppers. While Master Lock might measure their stopwatches in minutes, even seconds, and Verizon in, at most, days, painstaking marketers think in terms of stopwatches that tick for years. The appropriate imagery might even be calendar marketing, rather than stopwatch marketing.

Those calendars take on relatively greater importance wherever the largest number of customers follow the same shopping rhythm; but consistent rhythms—everyone shops for Thanksgiving turkeys at pretty much the same time—do not, by themselves, make shopping painstaking. What makes a long-term shopping decision a painstaking one is fear. Because the consequences of a wrong decision in this quadrant are often frighteningly high, the experience is generally not an entertaining one. As a result, the painstaking quadrant, uniquely in our model, contains not only *primary* marketers of products and services, but vital and often even more profitable *secondary* marketers: businesses whose value proposition is the elimination of shopping anxiety. A kitchen renovation is not only a frighteningly expensive prospect, but just plain frightening as well ("did I leave enough space for the refrigerator door to open?") . . . which is why most people hire kitchen design firms, instead of buying cabinetry, appliances, and flooring on their own. As we shall see below, entire industries have grown up around the desire of painstaking shoppers to find everything from the perfect night's sleep to the perfect college.

In point of fact, any business where the customer's hoped-for result is, even hyperbolically, "perfect" is very likely to depend on painstaking shoppers, and to use the same touchpoints in approximately the same manner. In all the examples that follow, from Lexus automobiles—"the relentless pursuit of perfection"—to a college degree, these exemplary painstaking marketers have shown a remarkably consistent willingness to focus on touchpoints during the months and even years during which a potential sale gestates, and to use those touchpoints as a means to reduce or eliminate customer anxiety about decisions that they will have to either remember, or live with, every day for years to come.

Or, sometimes, every night.

The Business of Sleep

They have no moving parts, but their prices start at $1,500, and can climb as high as $10,000 or more. Their owners use them for at least half a dozen hours out of twenty-four, seven days a week. And, in the words of the bible of American shopping, *Consumer Reports*, acquiring one provokes more anxiety than buying a car.

We're describing a premium mattress. (No points for guessing "plasma screen television.")

The business of buying a place on which to lay one's weary head obliges a mattress shopper to figure out whether the Sealy Posturepedic Warrington Limited Ultraplush Europillow sold by Sleepy's is comparable to the Sealy Posturepedic Antebellum Plush Box Top sold by U.S. Mattress. And they must do so while juggling such information as number and gauge of coils and the thread count of the damask (or satin) cover. And then, of course, obedient to the shopping advice given out by friends and strangers alike, to spend at least fifteen minutes in-store lying on any mattress under consideration. Perhaps the most remarkable thing about this $5 billion industry is that, despite these incredible demands on the shopper's time, most buyers actually report a high degree of purchase satisfaction.

The reason, of course, is that virtually all mattresses that compete for the $1,500+ sale are pretty much identical in use, even with the assortment of names, pillow tops, Ultrasuede, coated coils, and so on. They're even similar in manufacture: Most of the business ends of every innerspring, box spring, and even bed frame made by Sealy, Simmons, Stearns & Foster, King Koil, and Serta are actually made by a Carthage, Missouri, company called Leggett & Platt. As with many consumer durables—those household items intended to last for five years or more—a good bed might require a lot of search time, but the companies that manufacture them have a good idea what their buyers want . . . even when the buyers don't know themselves. In the words of Warren Shoulberg, editor of *Home Furnishing News,* "You only buy [a mattress] once every 10 or 20 years, so you are woefully unprepared and uneducated. You are confronted with this police lineup of white boxes that all look remarkably similar. The one that's $500 doesn't look all that different from the one that's $5,000."[2]

And, in return, their buyers not only spend a *lot* of time shopping for mattresses; they contribute some of the most attractive margins in the consumer durables category—45 percent gross margin, to be precise. In furniture stores, bedding turns six times annually, with 8 percent of selling space returning 11 percent of sales; by contrast, sofas have the same gross margin, but turn only four times annually and use up 27 percent of selling acreage for 23 percent of sales. Premium-mattress buying, with its combination of high willingness to spend time, and high profit margins (to both manufacturer *and* retailer), is firmly fixed in the painstaking-shopping quadrant. That is, after all, the very definition of the painstaking quadrant: high margin/touchpoints and high time value.

The industry is also dominated by extremely well-entrenched competitors. The business's top ten companies control three-quarters of the entire industry, and the Big Four—Sealy, Simmons, Serta, and Spring Air; something about mattresses favors the nineteenth letter of the alphabet—

controlling 58 percent. With established manufacturers dominating a relatively fragmented retail channel—the top twenty-five retailers comprise only 40 percent of sales—a new company that could enter the bedding industry's painstaking quadrant, and succeed, has something to teach anyone with a similar challenge.

Meet Tempur-Pedic.

Founded in 1991 by a onetime Lexington, Kentucky, horse breeder named Bob Trussell, Tempur-Pedic—in company legend, anyway—turned the heat-sensitive foam developed by NASA in order to relieve the acceleration forces experienced by astronauts into a consumer product that, in 2004, generated nearly $700 million in sales . . . and a compound annual growth rate of 46 percent over the preceding years, with net operating margins of 22 percent.

Creating and executing a marketing plan for a truly better mousetrap would seem to be a trivial challenge, what with the world beating a path to retailers eager to stock said mousetrap. As is often the case, though, first impressions are wrong. When mousetrap buyers have to shell out thousands of dollars for a better one, shop for one every ten years or so, and were pretty happy with the last one they bought, selling a mousetrap that not only costs more, but looks nothing like the familiar and reliable spring-loaded version, is a daunting prospect.

And, despite the unusual claims made for it, Tempur-Pedic's "memory foam," which changes its elasticity when it comes into contact with body heat and so molds itself to the sleeping body, is not exactly a perfect product. Because of the heat sensitivity of the "Swedish sleep system" (it's actually manufactured in Denmark and Virginia), it can't be used with electric blankets or heating pads. It is highly sensitive to environmental temperatures, and owners are advised to keep bedrooms at a constant 65°. Sleepers find it difficult to turn, read in an upright position, or—presumably—engage in other bed-traditional activities. And, the mattress smells bad.

Add to these considerable disadvantages the need to attract the attention of a respectable percentage of the 10 million or so American households who go mattress shopping every year, typically spending two or more days in the search. Since this is more shopping time than is historically spent on a high-end television, and nearly as much as on an automobile, grabbing an additional quarter-hour of the shopper's time was the *sine qua non* of success.

Many of the tactics pursued by Tempur-Pedic in service of this objective were classic old-time marketing: convincing the retailing community to tell the tale by giving away thousands of free beds to store personnel; wide distribution of promotional material, including not just DVDs and videotapes that describe the "weightless sleep" or "Swedish sleep miracle" but samples of Tempur-Pedic's memory foam, as well. The company pursued not only traditional consumer testimonials and used the NASA connection shamelessly (though the value to consumers of the space program's implied endorsement has declined considerably from its Tang and Space Pen peak) but actively marketed to hospitals and health care professionals, reasoning that the public's belief that firmer sleep surfaces helped to avoid and reduce back pain needed correction.

But the most unusual, and effective, tactic used by Tempur-Pedic in grabbing their share of the shopping time potential mattress buyers were willing to spend thinking about their innovative product was to expand the time itself. Tempur-Pedic turned its entire product line into a long-term product test by selling "viscoelastic" pillows, mattress toppers, slippers, even sleep masks, each of them at a price that represents only a tiny fraction of the cost for an entire system, which includes a mattress, platform, and frame, at a cost of up to $6,000. The result is that they placed their most effective touchpoints in the stopwatches of customers who don't even know they are customers. Tempur-Pedic isolated a significant fraction of the potential buyers long before they were even in buying mode.

Consider the following: While Tempur-Pedic's pillow unit sales over the three years 2001–2004 more than doubled from 1.4 million to 2.9 million, over the same period the share of sales represented by those pillows had *dropped* from 34 percent of Tempur-Pedic's sales in 2001 to 21 percent in 2004. The inference is clear: Tempur-Pedic has won the battle for the painstaking mattress purchase by turning pillow buyers into mattress buyers. A typical shopper is a lot more likely to take a chance on Tempur-Pedic's $3,000 Eurobed if she already owns at least one $100 Tempur-Pedic pillow. And, for those interested in the company's long-term plans to port its U.S. success into the sixty foreign countries in which it is now doing business, the signs are mostly positive: the company's international product mix in 2004 is almost the same as the U.S. mix in 2001, with more than a third in (relatively) low-margin pillows.

Tempur-Pedic has fundamentally altered the speed of the shopping stopwatch, preselling mattresses every time someone buys a travel pillow. And why not? The cost of preselling is a very small percentage of the value of a customer, particularly when the customer can be expected to pay up to $6,000, the list price for Tempur-Pedic's top-of-the-line Grand Bed*.[3]

And an even smaller percentage when the price gets closer to $50,000.

Pursuing Perfection

Years ago, one of our clients was working for one of the big three Detroit automakers (enough years ago, in fact, that Detroit was home to the world's big three). Try as we might, with truckloads of consistent and un-assailable consumer research, we simply couldn't convince the marketing team from Detroit that the day the average consumer walks into a dealer-ship was *not* the biggest day of his or her decade. The Detroit team hon-estly and adamantly believed that consumers thought it to be a very, very, very good time when they (the consumers) "got the opportunity" (De-troit's words) to go into a dealership and haggle.

Readers may draw their own conclusions from this observation. An obvious one would be that this particular automobile manufacturer was delusional. Another would be that our client was not Lexus.

Entering a Lexus showroom is a lot more like visiting a luxury hotel than a car dealer; this is not entirely a surprise, since Lexus famously models its training program for employees on that given by the luxe hotel chain Ritz Carlton. In the search for new ways to surprise and delight its owners, Bob Carter, Lexus Division General Manager, looks to companies like Four Seasons Hotels, Tiffany, and Nordstrom. "When you purchase a Lexus, the ownership experience will be better than anywhere in luxury retail."[4] *Nothing* is regarded as excessive when it comes to pampering cur-rent and potential Lexus owners. Free refreshments are offered, of course, and not just coffee, but imported teas and pastries as well. Picture win-dows look out onto spotlessly clean service bays. Loaner cars. Free car

---

* Even this impressive number barely opens the door for what might be called the super-premium-mattress business, where products from Duxiana, Hollandia, and Hastens can eas-ily top $20,000. As the boomer demographic grows ever older and more affluent, they seem ever more willing to spend unthinkably large sums on the promise of a good night's sleep.

washes. Business centers, complete with fax machines and Wi-Fi Internet access. Gift shops. Playrooms for the kids. Indoor putting greens. *(Indoor putting greens!)*

That showroom experience, as mind-blowing and as important as it is, is only the end of a very long marketing path, one that has made Lexus one of the most profitable brands in America. Its parent company, Toyota, now the largest automobile manufacturer in the world and by far the most profitable, doesn't break out Lexus sales and profit in any reliable way. But since the United States accounts for 40 percent of Toyota's profit, and more than 80 percent of Lexus sales are in the United States (300,000 units in 2005), it's a safe bet that the brand is delivering something north of $1 billion in profit every year.

Lexus has been a success story ever since 1989, when the first Lexus LS400 was sold, six years after Toyota's then-chairman Eiji Toyoda signed off on a project to create a luxury vehicle that could compete with Mercedes-Benz, BMW, and Volvo (and Honda, which had launched the Acura luxury brand three years previously). Toyoda/Toyota's secret product, originally code-named F-1,* was, from the beginning, a different sort of luxury automobile, one that would benefit from all of the profit potential in the painstaking quadrant, without incurring the usual costs.

The problem with painstaking shoppers is that they don't merely *take* pains in finding the perfect hotel room/luxury automobile/stereo system, they frequently *become* pains as well. Given the time and money associated with most painstaking purchases, it should surprise no one that when consumers find themselves in this quadrant, too much is never quite enough. A manufacturer or retailer attempting to compete in this quadrant—and, given the profits to be found here, there is never a shortage—must be prepared either to anticipate all possible problems at all steps along the shopping continuum, or to have a constant stream of dissatisfied customers.

A special sort of painstaking trap lies in wait for a luxury automobile manufacturer: the better your product performs in ways that can be quantified, the more demanding your customers become. A car that goes

---

* It apparently took some persuading to get the company to use a name other than Toyota on the new car. Reportedly, Saatchi & Saatchi tested more than 200 possible names before coming up with the winner, including such also-rans as Vectre, Chaperel, and Alexis, and up until 2005, the cars were still sold in Japan under the Toyota marque.

0–60 in 6.9 seconds in 2000 had better be even quicker by the 2002 model year. Lexus divides the luxury segment into three subgroups,[5] which they call *informed* luxury (demographically, affluent and educated buyers in their early forties, representing approximately 36 percent of the market); *status* luxury (average age thirty-eight; 36 percent); and *conservative* luxury (fifties; 26 percent and declining). For good or ill, the most desirable of these—those willing to pay the largest premium—constitute the informed segment, for which Lexus competes against such marques as Mercedes and BMW, and who want the newest and sexiest, the most cutting-edge design and the highest of tech. The need to constantly top not only one's competitors, but oneself, is what keeps manufacturers in this segment up nights.

Lexus's response to this challenge has been to use their touchpoints—to reinforce the *qualitative* advantages of the brand.* Remember, in this category, you can afford to plant a *lot* of touchpoints at interaction points up to a year before purchase. Lexus's painstaking touchpoints are not designed to exploit customer's anxieties, but to soothe them.

To understand this, it's best to know something about how Lexus differs from its competitors in the allocation of marketing resources. Those competitors constitute one of the advertising industry's biggest customers, spending more than $6 billion annually in the United States. Traditional auto marketers spend about two-thirds of those funds on the last ticks of the shopping stopwatch—sponsorships, dealer cooperative ads, and especially buyer incentives—with only one dollar spent on the earlier-stage brand-building. It is estimated that Lexus, however, spends 50 percent of its marketing dollars on brand-building, half again as much as most car companies.

A big chunk of Lexus's spending—and a rapidly growing chunk—is spent on online communications. It has to be: nearly two-thirds of new-vehicle shoppers now do at least some of their shopping research online before purchasing. This translates into 38 million unique visitors, clicking onto 40 million sites, and spending time on 1.5 *billion* pages, typically starting about thirty days before making a purchase decision. With the

---

* Even when they focus on a quantitative advantage, it is frequently intended as anxiety relief. The famous Lexus production line at Tahara, Japan, appears in the company's marketing literature not because they make the world's fastest cars, but because it has the fewest manufacturing defects of any factory in the world.

unique ability of the web to record shopping time,* researchers can record a very high order of correlation between site activity and what we might call checkbook activity; for example, when online visits for Buick Rendezvous declined 24 percent from March to April, sales declined 33 percent April to May; when visits for Jeep Grand Cherokee increased 16.5 percent in the same period, sales increased 19.2 percent. (For the mathematically inclined reader, this means that site activity correlates with sales at an R^2 of 93.4 percent.)[6]

Lexus is an "industry leader in interactive online marketing,"[7] producing podcasts, investing millions in websites, and creating the industry's best do-it-yourself feature, their "design-your-own-Lexus" website. For the launch of the new IS model, the company ran an online sweepstakes that invited visitors to submit personal photos (only occasionally including the actual car), which they then used to produce a "photomosaic" on what the company called the world's largest digital display on the sixty-foot Reuters billboard in Times Square.

But online marketing, to Lexus, is simply a piece in a multidimensional painstaking marketing plan with touchpoints at every step along the months-long path that leads to the dealer showroom, each of which represents an increasing amount of customer interaction. "The depth and complexity of multi-touchpoint marketing," which was explicitly aimed at more involved—often younger—potential customers, "is what made the IS launch both unique and successful" according to Robert Pisz, national interactive and relationship marketing manager for Lexus.[8] It was during the IS launch that Lexus expanded the interactivity of their touchpoints by placing laser equipment inside empty New York City and Los Angeles storefronts, and then inviting passersby to build their own "holographic" Lexus, changing options, colors, and models on a full-size (though immaterial) model car.

Perhaps the most consistent lesson of marketing in the painstaking quadrant is that painstaking shoppers want to participate in the selling process . . . that they want, in fact, to sell themselves. In a study led by Simon Arbuthnot, national marketing manager for Lexus of Great Britain, the cumulative impact of Lexus's multidimensional marketing— television advertising, print, direct mail, Lexus's website, and, of course,

---

* For more about this capability, and putting it to work, see chapter 8.

their showrooms—was shown in high relief.[9] By taking reported satisfaction levels for consumers at specific touchpoints, and comparing them with a variety of actionable measurements—such as "propensity to purchase or recommend"—Arbuthnot's team discovered that the interactive touchpoints (website, showroom) had significantly larger impact than noninteractive (direct response, television and print advertising).

No huge surprise there. However, mapping the results against time-to-purchase, and comparing it with a simultaneous set of studies, the survey showed that different categories of touchpoints correlated with propensity to purchase depending on distance in time from the purchase. TV and print displayed the highest impact a year prior to purchase; direct mail was highest two to three months prior, and website and showroom were highest within days and weeks. High involvement within weeks of a purchase; low involvement within months . . . but the research clearly showed that a single misstep at *any* touchpoint—inappropriate print ad, website mishap—damages propensity to purchase along the entire shopping continuum. Painstaking shoppers want to *buy* (rather than to *be sold*), but they can't be rushed. They have to be reeled in, slowly, with a series of touchpoints that gradually increase the level of shopper involvement.

The company's focus on preselling, on making sure that potential customers have already been seduced long before they walk into one of those extraordinary showrooms, is not, however, a comment on the importance of the dealers; quite the contrary. Lexus invests in preselling *in order* to support their retailers, the automobile industry's most envied dealer network.

From its beginning, Lexus has been determined to have an outstanding relationship with their dealers. The relationship between automobile manufacturers and their dealer networks has historically been a stormy one. Though the automobile industry has always been relatively concentrated since GM merged a half dozen formerly independent manufacturers into the world's largest company, the dealers, almost all independent, are very fragmented: The top twenty-five dealers in the United States control less than 8 percent of market. This relationship, which had historically been used by manufacturers to force inventory onto dealers' lots whether they were able to sell them or not (and thus improve their own earnings), bred a long-standing hostility between manufacturers and dealers. Over time, and in order to improve their bargaining position, dealers more often than not opted for nonexclusive relationships, so much so that today the average dealer sells 2.4 different automotive brands.

That same relationship of unequals put a lot more margin in the pockets of manufacturers than their dealers, who usually derive most of their gross sales from vehicle sales, but most of their profit from parts and service.

Lexus has changed this relationship by showing potential dealers a better way, using brand-building rather than incentives to deliver not only gross sales, but the highest profitability in the industry. The company drives several dealer training and recognition programs with names like "Lotus Benchmark Service" and "Elite Dealers." Among the features of these programs are visits to the U.S. dealerships by personal trainers from Lexus headquarters and visits to Japan by U.S. dealer personnel for months of training and indoctrination.

And dealers line up for the privilege. Lexus is so selective, in fact, that they accepted only 72 out of 1,500 applications in the most recent year for which they have reported results. Those seventy-two are well suited for Lexus's focus on eliminating every point that an anxious, painstaking shopper might find as a reason to delay or forgo purchase. The one enduring criticism of the Lexus has been that it is boring, at least as compared with BMW, or Jaguar, or Audi, or other brands with more quantifiable performance benchmarks. Articles from *Car and Driver* to *Marketing Week* have hammered on this but they miss the point. The character of BMW is precisely what Lexus promises buyers they won't need to worry about: You don't buy a Lexus in order to stretch your driving skills; you buy it to enjoy the luxury of an outstanding automobile backed by an outstanding service experience. The success of the brand has shown, better than any survey, that you can achieve more with painstaking shoppers by smoothing their paths than by asking them to break new ones. Lexus has demonstrated that the real sweet spot in the painstaking quadrant is the property of companies that do the best job at simultaneously calming and engaging shoppers who are rich in time and money.

Admit One

Shoppers might take weeks to decide upon a memory foam mattress; they might take a month or two shopping for just the right Lexus GS350: the one in Mercury Metallic, with Red Walnut trim and the DVD navigation system. A bride will spend a year planning every detail of her once-in-a-lifetime wedding.

How impetuous.

Year in, year out, the longest shopping cycle in America begins with hundreds of thousands of middle-class families realizing that their newly minted sixteen-year-old high school sophomores have started what may be the most important, and certainly the most expensive, shopping trip of all: picking a college. This painstaking effort typically does consume years. By comparison, planning a wedding consumes a mere six to eight months, according to *Bride's* magazine.

Few things are clearer than the long-term value of a college education: the most recent data from the U.S. Census Bureau suggests that the value of a bachelor's degree to an American who received one in 2005 might be as much as $2 million over an individual's earning life.* Just as clear are the costs of that degree. The average annual costs for tuition plus room and board at a public university currently approach $9,000, and at a private school just shy of $19,000. Even so, at any reasonable assumption comparing present cost versus future value, the investment in college is as close to a sure thing as any, though complicated by the fact that many of the costs are borne by family, while all of the return is received by the student.

Less clear than the value of *any* college degree is the value of a *particular* degree; despite the widespread belief in the premium value of degrees from prestigious institutions, researchers find it difficult to find it outside the dozen or so schools at the highest end of the SAT/GPA recruitment scale. Many other things conspire in the future income of the graduates of even Ivy League schools. George W. Bush isn't the president of the United States because he graduated from Yale any more than Bill Gates is the world's richest man because he dropped out of Harvard. Variability in earnings potential is far larger *within* graduating classes than *between* the class averages of any two universities. So far as the numbers indicate, what matters is college, not the perfect college.

As with so many other things in the life of modern American consumers, however, perceived value matters as much or more than real value.

---

* Based on fairly conservative assumptions, the holder of a B.A. or B.S. can be expected to earn $3.907 million versus $2.050 million for someone with a high school diploma.

For every study that demonstrates the negligible added value of degrees from prestigious colleges, another shows that students—and, perhaps more important, their families—*over*value them. It is, moreover, no coincidence that colleges and universities attach a higher value to the students who most overvalue *them;* in addition to the nonfinancial competition in which institutions of higher education are engaged—to recruit not only the brightest high school seniors, but the best athletes and the most talented musicians—there are clear financial advantages in the pursuit of the most avid potential students: they are the students who are most likely to pay retail prices for that diploma.

This is no small objective, and it gets larger every year. In 2004, the list price for a single year at Yale University—including tuition, room and board, but not including books, travel, and incidentals—was $38,432. The average out-of-pocket expense for the incoming first-year class, however, was only $15,759, with the difference made up from scholarships, loans, and work-study programs. At America's most elite universities, the revenue difference, over four years, between a student that the school recruits and one that recruits the school—between the reluctant and painstaking quadrants—is approaching $100,000, and though the difference is smaller at public schools (and at private schools without a Yale-size endowment) it remains very large indeed. Hardly any shopping decision of this magnitude better illustrates the power of Alchian and Allen's theorem.

A midwestern state college may not be marketing itself nationally like Stanford, Harvard, or Yale—or, in their own niches, Annapolis or Caltech—but it is still competing for both the best local applicants and those most likely to pay their way. Given the extraordinary potential value of painstaking decisions to *any* college, one might expect to find, on the part of college recruiters, a careful attention to consumers' shopping stopwatches. One would not be disappointed.

In fact, the college shopping experience is very nearly a perfect laboratory for seeing the stopwatch in action, because shoppers in the category are not merely driven by the calendar, but are all on the *same* calendar. In 2005, at least a third of America's 4 million or so high school juniors showed enough painstaking interest in college to take one of the two national college entrance examinations and about half of *them* had already taken a preliminary test whose only value is the number of scholarship dollars available to those who score well.

The decision to attend college, and to refine the choices available, starts even earlier; during their ninth and tenth grades, 15 percent of students, and 27 percent of their parents, have investigated college costs; by the time those same students are eleventh graders, more than half have done so (52 percent of students, 54 percent of parents).[10] But SAT/ACT season is what starts the largest number of those painstaking stopwatches ticking. Scores for each test, which are given on a rolling schedule, arrive three to four weeks after the test date, and it's a toss-up which is more wrenching: taking the test, or seeing one's score, since the latter is a key moment in the selection process . . . in the painstaking-shopping experience. A student, or her family, may have her heart set on one school, but her ability to satisfy that desire depends on grades, test scores . . . and money, since scholarships that are not need based tend to be a lot easier to find for applicants with scores in the top quartile.

The stopwatch continues to tick throughout the summer between junior and senior years, which is the season with the largest number of campus visits. During the senior year it ticks not only more frequently, but louder, with applications due in November of the senior year for those students interested in declaring their sole-and-undying interest in a single school. Though the procedure known as "early decision" (in which applicants agree to accept an offer for admission, in return for both an early response and improved chances; a less binding version, known as "early action" is not binding) is no longer as prevalent at America's top colleges as it once was, it isn't likely to vanish any time soon, probably because it maps so neatly onto the characteristics of the painstaking quadrant. That is, it gives the highest priority to the customer willing to start the shopping process at the earliest date. Since the applicant decides on a school before knowing what, if any, financial aid might reduce the real cost, it disproportionately attracts the high-margin students who are able, if not willing, to pay full fare. For everyone else, regular admission applications are due between January and mid-February, as are financial aid applications. In April, acceptance letters are mailed, and by May, applicants are obliged to either accept or reject acceptance; as a result, another burst of campus visits occur every spring.

This schedule will be familiar to every reader who has either been through it, or—more likely—has observed it at secondhand, through the eyes of their children. But it is even more familiar to the other side of the transaction: to the admissions officers at America's 2,500 four-year and 1,000 two-year colleges.

The art of college admissions, whether at Anonymous State or at Harvard University, is more than simply attracting students with the highest SATs or fastest times in the forty-yard dash or (more cynically) the best chance of paying retail price. Every college has a slightly different set of objectives, ranging from raising the school's profile in national rankings to filling a needed place in the school's marching band; flugelhorn players, like National Merit Scholars, do not grow on trees. But whatever the criteria, whomever they are recruiting, *all* colleges try to place their most powerful lures—their best touchpoints—at those points in the shopping process where they are likely to do the most good. Studies show that, for nearly nine out of ten applicants, this painstaking process takes place during the two years between taking either the SAT/ACT at the beginning of junior year and the receipt of acceptances at the end of senior year.* It is there that institutions of higher education, quite properly, invest their marketing resources.

Those resources are small by the standards of many of the businesses profiled in this book. But they are not insignificant. In for-profit higher education, institutions spend 20 percent of their total budgets on marketing[11]; in the much larger not-for-profit sector, the marketing budgets are closer to 5 percent. Not surprisingly, the cost of recruitment is directly proportional to the cost of tuition; private four-year institutions, whose median cost for annual tuition exceeds $30,000, pay more than $2,000 in recruitment costs for every accepted student; four-year public colleges, on the other hand—with a median annual tuition cost of $10,000—pay $455.[12]

Despite this significant dollar investment—or, perhaps, because of it—colleges have been slow to apply real rigor to analyzing the effectiveness and cost/benefit trade-offs of the specific programs. Only since the early 1990s have they been engaging in post hoc evaluation of each marketing and recruitment strategy,[13] taking their high school visits, targeted advertising, and campus visits, and mapping their effectiveness against their costs. They now know, for example, that, as the *Chronicle of Higher Educa-*

---

* About 11 to 12 percent are either early planners (in the case of a small number of loyal alumni, i.e., less than 1 percent, from birth on) or applicants who decide on college after the senior year.

tion put it, "guidance counselors often have some of the least influence on the college decision-making process."[14]

If high school guidance departments are not where a smart painstaking marketer would place touchpoints, where?

Founded in 1891 as a women's college with the unwieldy handle the North Carolina State Normal and Industrial School, the University of North Carolina at Greensboro—as it is currently known—is the sort of college on which the United States is truly built. America's college graduates are far more likely to have attended a school like UNC–Greensboro, a midsize public institution with 16,000 students overall, about 12,000 of them undergraduates, than schools better known because of their ivy-covered walls or Division 1A football champions. And their graduates are well-served; trusted sources like the *Princeton Review* and *Kiplinger's* give the school high points both for quality and for value. Its undergraduate faculty in accounting and business, and its graduate faculty in education and nursing are first-rate, as is the education they give to their students. The campus is attractive (and fully equipped for wireless networking), the library good, and the climate pleasant.

Nonetheless, UNC–Greensboro, like most of the schools it resembles, must recruit aggressively for the best students in a particular region, in Greensboro's case, North Carolina and the Southeast. Jim Brown, the Associate Provost for Enrollment Services at the university, manages more than twenty annual on-campus recruitment events, sends representatives on several hundred high school visits, and publishes twenty-two recruitment publications every year. The "marketing department" at UNC–Greensboro authors hundreds of web pages, distributes nearly 60,000 CD-ROMs extolling the wonders of the campus, and communicates with top prospects as many as forty times over a two-year period.[15]

The information that is presented in all these interactions—all these touchpoints—seems almost obsessively rational in their content. Students are advised to create checklists containing quantitative data on everything from average SAT scores to the ethnic profile of the student body to the job prospects—frequently calculated to several decimal points of precision—of the college's graduates. Students are told everything they need to know about undergraduate majors, housing subsidies, and, of course, tuition costs. Nonetheless, at the most analytical admissions departments, all of these activities are focused on a single decisive moment. Echoing the extraordinary efforts that Lexus dealers invest in showroom interactions, the pivotal event for UNC–Greensboro's recruitment strategy is the campus visit. Like buying a mattress or luxury automobile, the decision to attend a particular college is an emotional one and it is often made in something less than thirty minutes.[16] As a result, best practices for marketing a particular college to painstaking shoppers during that visit include offering hotel discounts, flexible visit times . . . even such less-than-obvious activities as investing in special signs and directions and campus maps targeted at the first-time visitor. It is scarcely a surprise then, with campus visits the key closing moment for most colleges, that campus tour guides are the single most important link in the painstaking chain. Franklin and Marshall College even rates their guides monthly on "professionalism and engagement."[17]

The decision to attend a particular college, therefore, is pretty clearly another place where stopwatch principles are precisely on point; as with the selection of a luxury automobile, anxiety about making a less-than-perfect choice dominates the shopper's mind for a period running into years. As with all consumption within the painstaking quadrant, a dozen or more touchpoints, when properly mapped, lead key shoppers to a decisive moment when an emotional calculus tips the decision one way or another. This key moment, and the buildup to it, is, perhaps, the defining characteristic of all painstaking shopping. The margin-growing strategies so successfully employed by companies operating in the painstaking quadrant are illustrated in Figure 6-1.

Moreover, the painstaking quadrant demonstrates the power of applying stopwatch marketing principles. This quadrant, after all, is the northeast corner of the matrix—every player in this quadrant is already in a high-margin category and is already dealing with customers who are willing to take the time to research and/or be sold. What Lexus, UNC–Greensboro, and Tempur-Pedic demonstrate so brilliantly, then, is that diligent marketers can move northeast even *within* the painstaking quadrant. The stopwatches of even painstaking shoppers can be slowed down and sales can be closed at an even higher margin.

More broadly, the painstaking quadrant is a good place to summarize the matrix construct, because, everything else being equal, marketers should nearly always desire to move their product or service east—more time to close the sale because of a more slowly ticking stopwatch—and

PAINSTAKING QUADRANT

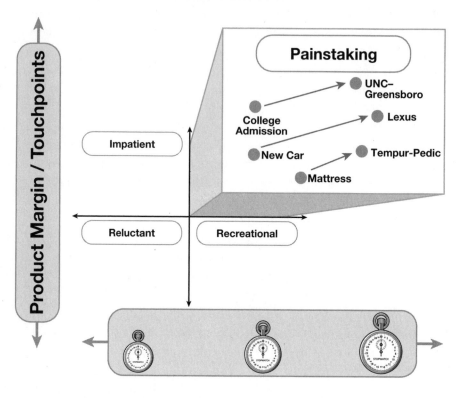

Figure 6-1

generally north—higher margins. We have argued throughout the preceding pages that the key challenge for marketers is either to slow down the target customer's stopwatch to allow for more time to close the sale or to stop the ticking right now and close the sale right now. Whole Foods Market, Charles Schwab, and Lexus are superior examples of the "slow down and enjoy yourself so we can sell you" approach while Microsoft and Master Lock are perhaps the best at "stop right now, we've got what you want, don't think about it anymore" approach.

We do suspect, however, that most marketers probably think their target customer has a more slowly ticking stopwatch than they do, in fact, exhibit in the real world. With all the brainpower and marketing knowledge aimed at copywriting, advertising, POP (point-of-purchase) materials design, creating the perfect media plan, and so on, one might begin to believe that customers do, indeed, spend a great deal of time internalizing it all. The challenge of actually determining where any given company's or brand's consumption patterns lie on the matrix and, of course, developing some strategies to deal with that placement is the focus of the next section of this book.

Part Three
Putting It All to Work

Chapter Seven

Discovery: Identifying Your Selling Quadrants

Discovery Defined: Identifying the Target and the Purchase Decision

 This chapter is about change. Specifically, this chapter is about changing the way you think about marketing your product or service. It is about beginning the process of stopwatch marketing for your company by identifying the quadrants in which the consumption for your products and services lie. After all, it is insufficient to simply view the matrix as an interesting concept; it is now time to define—with as much basis in fact, quantification, and specificity as possible—how the stopwatch matrix concept can better inform the management of your business.

Change, however, is hard. It's hard for reasons of human temperament, but also for what might be called the underlying laws of the universe. The same four-century-old logic that explained to Isaac Newton why things tend to travel in a straight line unless acted upon by some outside force explains the tendency of business organizations to perceive the world using the same tools year after year. In fact, the very names of these business tools indicate their repetitive natures: *quarterly* tracking studies, *interim* budget reviews, *annual* planning processes, and so on.

This inertia, to give the phenomenon its proper name, is especially pronounced in successful businesses. And since the unsuccessful ones tend to disappear over time, in any given year most businesses are, by definition, successful ones. While this is a testimony to their survival skills, it is also a problem: In a successful business organization, just about everybody, from the rawest intern to the most seasoned CEO—and especially sales and marketing executives—*loves* their product or service. They are entranced by every aspect of it. They eat, drink, and breathe it. They talk about it and they read about it. In our parlance, their behavior most closely mirrors that of recreational shoppers . . . the sort of people who will take time during vacation to visit a hardware store, or tire dealership, or mattress factory. They aren't called "busman's holidays" for nothing. And nothing adds to marketing inertia—the tendency to do things the way they've always been done—more than total immersion in the product or service being marketed; nothing mislabels your customer's shopping behavior more reliably than your own preconceptions.

Remember our onetime Detroit-based client who believed that their showrooms held an attraction to car buyers comparable to what Santiago de Compostela offered pilgrims? According to the highly paid marketers at this particular auto company, a day at one of their dealerships, haggling over price, choosing between owning and leasing, filling out credit applications, deciding whether to sign up for the extended warranty, rust protection, or antitheft window etching, calculating the taxes and licensing fees, was, apparently, a Good Time . . . in short, recreational shopping.

The results of this, ahem, misperception (the average car buyer would rather visit a dentist than an automobile dealer) should be obvious to anyone who has followed Detroit's fortunes over the past several years. The fact that more than half of all buyers report that they paid more and received less than they wanted (and these were the people who actually *bought* something) is predictable. Because GM, Ford, and pre–Daimler Chrysler were so convinced that their customers' stopwatches were, essentially, turned off while they were inside the doors of a dealership— time, after all, does fly when you're having a good time—they consistently placed their touchpoints at the wrong spot on the shopper's time continuum. Believing that potential buyers of Buicks, Dodges, and Mercurys were so eager to buy one or the other that the key marketing objective was simply guiding them into one rather than the other, they invested far too much time, effort, and money on the consideration touchpoints found outside the dealership and on dealer incentives. As the Lexus case study demonstrates, they also spent far too little on actually improving and enhancing the consumer's experience at the dealership.

It is, therefore, absolutely critical for marketers to take a brutal, clear-eyed approach to determining the quadrant in which their current customers occupy when shopping for their product or service. This is the process marketers call "Discovery," the utterly essential first step in stopwatch marketing, where the most important elements of the consumption mix are assigned to the most appropriate quadrants. A quick look at the summary matrix in Figure 7-1 makes this clear: who wouldn't rather lead the well-known, branded institutions listed in the matrix (Goodyear Assurance with TripleTred, Whole Foods Market) than the generic category descriptors ("Replacement Tires," "Traditional Supermarkets," and so on)?

THE MATRIX: Summary of Examples

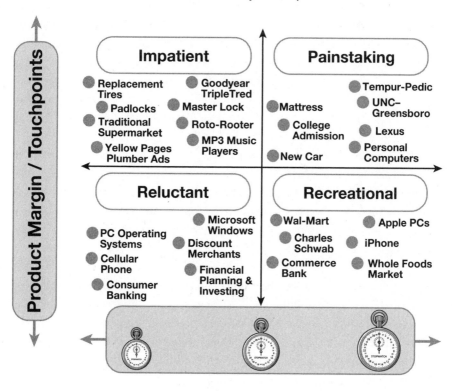

Figure 7-1

Perversely enough, and despite their own emotional engagement in their products or services, many managers, unfortunately, ignore the emotional element of buying decisions when pursuing the Discovery process, much less planning a marketing campaign. Not all, to be sure; some categories, such as perfume, liquor, and fashion, are so dependent on emotional appeals that they absolutely demand emotional thinking. But even there, we frequently find that clients fail to attach enough importance to the emotional side of buying. And since time perception is one of the most subjective of all phenomena, they miscalculate the rate at which their customers' stopwatches are ticking away. We suspect that the nature of graduate business education is partly to blame; it's far easier to teach a marketing MBA how to use multiple regression, factor analysis, and statistical modeling than how to recognize a happy customer. Even so, any disciplined, deliberate approach to locating a product or service in a given quadrant must take into account the emotional drivers ("This is fun") of purchase and preference as well as the rational ("It's on my way home").

This is particularly true in business-to-business markets. After all, in a B2B transaction, we're often asking shoppers to bet their yearly targets, their bonuses, and quite possibly their jobs, careers, and reputations. You don't really think all those years of "nobody ever getting fired for buying IBM" was driven by a purely rational cost/benefit trade-off with the *company's* interests held paramount, do you? Or, more recently, you don't think middle managers *rationally* spend up to three or four times the price of overnight mail to use FedEx when it absolutely, positively has to be there overnight? Or that all those designers and artists (who were long-haired rebels in college and didn't take the GMATS) are buying Apple PowerBooks rather than Dells because the screen has a few more pixels?

Being blind to the fact that consumers are rarely if ever as fascinated by the product as are its creators seems almost forgivable; it is certainly almost inevitable. So is an over-reliance on the quantitative techniques mastered in graduate school. The same cannot be said for the other common reason for misreading stopwatches we find in our practice: simple territoriality. An admiral testifying before a congressional committee about the imperative need for yet another aircraft carrier battle group is no more impassioned than a product manager fighting for her budget, or a sales director supporting his field force. And the results are, not surprisingly, similar: The Navy gets its own pilots and planes, no matter what the Air Force wants, and the Sales Department keeps its territories and the product manager keeps her TV budget, to keep peace in their respective families; avoiding, thereby, the need to change how they are organized and prepared to attack the target.

The combination of affection for the product, discomfort with the fuzziness of emotionally driven choice, and protectiveness for turf, tends to constrain most companies into doing what they've always done, with change occurring only at the margins. This may be acceptable for successful companies—remember, these are survivors; it is wise to remember that natural selection in business, no less than in evolutionary biology, conserves useful adaptations, and that change-for-the-sake-of-change isn't especially helpful. The dinosaurs ruled the earth for a hundred million years, after all, and showed a pronounced aversion to change.

Until an asteroid strikes, that is. The asteroid can take the form of new competitors, a drastic fall-off in share or profits, a sea change in consumer preferences, and—most terrifyingly—the introduction of a completely new solution to the problem that defined your core consumer; petroleum was to the whale oil trade in 1870 what scientific calculators were to the slide rule industry in 1970. Even then, the traditional answer is usually the same: "Do what we've always done, only better/faster/harder/cheaper" and "Get back to basics"; in 1969, the Pickett Company, America's premier slide rule manufacturer, invested in a new technology to make the lines on the N600 logarithmic slide rule—the one that, the company boasted, flew to the moon on Apollo 11—"finer than a human hair." Had the slide rule makers realized that what they sold was not a few pieces of finely machined wood, plastic, and metal, but solutions to mathematical problems, the label on your calculator might say "Faber-Castell" instead of "Hewlett-Packard."

It's too much, of course, to blame the decline of America's slide rule manufacturers—to say nothing of her automobile industry—on difficulty in implementing stopwatch principles. No matter how well Pickett Inc. recognized that the market for their beautifully made calculating machines had gone from a medium-size group of painstaking shoppers to a tiny number of collectors in the far reaches of the recreational quadrant, their business was still going to vanish. But for companies with more manageable problems, understanding those customers is the first step to a solution.

The first crucial activity in stopwatch marketing is to identify the *real* consumer of your product or service. Federal Express has become a $29-billion-a-year giant for many reasons, but one is surely their understanding that the target for their service was *not* the managers of America's corporate mail rooms, but the middle managers who, in a crisis, will *tell* the mail room guy to "FedEx it," regardless of policy, preference of the supply chain manager, or good common sense. Our experience is that most companies or marketing departments do a poor (or at least insufficient) job of defining their target market. Most big companies are good at defining a *media target* such as "women aged twenty-five to forty-four." Companies are even very good at detailing the demographics of their target: "upscale, suburban, working mothers aged twenty-five to forty-four." What companies are, in our opinion, less disciplined about, is defining the target market in emotional and payoff terms that you can affect in ways that permit effective marketing actions . . . ways that lead to a sale, which is, after all, the point of the entire exercise. It isn't terribly helpful to paint a bull's-eye on a piece of cardboard unless you can also aim and fire a rifle in its direction. In the FedEx example, the company's great insight was to define the target market as "deadline dependent managers." In three short words, they had defined exactly whom they should target and the benefit they should promise.

In the FedEx example, the payoff to the target market—the benefit— was also quite straightforward: "You won't get fired." That is, middle managers (a career-preserving lot if ever there was one) were quite willing to spend up to five times the cost of using the U.S. Postal Service to be absolutely, positively certain that their package or letter or invoice would get there overnight. The tagline, and ad campaign, "When it absolutely, positively has to be there overnight," of course, captured this brilliantly and became a long-remembered classic. The insight, however, that led to this was the determination that "deadline dependent managers" were the target and their deep emotional concern was "not getting fired."

So, the second crucial element of the Discovery process in stopwatch marketing is to identify the three elements that define the purchase decision for your product:

1. Is it an important purchase or not? What are the needs, problems, hopes, and dreams that are entangled in this decision?
2. Is there a risk in making the wrong decision? What are the trade-offs that your consumer is willing to make between risk and benefit?
3. How much time and trouble do key buyers really invest in planning, researching, and shopping?

A Better Focus Group

These are fundamentally subjective issues, and they are best answered in a qualitative manner. We have found that the most effective technique with our own clients is to begin with a series of focus group interviews well in advance of any quantitative research. So, indeed, do most marketers with the budget to do research. However, a focus group intended to elicit the sort of issues needed for stopwatch marketing has a special character, focusing on the time when your customer decides to buy. In addition, we again emphasize the emotional side of the purchase decision. Remember how we described the mind-set of participants in the recreational quadrant: "I just can't wait to go back . . . this is really fun." Or in the impatient quadrant: "I just can't wait to get this over with." Consequently, the focus group exercise is intended mostly to get at those emotional hot buttons. We ask questions like "What would you do if (fill in the blank) didn't exist?" and "How did you feel at the end of that shopping day?" and "If you could get rid of some aspects of this experience, which aspects would those be? To whom would you dump off those tasks? How is that likely to make them feel?" In addition, we often give the respondents multiple homework assignments in advance of the group on product or user imagery, asking them to bring to the focus group an article from their home or a magazine ad that best represents how they feel when they shop for whatever it is we're researching at the moment. In the homework we may ask them, for instance, to bring in magazine ads representing how they feel today (about the product we're researching) and how they would like to feel in the future. The contrast-and-compare exercise can lead to quite frank discussions about the real emotional needs.

What *we* bring to Discovery focus groups (the starting point for creating a stopwatch marketing plan) is many years of experience with the process, as well as access to research professionals who can handle the nitty-gritty of recruiting, moderating, creating stimuli, and reporting out on the groups. Sometimes these professionals take the form of other, specialized consulting services; sometimes they are provided by the client's own research department. If you lack similar access (or at least some familiarity with the process) yourself, what follows may seem somewhat confusing, but if a primer on these issues is needed, we've listed several good market research textbooks and guides in Appendix A.

The primary purpose of the focus groups is to identify the quadrant in which the target customers for a given brand, or company, or product take the time to decide to buy. To do that, we use the process to explore the three basic questions:

1. Is it important?
2. Is it risky?
3. Does it take time and trouble?

The general answers to these questions, which can identify the quadrant in which most of the shopping behavior occurs, determine the path of the second half of the focus group, which consists of quadrant-specific questions.

Among the general questions we would always recommend asking are:

1. Is this purchase an important one or not?
2. Is it routine or rare? How rare? Twice a year? Once a decade?
3. Do you find yourself putting off the purchase? Do you put off even thinking or researching about it?
4. If you do put it off, why? Because you don't really want to do it? Because you think you'll screw it up? Because you think the whole thing is an unpleasant process?
5. Is it worth it to invest a little more time in studying up, comparison shopping, and so on to make sure you make the right decision? How do you, personally, define "worth it"?
6. Where do you go for information—magazines, *Consumer Reports*, friends and relatives, and so forth? How much time do you take in this information-gathering process? Do you spend more time thinking about this purchase, making the purchase, or using the product?
7. If you make the wrong decision, what are the repercussions? Does it affect only you or are others (boss, client, spouse, coworker, kids) going to know about it? Are you going to have to live with your screw-up for a long time?
8. Do you look forward to shopping there? Looking for this product or service? Reading about it before shopping?
9. Is this "fun" or a "pain"?

Having completed this overview on the customer's shopping style according to the three key questions (Importance, Risk, Time and Trouble), we then move on to the "quadrant identifiers"—specific questions that pigeon-hole respondent consumption behavior and buying decisions into one of the four quadrants (see examples in Figure 7-2).

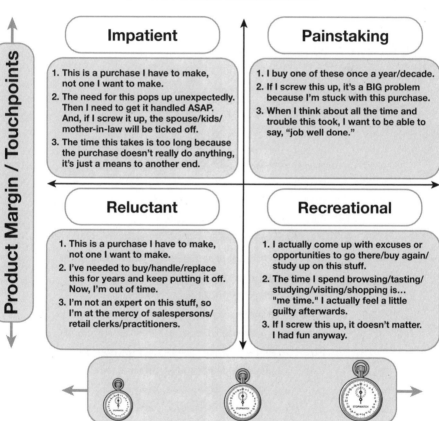

Figure 7-2

In the actual, relaxed focus group setting, we often find it best to phrase the specific quadrant identifier questions in true–false format; for example, "True or false: If I screw this up, it's a BIG problem because I'm stuck with this HDTV for the next ten years."

To bring this all to life, imagine conducting focus groups to understand the differences between Whole Foods Market and Goodyear Tire stores, two different experiences we discussed in the chapters on recreational and impatient shopping. This is not far-fetched, by the way; we are often asked to help clients operating in the reluctant or impatient quadrants to help them find ways to make the customer experience more pleasant, fun, rewarding, and the like. The following is a sample discussion guide for such Discovery focus groups.

EXAMPLE DISCUSSION GUIDE

Natural Foods / Replacement Tires Focus Groups
Discussion Guide

Timing	Topics

0:00–0:10   **Focus Group Basics, Introductions, etc.**
- Welcome/thanks for coming
- Purpose of discussion
  - Attendees need to be incredibly honest
  - No right/wrong answers
- We are going to talk about shopping today—shopping for two very different kinds of products—food and tires

0:10–0:20   **Information Sources, Media Habits, and Topics**
- We are all bombarded by all sorts of media—some of it is entertaining, some purely informational. I'm interested in the specific media that you feel you consume on a regular basis: that is, what TV do you watch regularly, what magazines or newspapers do you spend some time with, what kinds of things do you stop and read (e.g., newsletters from stores, daily info shots from websites)
- When you think about all of that media—where do you feel you get most of the information about the products you buy?
- How does that vary from product category to product category? Thinking about the two areas we're talking about today, how is that different for food versus tires? (Are some from TV, others from the web, etc.?)
- (If the group fails to mention either, a question that asks directly about

food and beverage is a reliable fallback): There is a lot of buzz out there about certain benefits of different types of foods/beverages. What have you heard about recently?

0:20–0:35   **Food-Shopping Habits**

- Where do you shop for the foods and beverages you and your family eat at home?
- How did you happen to choose these places?
- How do you divide your shopping between these places?
- Do you approach shopping at each place in the same way? If not, how/why? Do you, for instance, browse at one and "just rush through" at another?
- If you could give the task of shopping at one place to someone else, what place would you like to give up? Why?

0:35–0:50   **Discuss the Whole Foods experience.**

Recall that attendees have been asked to bring in an item that evokes the "Whole Foods shopping experience." Here is the place to discuss their homework:

- How does this item represent Whole Foods? What makes Whole Foods special?
- How long have you shopped there? Why did you first go there?
- What store did it replace? Or was it incremental?
- When/how often do you shop there? If not every week, what motivates the visit?
- What kind of products would you buy only at W.F.? What would you never buy there? Why?
- Probes on natural foods:
  - What are "natural foods"?
  - Why are they important to you? How long have you used/sought them?
  - What foods/beverages *must* be natural for you? Which do you *not* care about?
  - Complete these sentences: For something to be "natural" it has to have/be _____.
- When I walk into Whole Foods, it makes me feel like _____.
- People who shop at Whole Foods are the kind of people who _____.
- Cutting through all of it, Whole Foods is really all about _____.

- The one thing I expect from Whole Foods that no place else delivers is _____.
- I know that a product sold at Whole Foods is one that is _____.

0:50–1:15 **Whole Foods Quadrant Identification**

So, thinking about an average week or month . . .

- How important is your typical visit to Whole Foods?
- On a scale of 1 to 10 where 1 is "I dread it and I really am putting it off" and 10 is "I am really looking forward to it," how would you rate your feelings about your next visit to Whole Foods?
- If you do put it off, why? What are some of the factors that make you not want to do it? What makes the visit an unpleasant or a pleasant process overall? Is it ever better or worse? Why? Can you really screw up a visit to Whole Foods? If so, how? Then what happens?
- Is it worth it to invest a little more time in studying up, comparison shopping, and so on to make sure buying food at Whole Foods is the right decision? How do you, personally, define "worth it"?
- When, if ever, is shopping for food at Whole Foods the wrong decision? If you make the wrong decision, what are the repercussions? Does it affect only you or are others, such as your spouse and family, going to know about it? Are you going to have to live with your screw-up for a long time?
- Do you look forward to shopping there, reading about it before shopping, and so forth?
- Is shopping at Whole Foods fun or a pain?

So, please answer three "True or False" questions about your feelings about and recent shopping experiences at Whole Foods for me: (Assuming the discussion to date has led us to presume Whole Foods is in the recreational quadrant.) **True or False:**

- I actually come up with excuses or opportunities to go there, buy again, study up on the stuff, and so on.
- The time I spend browsing, tasting, studying, visiting, shopping, and the like is "me time." I actually feel a little guilty afterward.
- If I screw this up, it doesn't really matter. I had fun anyway.

1:15–1:25 **Replacement Tires**

Now, as promised, we're going to switch gears entirely and talk

about a different shopping experience. We're going to talk about the last time you bought replacement tires for your car.

- What brand/model car do you own and drive most often? Did you drive here today?
- How long have you owned it?
- What accessories did you buy the vehicle with? Any upgrades? Which one(s)? Why the upgrades?
- Why did you buy this brand/model of car? What factors were important to you? What benefits were you looking for?
- What do you particularly *like* about your car? How would you describe the role your car plays in your life?
  - Just transportation
  - Part of family
  - Self-image enhancer
  - Other (what exactly)

  Why?
- Could you share with me what you brought in for your homework? Why did you select what you selected? Did you have an easy or hard time finding these photos? Why?
- What role(s) do tires play for you in terms of the earlier discussion?
- That is, how do you view or perceive them?

1:25–1:45   **Recent Tire-Buying Process**

- Let's walk through the steps that you went through for the tires that you bought most recently. How long ago was that?
- How did you know you needed new tires? Did *you* come to that conclusion yourself or did *someone else* tell you tires were needed? Which option? If someone else, who?
- At this point what were you thinking?
- Did you do anything from a research point of view after you discovered that you needed tires? Did you look for any information, check any ads/specials, ask anyone for advice, check websites, and so on? If yes, what? If no, why not?
- How quickly/fast did you go to a store after realizing that you needed tires? Why that time?
- Which store did you go to? Why that store? What happened in the store?
- What were you looking to accomplish? *What factors were important*

to you in deciding what tire brand to buy? That is, what were you looking for? How did you decide what to buy?

- Where did you make the brand decision? Why there? Did you walk in the store knowing the brand? Why? Why did you know or want the specific brand of tires ahead of time?
- What type of communications occurred with any store personnel?
- Did the dealer encourage selling you any certain brands? If yes, which one(s)? Were they brands you had heard of previously?
- Which brand did you end up buying?
- What was your experience in the store where you bought the tires? Good/bad? Why? How did you feel?
- Having got your new tires how did you feel? Why? How did you feel now versus before?

1:45–2:00   **Replacement Tires Quadrant Identification**

So, thinking about your shopping trips for tires . . .

- Is your trip to a tire store an important event in your week, month, or year?
- Do you find yourself putting off the next visit to the tire store? Do you put off even thinking or researching about it?
- If you do put it off, why? Because you don't really want to do it? Because you think you'll screw it up? Because you think the whole thing is an unpleasant process?
- Is it worth it to invest a little more time in studying up, comparison shopping, and so forth to make sure buying tires at a particular dealer is the right decision? What is the payback, or benefit, from taking the time to comparison shop?
- When, if ever, is shopping for tires at a particular dealer the wrong decision? If you make the wrong decision, what are the repercussions? Does it affect only you or are others, such as your spouse and family, going to know about it? Are you going to have to live with your screw-up for a long time?
- Do you look forward to shopping there, reading about it before shopping, and so on?
- Is shopping for tires fun or a pain?

So, please answer three questions about your recent shopping experiences for replacement tires for me. (Assuming the discussion to date has led us to presume Replacement Tires is in the impatient quadrant.) **True or False:**

- This is a purchase I have to make, not one I want to make.
- If I screw this up, it's a big problem because someone else (spouse, kids) will be quite ticked off and I'll pay for it.
- The time shopping for/buying/installing these takes too long because tires themselves don't really do anything; it's just a means to another end, such as driving to my kids' soccer game, work, and the like.

Thank you very much for your time and participation.

Discovery Quantified: Survey Research

With the target identified, and the three key questions about shopping style answered or approximated, the more detailed process of Discovery can begin. At this point, you should be able to make a solid guess as to which quadrant best defines the shopping style of your target customer. Sometimes, of course, the qualitative efforts described above represent a sufficient—or the only affordable—approach. In this case, you'll need to be able to build marketing plans and strategies based on them. And we reiterate that even an overbroad determination of quadrant (and the corollary implications about stopwatch behavior) is still worth a lot more than complete ignorance of it.

However, as with all analysis, more fact-based and quantitative detail is usually welcome, and normally yields better results for decision making. Assuming you and your organization have the budget to continue to quantification of the quadrant determination, the following provides some critical guidelines on how to do so.

A key reason to quantify customer behavior—the time when your customer decides to buy—in the Discovery effort is: Not every customer, not every product category fits securely, solely, always, and everywhere in one quadrant. The quadrants, in their two-dimensional graphical representation, appear discrete and mutually exclusive. They are not. In the real world, we must deal with probabilities. You, as a marketer, have to assume a dynamic marketplace in which consumers shift from quadrant to quadrant depending on the situation. For some people, shopping for and researching replacement tires *is* fun. In the graphic we used to introduce the quadrant concept, we purposely placed wine buyers in all four quadrants in order to emphasize this point—their placement in the matrix is dependent on the detailed definition of the target consumer and the specific occasions of purchase and use. What we are really interested in, then, is "What proportion of customers and what proportion of the dollars they spend lies in each quadrant?" Armed with that knowledge, we can then determine in which quadrant-defined segment we are best advised to invest marketing resources.

Market research purists would say that what we are talking about here is "occasion-based segmentation." They would be mostly, but not entirely, correct. What we are suggesting is an entirely new way to look at market segmentation—one based on the customer's stopwatch. Traditional segmentation focuses on either price segments (discount, mass, premium), product segments (light beer), or consumer needs–based segments (beer drinkers who are conscious about their weight). Before developing our thinking on stopwatch marketing principles, we were first in line to support consumer needs–based segmentation: If marketers can define a sufficiently large and promising segment of consumers with consistent needs, those marketers should be able to develop marketing strategies to fill those needs profitably. Stopwatch marketing principles, in effect, build on and extend this consumer needs–based approach to include shopping *style*. That is, consumers in the recreational quadrant have a need for something (fun, fulfillment, self-gratification) and a revealed shopping style that recognizes and exploits the self-imposed constraints on the consumer's time—the time they are willing to devote to gathering information and completing the purchase. When cross-tabbed against the margins/economics of the category itself, segmentation by stopwatch marketing principles results in the matrix shown in Figure 7-3.

From where/whom is it easiest to get the most future volume and profit? Regardless of the marketing segmentation jargon and graphics, the question we need to answer is "What proportion of our target market and what proportion of dollars spent/profits realized lie in each quadrant?" or, even more simply, "How many consumers are in each quadrant and how much spending on our product do each of them represent?"

To properly define and populate the matrix, identifying the most promising quadrants for marketing investment, you'll need the raw inputs from the ensuing quantitative market research. In fact, you'll need three sets of research findings and analysis:

THE MATRIX: Example Products and Services

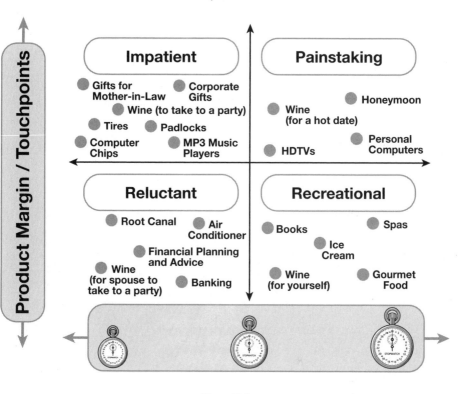

Figure 7-3

1. The customer's needs gaps: This is the gap between what the customer claims is important and the level of his or her satisfaction with whatever is his or her current solution. For example, when flying to Chicago, both safety and on-time arrival are likely to be highly important needs but the level of satisfaction with on-time arrival is likely to be quite low. The difference between importance and satisfaction is the needs gap.

2. The customer's stopwatch: This is the percentage of the day, week, hour, or year (depending on the quadrant) the target customers spend on problem recognition, information searching, evaluation of possible alternatives, making the purchase, evaluating the purchase after the fact, and so on.

3. The customer's value: This is all of the above modified by at least two

dimensions: Percentage of Decision Influence and Percentage of Actual Volume/Profit.

Discovery Quantified Step 1: Needs Gaps

Identification of needs gaps is a traditional quantitative research technique. (We again assume here that you have access to research suppliers or managers with experience in needs gap exercises, so we will treat this very quickly, reserving more detail for Steps 2 and 3.) Essentially, all you need to do is to expose respondents to a battery of twenty-five or more "Needs Statements" and then ask two questions: "How important is it?" and "How satisfied are you with it today?" These are generally rated on a five-point scale. So, in our replacement tire example, we might ask:

On a scale where the number 1 = "not important at all" and 5 = "extremely important," how important is it to you that your *next set of tires* . . .

- Are recognized by *Consumer Reports* as very safe?
- Last more than forty thousand miles?
- Really look good on your car?
- Provide very good traction in all weather?
- Are purchased in a store that is fun to shop in?
- Are purchased because you researched them and decided they were the best?
- Are purchased because the salesperson gave you a deal?
- Are purchased from a store where you know you can get in and out in less than an hour?

How satisfied are you that your *current tires* . . .

- Are recognized by *Consumer Reports* as very safe?
- Last more than forty thousand miles?
- Really look good on your car?
- Provide very good traction in all weather?
- Were purchased in a store that was fun to shop in?
- Were purchased because you researched them and decided they were the best?

- Were purchased because the salesperson gave you a deal?
- Were purchased from a store where you knew you could get in and out in less than an hour?

The resulting analysis of the responses to this battery will provide you with:

1. A rank order of Importance: Is "deal from a salesperson" more or less important than "reputation for safety" or "store you can get out of in an hour"? This is usually expressed as a top two box average score.
2. A rank order of Satisfaction: Is your target customer more or less satisfied with what she is currently getting in terms of "deal from a salesperson," versus "reputation for safety," or "store you can get out of in an hour"?
3. A rank order of the Needs Gaps: Importance Score minus Satisfaction Score for each. Any statement where Importance is high and Satisfaction is low, therefore, represents a big marketing opportunity.
4. The raw material for a needs-based segmentation: This can be done very simply by arraying the responses in a three-by-three, High/Medium/Low matrix of importance versus satisfaction—identifying, for instance, how many consumers lie in the high importance/low satisfaction cell. Assuming you have the time and budget, you should use some data reduction technique, such as factor analysis, to reduce the data set of responses here to a manageable number (four to six) of needs-based segments. These revealed segments might be defined as "convenience," "time-starved," "prestige," "safety," "conservative," and so on.

As noted earlier, this is where traditional market research analysis or, indeed, segmentation, usually ends. More precisely, this is often, unfortunately, where the research and analysis stops and marketing strategy takes over. Marketing management says, essentially, "I got it . . . 48 percent of the target market is in the 'safety' segment, I know how to get an ad agency to make a commercial about safety, thank you very much, let's get the agency in here and take some pictures of cute little babies playing with our product."

This quantification of the customer needs your product could satisfy, or the gaps that it could bridge, provides much more, however, than targets against which you and your company's brand managers and product developers can invest resources. Properly constructed, this analysis can heavily inform the essential, emotional element needed to begin defining the quadrant for your product or service. Put simply, a large number of large needs gaps, especially if at least some are emotionally (or irrationally) defined, means that your customers define your category further to the east (willing to spend time shopping, searching, and gathering information) and north (willing to spend money).

Discovery Quantified Step 2: The Stopwatch

To really capitalize on the time when your customer decides to buy—to get the most out of your market research investment according to stopwatch marketing principles—you'll want to extend the analysis to the next step: understanding in deep, quantifiable detail, the amount of time that these consumers are willing to spend in shopping for this particular commodity . . . the size of their stopwatches. With a sufficiently large sample of respondents, we can ask them to self-report, with a battery of questions like the following.*

Thinking about the last time you bought _____, please tell me:

1. When did you first think about the need for new _____?
   - A. One hour before your purchase
   - B. One day before your purchase
   - C. One week before your purchase
   - D. One month before your purchase
   - E. More than a month before your purchase (whatever is relevant).
2. Please indicate which, if any, of the following brands of _____ you were aware of prior to that moment when you first thought about purchasing _____.
3. What caused you to first think about the purchase?
4. What sources of information did you consult? (Here we list a long sub-battery that might include newspapers and magazines, books, relatives, experts, salespeople, coworkers, etc.)

---

* Please note, for this to be a truly useful quantitative assessment, these questions must be done in forced-choice format, as we are showing in Question 1. For ease of reading at this point, for the subsequent questions, we show the question only, not the forced choices.

5. For each of the above that you actually did use, please tell us as best you can remember,
   A. What prompted you to use/consult them (advertising, word of mouth, Internet search, etc.).
   B. When you first consulted them.
   C. How often you consulted them.
   D. How much time you spent with them.
   E. Was this more or less time than you had expected/planned to spend on this step?
   F. Did using/consulting these change your perception of _____?
   G. How important was this step in influencing your final purchase decision?
6. Had you ever seen or heard advertising for _____? When and in what form?
7. Before you made the actual purchase, what alternatives did you consider?
8. When and under what conditions did you consider those alternatives?
9. When you actually made the purchase, how much time did you spend at the store?
10. What time of day did you visit the store for the actual purchase?
11. How much time passed between the purchase and your actual use of the product?
12. After making the purchase, how often have you thought about how it might have been done differently or better?
13. Thinking about the NEXT time you will be buying _____, please answer the following TRUE or FALSE questions:
    A. This is a purchase I have to make, not one I want to make.
    B. If I screw this up, it's a big problem because someone else (boss, spouse, mother-in-law) will be quite ticked off and I'll pay for it.
    C. The time this takes is too long because (researching alternatives, the shopping process, and the ultimate product) doesn't really do anything; it's just a means to an end.
    D. When I think about this after the purchase, I want to say about myself, "job well done."
    E. The time I spend (browsing, tasting, studying, visiting, shopping, etc.) is "me time." I feel a little guilty afterward.

F. The need for this pops up unexpectedly . . . and then I need to get it handled ASAP.

G. I'm not an expert on this stuff, so I'm at the mercy of others . . . salespeople, retail clerks, "practitioners," and so on.

H. If I screw this up, it doesn't really matter. I had fun anyway.

14. Thinking about the NEXT time you will be buying _____, please answer the following MULTIPLE-CHOICE questions:

A. I buy one of these (once a day, week, month, year, decade).

B. I actually come up with excuses to (go there, buy again, study up on the stuff).

C. If I screw this up, it's a BIG problem because I'm STUCK (with this HDTV for ten years, won't get another chance with this hot date, etc.).

Analysis of the above should provide specific information to begin plotting the horizontal axis of our matrix—the size and complexity of the customer's stopwatch. We should be able to array the proportion of consumers easily along some time-defined measure.

We will now introduce the concepts of time segment analysis and stopwatch leverage, to be more fully developed in a subsequent chapter on allocating resources. Marketers have for some time used a generic continuum of consumer action steps to describe purchase behavior:

Awareness
Consideration
Trial
Initial Purchase
Usage
Loyalty

Stopwatch marketing is based on the core belief that the decisive factor at each of these steps is the tyranny of the consumer's available time. Consequently, we refer to these steps as "time segments." For purposes of this chapter, we will use these generic descriptors. We would emphasize, however, that one of the key objectives of the stopwatch research outlined above is to identify the *specific* time segments that are unique to your product or service and the quadrant in which your product and consumers live. That is, for your specific product, we would expect that the generic time segment "Consideration" might be replaced with "Consult information sources," "Seek advice from experts," "Visit three different stores" —whatever the research reveals. That's why some of the questions we recommend above include "What caused you to first think about the purchase?" and "What sources of information did you consult?" and "When did you first consult them?" and "How much time did you spend with them?"

Questions 1 through 14, above, are intended to identify both (a) the quadrant location for your product or service and (b) define these time segments (Awareness, Consideration, etc.) specifically for your product or service.

The fundamental insight of stopwatch marketing is that every buying decision can be measured by a stopwatch that is ticking continuously. But it isn't always ticking at the same rate. At specific points—those moments that separate one time segment from another—those consumers make a decision (sometimes deliberately, sometimes reflexively) to move on to the next time segment. Thus, *the critical effort in applying stopwatch marketing principles is to either (a) slow down the ticking at important time segments in order to increase the number of people in our target moving on to the next time segment and ultimate purchase or (b) close the sale right then and there.* A simple example: If 75 percent of those who are Aware of our brand move on to the Consideration time segment, and 40 percent of those who Consider move on to Trial, then 30 percent (40 percent × 75 percent = 30 percent) of the total is still ticking at the Trial time segment. Questions 3 through 6, above, are intended to give insight into the ability of marketing activities to affect consumers at each time segment, that is, to either extend the stopwatch (time spent by consumers at each time segment) or increase the number of target consumers moving on to the next time segment (stopwatches still ticking).

Increasing the number of stopwatches that are still ticking at each time segment is what we refer to as stopwatch leverage. That is, stopwatch leverage is the ability to positively affect consumer behavior at each time segment. In the example above, if marketing activities at the Consideration time segment can increase the proportion moving from Consideration to Trial from 40 percent to 45 percent, the number of target consumers still ticking at the Trial time segment is 33.75 percent, not 30 percent (45 percent × 75 percent = 33.75 percent). This is emphatically NOT a 3.75 percent increase: It is a 12.5 percent increase in the number of people still ticking;

that is, 12.5 percent more target customers are trying your product (3.75 / 30 percent = 12.5 percent). *This* is stopwatch leverage.

As noted above, understanding these time segments will play an important role in the allocation of resources in a subsequent chapter. For now, we return to the subject of this chapter, locating the most promising or valuable target customers for your product or service in the appropriate quadrant, in order to give guidance to overall marketing strategies.

Discovery Quantified Step 3: The Customer's Value

To complete the process of Discovery, which began with evaluating your customers' needs gaps, all that you still require is a determination of the *value* of your customers. The respondent's *behaviors* regarding time, identified in the battery above, must now be mapped against some measure or set of measures of the *value* of that time to your company. The easiest and quickest way to get at this, of course, is to simply ask: "How much did you spend on ____ last year?" Such self-reporting is generally accurate when the sample size is sufficiently large. Depending on the category involved and the data available, you may already know the dollar value of the respondent from other sources, including customer lists, direct marketing efforts, or diary panels.

But, somewhere along the line, unless you already know the answer, you need to ask the respondents about their actual spending levels—that is, the dollar value of the customer's decision to buy. Recall the purpose of this Discovery exercise: to identify the quadrants in which the consumption for your product or service lies. The matrix that defines those quadrants has two axes. On the horizontal axis is the customer's stopwatch and on the vertical axis are the margin and/or touchpoints available to you as a marketer. An effective time segment analysis should provide specific, detailed quantification of the horizontal axis—the customer's stopwatch—of your matrix. The percentage of customers and their attendant percentage of annual spending can be plotted along some time dimension–defined measure.

What you need to add to the analysis now is some quantification of the customer's spending or value so as to array them along the vertical axis— margin/touchpoints. With specific, detailed numbers on total money spent, the number of customers spending it, and a curve that describes the distribution of both, you can locate the customers that represent the bulk of your sales and the gross margin you can collect. It should at least be apparent from the answers to the above whether the product or service represents a fun—recreational—purchase to a significant number (Whole Foods) or an unpleasant, reluctant one (retail banking).

To further the effort at arraying customers along the vertical axis, we usually advise using a technique called "Derived Importance" or "Decision Influence." Remember the notion of the twenty-five-plus needs/gaps (importance minus satisfaction) statements? In our questionnaires we ask a third question for each: "Which brand (or product, or service) is most associated with this statement?" In another section of the questionnaire, we ask, "Which brand would you most likely purchase?" We can then do another rank order comparison of *stated* importance versus *derived* importance. An oft-used illustration:

Q: What's the most important consideration in buying a car?
A: Safety.
Q: What's less important?
A: Image—people will think I'm successful.
Q: Which brand is most associated with image?
A: BMW.
Q: Which brand is most associated with safety?
A: Volvo.
Q: Which brand are you going to buy with your big Christmas bonus?
A: BMW.

By comparing stated importance (safety) with actual behavior (buying a BMW), we can infer that, in this example, at least, image is the most important need. We call this Decision Influence. That is, the *influence* of image, in this example, on the purchase *decision* is higher than the original, stated importance of image. Armed with Decision Influence, we can begin a more accurate plotting of the vertical axis. If we know what *really* influences decisions for our population of research respondents, we can then more accurately determine whether they perceive a given shopping experience as recreational, painstaking, impatient, or reluctant.

To complete plotting of the vertical axis, all you will need from here on is intelligent economic analysis. For example, you must identify the various touchpoints whereby target customers can be addressed; the customers' various alternatives must be fully detailed. Finally, most important, your brand's relative margin must be objectively assessed. (The definition of our generic vertical axis, after all, is "Product Margin/Touchpoints.") And these factors, especially relative margin, are resistant to general principles, and must be plotted on measures that are appropriate to your specific industry or category, and in a directly competitive context. In an ideal world, you would build an array of (a) all possible "things" the target customers could spend money on as well as (b) a comparison of your product to the top three competitors.

A reminder: Before moving on to developing the actual marketing plan, the wise marketer (you), armed with the data and fully-fleshed-out matrix, should work to socialize the findings within your organization. Since the whole idea here is to change the way marketing is pursued, executed, and measured, this socializing is important. We encourage marketers just starting out on this socialization process to search for analogies to bring the ideas to life. In most big companies, you'll get a lot further with "It's recreational, just like Apple" than you will with "Our analysis indicates that 73 percent of the decisions are made on an emotional basis three to six months before actual purchase. Fifty-four percent of this emotion is driven by self-image while 23 percent is driven by peer pressure, making it what we call a recreational purchase."

Discovery Quantified: In Action

If you are one of the readers of this book employed by a company with a market research budget measured in the millions of dollars (such as Goodyear, Apple, or BMW) and/or millions of ongoing or returning consumers to survey (Whole Foods Market, Wal-Mart), you can probably stop reading here, and move on to chapter 8. If, on the other hand, you are working at a place with only a few employees, and number your customers not in the millions, but in the thousands—or even hundreds—we offer here a real-world example of how a small business might go about gathering the information necessary to determine its shopping quadrants. It remains our firm conviction, borne out, we hope, by the findings below, that even single-location, small businesses can better understand their customer base, revisit their marketing strategies, and revitalize their business by applying stopwatch marketing principles.

In the summer of 2006, we approached the owners of an upscale Manhattan wine shop (fortuitously named "Discovery Wines") to cooperate in proving this hypothesis. Like the proprietors of nearly every small business, the owners at Discovery Wines were interested not only in increasing revenues and profits, but also in understanding the usefulness of various marketing innovations in which they had heavily invested. These included informational computer kiosks in the shop, daily tastings, home delivery, and so on (all described in more detail later). The owner and key managers told us directly that they had made these investments in the hope of creating a truly differentiated consumer experience but really had little idea of their value. "Better understanding their customer base, revisiting marketing strategies . . . ," and so forth would be our (consulting) terms, not theirs. Nonetheless, the leaders at Discovery Wines were fascinated with the idea that they could take advantage of the tools generally thought to be available only to Fortune 1000 companies.

First, a little background: For readers unfamiliar with New York City, wine, by law, cannot be sold in supermarkets, drugstores, or any—yes, any—chain stores. It is also not sold in state-owned "ABC" stores as would be the case in Pennsylvania or Virginia. Consequently, all wine and liquor stores are independent operators, serving, by their very nature, a rather limited geography. However, competition within that limited geography is voracious, since there is no huge supermarket, Wal-Mart, or Whole Foods Market to suck up all the wine and liquor volume for miles around.

Discovery Wines is located in an area of New York known as Alphabet City, at the junction of the East Village, Soho, and the Lower East Side. The official New York City tourism website describes the area as follows:

> For more trend-setting street life, head east toward Alphabet City . . . still a little rough around the edges but with many reasonably priced, fun, and gamut-running places to eat, drink, and shop . . . and, if you're really getting into the scene, some very cool tattoo parlors.[1]

Because Alphabet City is also located conveniently near the corporate canyons of Wall Street and New York University, the pedestrians and residents around Discovery Wines can include corporate and financial heavyweights, wannabes in the Wall Street training programs, NYU professors, hippie and beat-generation refugees, artists and musicians, and proprietors of the many restaurants, shops, and tattoo parlors in the area. We belabor this to make an important point—the owners of Discovery Wines would be unable to take a traditional or demographic approach to identifying their marketing strategies. Alphabet City and the customer base for Discovery Wines cannot be characterized as blue-collar, upscale, artistic, corporate, touristy, ethnic, or any other pigeonhole other than the stereotypical "eclectic." Wine and liquor shops in other parts of New York State may have the luxury of focusing on a demographic target market—they may literally be on Wall Street or across the street from an upstate Ford Motor factory—but Discovery Wines cannot. The Discovery Wines people must find a way to understand *shopping behavior* for their current and future clientele: In which quadrants are their current customers most heavily represented? How long will their stopwatch keep ticking? When do they make the final purchase decision? What is the opportunity to leverage this knowledge to increase frequency of purchase, transaction size, and loyalty?

Before delving into how we went about answering those and other questions, we offer here a little more background on the shop itself. Recognizing both the need to differentiate their shop from other such individual wine and liquor stores in Manhattan, and the eclectic nature of their clientele who are expressly *not* interested in mass or run-of-the-mill shopping, the proprietors of Discovery Wine set out to make sure that prospective shoppers would understand that they are also not interested in marketing to masses. The Discovery Wines website (www.discoverywines.com) opens with the following:

WELCOME TO DISCOVERY WINES

Discovery Wines is not interested in selling you mass market bottlings available at so many other stores in New York. Our managers, Matt and Scott, have personally selected every wine in our store, with a focus on quality and value. Many are from small producers not widely available. The high quality of our wines does not mean high prices—60% of our wines are less than $20. Just ask Scott or Matt what kind of wine experience you are looking for. Whether you're interested in learning about a new region of the wine world, or trying to find something other than the old standby, we can help find the wine or wines that are right for you. Come in and discover the world of wine with us.

Key features of Discovery Wines' marketing strategy include:

1. Stocking an array of little-known, new wines
2. Providing a knowledgeable and helpful staff to assist customers
3. Executing frequent in-store wine tastings
4. Following up with both high-tech and traditional community outreach (their website, newsletters, tastings, etc.)
5. Providing a proprietary twenty-first-century technology in the form of computer kiosks throughout the store that customers can use to learn more about each wine
6. Home delivery throughout New York State

To summarize, the leaders of Discovery Wines were interested in determining how best to increase revenues and profits, largely by increasing the number of shoppers, the frequency with which they shopped, and the dollars spent when they were in the store. In addition, the store's management was highly interested in determining whether their investment in such value-added marketing efforts as the computerized kiosks and community programs were paying off. We set out, then, to determine, in our terms, where the leverage points were for the shop's current and potential customers—the quadrant in which they lived, which time segments were leverageable, and how to evolve many of them to more profitable quadrants. In the shop owners' terms, we set out to find if the investment in kiosks, staff, delivery, tastings, and so on was paying back, and if so, whether it should be increased or decreased. Inherent in our approach was the assumption that while they may be demographically very eclectic, Discovery Wines' customers may share similar attitudes about wine and how they like to shop for wine (e.g., the joy of a new discovery) that makes Discovery Wines relevant/appealing to them.

To do so, we and Discovery Wines' owners and staff developed a plan to execute a survey of customers in the store. Customers were asked to fill out a simple, one-page questionnaire at checkout. In addition, the staff was asked to staple the receipt for the transaction to the questionnaire for our data analysis team to use in cross-tabbing answers to the questions to amount spent, number of bottles purchased, time of day and week, and other relevant measures.

To specifically address the issue of locating the quadrant for each shopper, we needed to define the horizontal axis (diameter/speed of stopwatch). We asked directly of the customer, "When did you *first* decide to purchase wine for this occasion?" and "How long did you spend in the store before making a purchase decision?" and "Once you decided to buy wine, how long ago did you decide to purchase at Discovery Wines?" (See Figure 7-4, Questions 3, 6, and 4.) For the vertical axis (Margin/Touch-points) we needed a good, quick proxy that could be captured in one or two questions. This is, after all, a one-shop retailer, not a billion-dollar manufacturer with a million-dollar research budget. So, we went with the customer-defined risk profile for this purchase. The specific question we asked was, "On a scale of 1 to 10, how important would you say your choice of wine is for this occasion? '10' means extremely important (for example, wine for a very special occasion or a wine that will make the right impression)." (See Figure 7-4, Question 11.)

Total respondents numbered 221, a sufficiently large sample from which to draw some inferences and make decisions. Interestingly, only 115 of the 221 completed questionnaires included a stapled receipt. The shop's employees simply stated that they were often "too busy" to staple the receipt. This highlights an important issue: the small business will often not be in a position to police the research effort to the same degree the high-budget firm will be. Too often, we believe, this fact is used as an excuse for failing to even attempt any data gathering on the part of small businesses. For this very reason, the small business that does take the time and effort to get some information and make information-based decisions will almost certainly have a leg up on its competitors.[*]

The Discovery Wines study yielded many important and interesting results. We'll discuss some of them now, but if you are interested in reviewing the complete results, see Appendix B.

First, we discovered that the current clientele is a loyal one, with two-thirds of the respondents claiming to have shopped six or more times. This loyal base first became aware of the store simply by seeing it—an important reality in a pedestrian-based location. The research purists in our organization have pointed out that we cannot say that the clientele is actually loyal; rather, they are only repeat purchasers. As marketing pragmatists, however, we would note that the difference between "loyal" and

---

[*] That said, the more diligent the data gathering, the better the data, particularly since the data is most reliable when there is a serious, concerted effort to make such a survey as "representative" of total customers as possible . . . reflecting things like balancing weekday versus weekend customers, and including more than just their "best" customers.

IDENTIFYING YOUR QUADRANTS:

Discovery Wines' Stopwatch Questionnaire

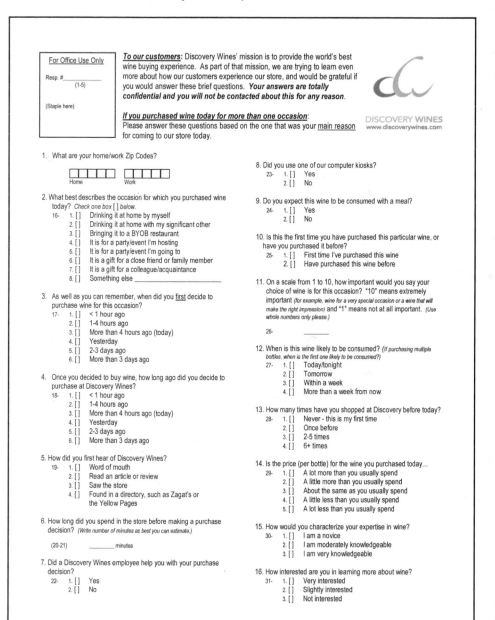

For Office Use Only

Resp. #_____
     (1-5)

(Staple here)

To our customers: Discovery Wines' mission is to provide the world's best wine buying experience. As part of that mission, we are trying to learn even more about how our customers experience our store, and would be grateful if you would answer these brief questions. *Your answers are totally confidential and you will not be contacted about this for any reason.*

If you purchased wine today for more than one occasion:
Please answer these questions based on the one that was your main reason for coming to our store today.

DISCOVERY WINES
www.discoverywines.com

1. What are your home/work Zip Codes?

   Home   Work

2. What best describes the occasion for which you purchased wine today? *Check one box [ ] below.*
   16- 1. [ ] Drinking it at home by myself
        2. [ ] Drinking it at home with my significant other
        3. [ ] Bringing it to a BYOB restaurant
        4. [ ] It is for a party/event I'm hosting
        5. [ ] It is for a party/event I'm going to
        6. [ ] It is a gift for a close friend or family member
        7. [ ] It is a gift for a colleague/acquaintance
        8. [ ] Something else _____

3. As well as you can remember, when did you <u>first</u> decide to purchase wine for this occasion?
   17- 1. [ ] < 1 hour ago
        2. [ ] 1-4 hours ago
        3. [ ] More than 4 hours ago (today)
        4. [ ] Yesterday
        5. [ ] 2-3 days ago
        6. [ ] More than 3 days ago

4. Once you decided to buy wine, how long ago did you decide to purchase at Discovery Wines?
   18- 1. [ ] < 1 hour ago
        2. [ ] 1-4 hours ago
        3. [ ] More than 4 hours ago (today)
        4. [ ] Yesterday
        5. [ ] 2-3 days ago
        6. [ ] More than 3 days ago

5. How did you first hear of Discovery Wines?
   19- 1. [ ] Word of mouth
        2. [ ] Read an article or review
        3. [ ] Saw the store
        4. [ ] Found in a directory, such as Zagat's or the Yellow Pages

6. How long did you spend in the store before making a purchase decision? *(Write number of minutes as best you can estimate.)*

   (20-21) _____ minutes

7. Did a Discovery Wines employee help you with your purchase decision?
   22- 1. [ ] Yes
        2. [ ] No

8. Did you use one of our computer kiosks?
   23- 1. [ ] Yes
        2. [ ] No

9. Do you expect this wine to be consumed with a meal?
   24- 1. [ ] Yes
        2. [ ] No

10. Is this the first time you have purchased this particular wine, or have you purchased it before?
    25- 1. [ ] First time I've purchased this wine
         2. [ ] Have purchased this wine before

11. On a scale from 1 to 10, how important would you say your choice of wine is for this occasion? "10" means extremely important *(for example, wine for a very special occasion or a wine that will make the right impression)* and "1" means not at all important. *(Use whole numbers only please.)*

    26- _____

12. When is this wine likely to be consumed? *(If purchasing multiple bottles, when is the first one likely to be consumed?)*
    27- 1. [ ] Today/tonight
         2. [ ] Tomorrow
         3. [ ] Within a week
         4. [ ] More than a week from now

13. How many times have you shopped at Discovery before today?
    28- 1. [ ] Never - this is my first time
         2. [ ] Once before
         3. [ ] 2-5 times
         4. [ ] 6+ times

14. Is the price (per bottle) for the wine you purchased today...
    29- 1. [ ] A lot more than you usually spend
         2. [ ] A little more than you usually spend
         3. [ ] About the same as you usually spend
         4. [ ] A little less than you usually spend
         5. [ ] A lot less than you usually spend

15. How would you characterize your expertise in wine?
    30- 1. [ ] I am a novice
         2. [ ] I am moderately knowledgeable
         3. [ ] I am very knowledgeable

16. How interested are you in learning more about wine?
    31- 1. [ ] Very interested
         2. [ ] Slightly interested
         3. [ ] Not interested

Figure 7-4

"repeat" is something for big budget firms to struggle with in their research. For a single retail store, the difference is less significant.

On the very first set of findings, we learn that the quadrant in which the bulk of Discovery's *first-time* shoppers reside is not painstaking (not when 80 percent of the shoppers became aware simply by seeing the store during their travels; see Figure 7-5). However, further questions are needed to establish which of the remaining three quadrants best describes the store's typical transaction, and whether the shoppers' behavior changes after their introduction to the store.

AWARENESS OF / PREVIOUS EXPERIENCE AT DISCOVERY WINES

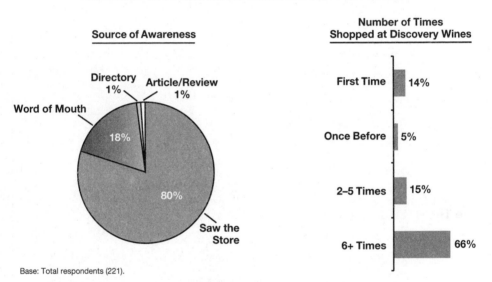

Base: Total respondents (221).

Figure 7-5

On an overall basis, the shopper's stopwatch cannot be expected to tick for very long—at most a day or two: Nearly all respondents expected the wine to be consumed the same day as purchase and only one in five decided to actually shop for wine more than a day before visiting the store. The majority of respondents were purchasing wine to be consumed at home, either alone or with a significant other. These findings are shown in Figures 7-6, 7-7, and 7-8.

The results in Figures 7-6, 7-7, and 7-8 make it clear that the vast ma-

CONSUMPTION OCCASION

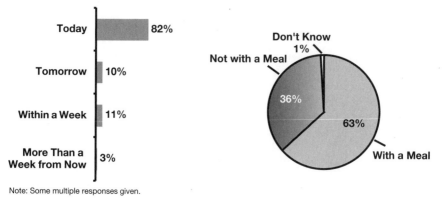

Today 82%

Tomorrow 10%

Within a Week 11%

More Than a Week from Now 3%

Don't Know 1%

Not with a Meal

36%

63%

With a Meal

Note: Some multiple responses given.

Base: Total respondents (221).

Figure 7-6

TIMING OF DECISION TO BUY WINE

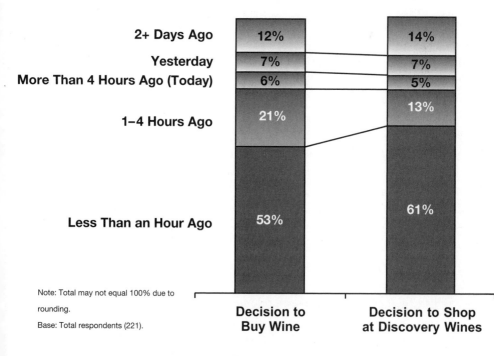

2+ Days Ago 12% 14%

Yesterday 7% 7%

More Than 4 Hours Ago (Today) 6% 5%

1–4 Hours Ago 21% 13%

Less Than an Hour Ago 53% 61%

Note: Total may not equal 100% due to rounding.

Base: Total respondents (221).

Decision to Buy Wine

Decision to Shop at Discovery Wines

Figure 7-7

PURCHASE OCCASION

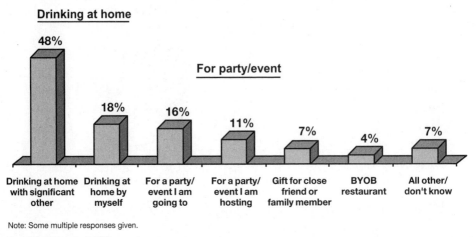

Note: Some multiple responses given.

Base: Total respondents (221).

Figure 7-8

jority of Discovery Wines' customers have a quickly ticking stopwatch—they make the decision to buy wine that day, often that very hour, and they expect to consume it that night, generally at home. These answers, in short, eliminate yet another quadrant: Most of the customers are not recreational shoppers. Not yet, anyway. See chapter 10.

One more question will establish the relative importance of Discovery Wines' two remaining quadrants: impatient and reluctant. How quickly is the stopwatch ticking once the customer is actually in the store? *Very* fast. On average, respondents spent 9 minutes on their purchase decision. About half spent five minutes or less, while only 22 percent spent more than ten minutes. The store and staff have less than ten minutes to create and satisfy a customer while turning him or her into a loyal one, as well. See Figure 7-9.

Facing such a quickly ticking stopwatch, Discovery's managers need to determine the nature and location (in time) of touchpoints that can accomplish two tasks that appear to be in conflict:

1. Quick in and out: For the customer who simply can't be slowed down (affected by staff recommendations, attracted to the kiosk, signed up for

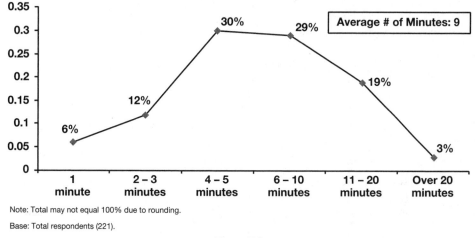

TIME SPENT ON WINE SELECTION

Note: Total may not equal 100% due to rounding.

Base: Total respondents (221).

Figure 7-9

newsletters, etc.) the store must be set up to allow that customer to quickly find something that meets his or her requirements and, just as quickly, pay for it and get on with his or her day.

2. Stretching it out: For the customer who can be affected by in-store activity, such actions that capture the customer's time segments and stretch out the stopwatch should be enhanced—more and more inviting kiosks; knowledgeable, trained staff to recommend wines; events and tastings, and so on, all come to mind.

That is to say, however, that the job of Discovery Wines' managers and owners must be to make the shopping experience at the store both fast and fun. We don't see these two as in conflict. Bookstores have been doing this for decades: If all you want is the latest Stephen King or John Le Carré, they're stacked up in the very front of the store, where you can see them from the sidewalk, parking lot, or mall. You can, literally, walk in, pick up the hot book, check out quickly, and be on your way in less than five minutes. If you want to browse, shop, relax, or all three, you can wander around for hours, stop at the cappuccino shop, meet a local author and get your copy of her book autographed, leave the kids in the children's books section for a time while you listen to some music in the CD section, and so forth. At Barnes & Noble's location in Santa Monica's 3rd Street Promenade, the benches surrounding the magazine section are occupied for hours every morning by readers who use the store as a public library, as they sip their coffee from the Starbucks next door. If you're there long enough, it will be hard to avoid getting signed up for the chain's loyalty program and co-branded Visa or MasterCard. Whole Foods Market, as noted earlier, does much the same: The front of every store is remarkably inviting, displaying a beautiful array of fresh produce, beckoning the shopper to come in and wander around, sampling food in several different aisles. Also near the front is an array of convenience items, such as beverages. If all you want is a cold fruit juice, you can duck in and out very quickly.

Before proceeding to populating the matrix, we want to share a few additional findings:

1. The purchase of wine was considered relatively important. On our key measure of importance/risk to determine the placement along the vertical axis of the matrix, the average rating was 6.2 on a 10-point scale (Question 11).
2. The average transaction was $24.30 and the average price per bottle was $14.30, making the average purchase 1.7 bottles. Two-thirds responded that this was "about what I usually spend" per bottle.
3. Sixty percent of respondents claim to be "very interested" in learning more about wine.

Now, to populate the matrix. Recall that our generic matrix, introduced in the second chapter, actually demonstrated that the purchase of wine could be made by customers operating in any of the four quadrants as in Figure 7-10.

Our challenge here, then, is to develop operational definitions of the axes and utilize the responses to the questions to populate the quadrants. Having done that, we can then use the quadrant analysis to develop more focused marketing recommendations. We created the Discovery Wines quadrants as follows:

1. Definitions used for Time Investment, on the horizontal axis:
   A. "More Time": Decided to buy wine more than an hour ago *and* spent at least six minutes deciding what to buy
   B. "Less Time": Decided to buy wine within the past hour *or* spent five minutes or less deciding what to buy

THE MATRIX: Example Products and Services

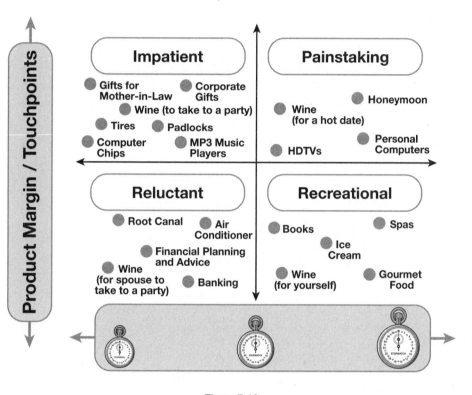

Figure 7-10

2. Definitions used for Importance/Risk, on the vertical axis:
   A. "More Importance/Risk": Rated the importance of their wine selection as "7" or higher on a 10-point scale
   B. "More Importance/Less Risk": Rated the importance of their wine selection as "6" or lower on a 10-point scale

The resulting, populated matrix for Discovery Wines is shown in Figure 7-11.

The indicated actions arising from this quadrant analysis are more fully developed in chapter 10, Activation. However, a few thoughts are in order here.

The most obvious and impressive finding is the aforementioned quickly ticking stopwatch. Fully 82 percent of the current customers are

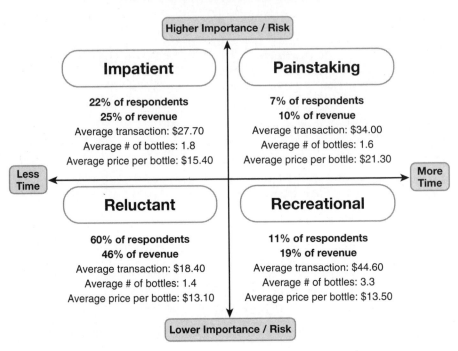

THE DISCOVERY WINES SHOPPING MATRIX

Higher Importance / Risk

Impatient

22% of respondents
25% of revenue
Average transaction: $27.70
Average # of bottles: 1.8
Average price per bottle: $15.40

Painstaking

7% of respondents
10% of revenue
Average transaction: $34.00
Average # of bottles: 1.6
Average price per bottle: $21.30

Less Time ← → More Time

Reluctant

60% of respondents
46% of revenue
Average transaction: $18.40
Average # of bottles: 1.4
Average price per bottle: $13.10

Recreational

11% of respondents
19% of revenue
Average transaction: $44.60
Average # of bottles: 3.3
Average price per bottle: $13.50

Lower Importance / Risk

CAVEAT: Some calculations within the quadrants of the matrix are based on extremely small sample sizes. These should be viewed as qualitative in nature.

Base: With receipt and all time/risk variables (113).

Figure 7-11

in the impatient or reluctant quadrants, with reluctants accounting for 60 of those 82 percentage points. Clearly the first priority for Discovery Wines must be to "do no harm"—in marketing jargon, protect that franchise. That means that any efforts to pursue "fun" cannot irretrievably damage the "fast" delivery by the store. These impatients and reluctants spend $13 to $15 per bottle. So, marketing should emphasize visible stacks upfront of such bottles, so that the impatient or reluctant shopper can know that he or she can get in, get a good bottle for $15, and get out quickly. In this recommendation, we are suggesting that Discovery Wines market more like a bookstore (best-sellers visibly stacked up front) than like a supermarket (disciplined traffic pattern forcing customers to traverse various aisles before chancing upon the frequently demanded items such as milk, toilet paper, bread, etc.).

The bookstore analogy offers more than an array of tactics for ensuring a fast transaction; it also suggests the value of fun (browsing, cappuccino, kiosks, chats with staff, etc.). The second critical finding from the quadrant analysis is staggering in its importance for the shop: recreational shoppers buy *two and a half times* as many bottles per trip and spend two and a half times as much as reluctants. Every effort (which doesn't violate the "fast" imperative) should be made to (a) appeal to recreationals and, more important, to (b) convert reluctants into recreationals. Just as Commerce Bank has proprietary change machines and play areas for children, and just as Barnes & Noble and Borders have cafés, Discovery Wines should consider "browsing drivers": reasons and excuses for the customer to spend more time in the store without violating the "fast" needs of the majority of impatients and reluctants. In chapter 10, we'll talk about how to do just that.

Having populated the matrix and identified the key finding—most wine buyers are impatient or reluctant but when they spend more time they spend more money—it is time to revisit the research for additional findings to reinforce our confidence and guide further marketing strategy development. In order to map out the location of key touchpoints, we set out, then, to find the drivers of increased dollars spent and bottles purchased. Recall that the average transaction was $24.30 and the average price per bottle was $14.30, making the average purchase 1.7 bottles. The results of our one-page survey can, indeed, quantify how slowing down the ticking stopwatch, leveraging the time segments along the face of the watch, and driving customers from reluctant to recreational can seriously increase revenue and profit. These additional results are shown in Figure 7-12.

The criticality of time could not be more obvious: a bigger stopwatch diameter, a more slowly ticking stopwatch, leads to higher revenue. Efforts to slow that ticking—trained and effective staff to engage the customer, fun activities like tastings, use of the kiosks, and so on—anything that drives customers from the impatient and reluctant quadrants to the recreational one will noticeably increase the shop's revenue.

We pursued one additional analysis to quantify the importance of time on spending at Discovery Wines. We were interested in determining how answers to the questions about *time spent* planning and shopping displayed an impact on the *dollars spent* in the store. To do this, we ran a logistic regression. (For readers bored by the details of statistics and regression

VALUE OF TOUCHPOINTS AT DISCOVERY WINES

Shopping Behavior	Average Transaction
Total Sample	$24.30
Spent 5 minutes or less in store	$20.40
Spent 6–10 minutes in store	**$26.30**
Spent 11+ minutes in store	**$37.70**
Decided to buy wine within an hour	$20.50
Decided to buy wine more than an hour ago	**$29.60**
Were not helped by an employee	$21.50
Were helped by employee	**$27.50**
Did not use the kiosk	$23.40
Used the kiosk	**$25.90**
Bought on weekday	$22.30
Bought on weekend	**$32.10**

Above-average transaction size shown in bold.

Base: Responses with receipts (115).

Figure 7-12

models, skip ahead to the next chapter. For those who want even more detail on our regression analysis, skip to Appendix B.) Among our key findings: If the wine is likely to be consumed *tomorrow,* there is a 73 percent chance that the consumer is a high spender (> $18). The customer is also more likely to be a high spender if the importance (risk) of the wine purchase is high and/or if this is his first purchase of this particular wine. Self-described "highly knowledgeable" wine drinkers and those who decided to shop "longer ago" were more likely to be low spenders. Impulse shoppers are higher spenders.

So, Discovery Wines' target consumer (if the objective is to increase dollars spent) is making a purchase on a short but not immediate timetable (for consumption tomorrow, not tonight). This target does not self-identify as knowledgeable about wine, understands the risk in screwing up for tomorrow's event, and is, therefore, open to trying a new (to them) brand or varietal. That is, the key target consumers reside in the north-west (impatient) quadrant: high importance/risk and a short/small stop-watch. This, then, implies the shop should pursue one of two strategies. The first would involve playing directly to the impatient-quadrant behav-ior pattern: encouraging the target consumer to "stock up" in advance of a currently unanticipated event. That is, "buy a bottle of something spe-cial today, because you know you are going to want to give it as a gift on short notice at some future occasion." In stopwatch marketing terms, this would mean *lengthening the stopwatch in advance of consumption* while recog-nizing the impatient consumer's desire to *shorten or eliminate entirely the stopwatch during purchase* via bundling. Such bundling would result in in-cremental purchases and spending *per trip*. The second, presumably more difficult but potentially more remunerative effort would be to encourage and incentivize consumers to shift their behavior from the impatient to the recreational pattern, making the experience of shopping at Discovery Wines a destination event.

And, to reiterate the rationale for the Discovery Wines effort in the first place: all of the above was developed from a one-page questionnaire and a few hundred responses. When confronted with the wealth of infor-mation that can thus be gained, we are often quite shocked when our smaller-budget clients claim inability to execute market research.

Chapter Eight

Web Analytics:
Timing Your
Stopwatch

 The most obvious criticism of the traditional methods used by Discovery Wines is that using survey questionnaires to measure the behavior of consumers over the time scale that matters—sometimes minutes, sometimes years—is too difficult, short of using the kind of hardware usually associated with prisoners under house arrest. Market research techniques, while powerful, provide only an estimate of consumer behavior. Market research is also not especially scalable; the bigger the business, the more time needed by customer-facing staff to collect questionnaires, when they should really be selling stuff. The advent of the Internet, however, has provided the capability to measure actual behavior literally down to the minute—the click. Since stopwatch marketing is about making the most of the time when your customer decides to buy, this ability to measure customer behavior at every moment and every action on your site can deliver a powerful competitive advantage.

For most of business history, you would have had to be satisfied with measuring not behavior, but behavioral proxies, like age and income. From decidedly unscientific beginnings—the database used by the first publishers of *Harper's Bazaar* were letters to the editor[1]—the discipline has matured to the point that some of the most gifted mathematicians in the world apply the arcana of Bayesian statistics, Markov chains, and diagonal multinomial probit models to predict which households are likelier to buy a particular brand of oatmeal.

All these tools of modern demographics (and the $255 billion advertising industry[2]) depend on the notion that group identity is behavioral destiny . . . that knowing the income, age, zip code, and education of an individual will predict the make and model of car she prefers. However, the idea turns out to be not nearly as powerful as one might think. For example, a 1998 study among magazine subscribers by Mediamark Research Inc. showed that pure demographic differences explained less than 2 percent of the variability in behavior.[3] If you're trying to launch, say, a new laundry detergent in the face of a dominant competitor, your chances of attracting a new purchaser on any given day depends a lot more on whether your target consumer just tried to clean a juice-stained T-shirt than whether she has three children, or a college degree. The best marker for one sort of behavior is another behavior.

Sensible, so far. But the idea of designing a sales pitch around what consumers *do*, rather than who they *are*, really got going only when those consumers started leaving a trail of their shopping behaviors behind on the Internet. That trail is, literally, marked by time stamps, making the implementation of stopwatch marketing principles not only possible, but competitively imperative.

The first recorded installation of what would come to be called "spyware" occurred sometime around 1994, but it wasn't until 2000, when the Aureate Company, the granddaddy of the spyware industry, started installing, on the computers of visitors to certain websites, programs that recorded a list of all the other sites visited. The business lay in selling that information to advertisers, who, it was reasoned, would be willing to pay for it. The web address of someone who was collecting online information on refrigerators might be of interest to a company such as, for example, Amana. And, so it proved. Programs like Aureate (which later changed its name to Radiate), Conducent, and, most important, Gator* were so successful at installing spyware packages that by 2004, the National Cyber Security Alliance estimated that three-quarters of America's personal computers had such spyware installed . . . an average of more than ninety programs per computer. A company like Lexus could segment visitors to its own website by the paths they took prior to their arrival there, whether by searching Google for information on SUVs or visiting a bank site for the purpose of comparing loan rates.

---

* Founded in Redwood City in 1998, Gator is one of the more controversial survivors of the Internet shakeout. A Google search matching Gator (or Claria) with the charming neologism "scumware" pulls up more than 35,000 pages.

They could. They can't anymore.

The golden moment for the use of computer programs for what marketers were already calling behavioral targeting (or contextual advertising) passed quickly. Actions generate equal and opposite reactions, and the reaction to the success of behavioral targeting was the explosion in methods to combat it, both technological—software programs like Opt Out, AdWare, SpyBot, as well as antispyware features for multipurpose computer security programs from Norton Utilities and Symantec—and legislative. As a result, the original suppliers of the service lost their appeal. Though Microsoft had considered acquiring Claria, the company that made the notorious Gator spyware tracking package, they retreated under the pressure of bad public relations. But while the third-party software providers were lowering their profile, behavior was still being tracked, this time by the portals themselves.

If ideas for new businesses were legally protected in the same way as inventions, Bill Gross might now be closing in on Thomas Edison's 1,093 U.S. patents.* IdeaLab, the business incubator he founded in 1996, has created a dizzying assortment of companies, including eToys, Tickets.com, NetZero, CitySearch, and Pets.com (well, not all of Edison's inventions were the lightbulb, either). In 1998, however, his fertile imagination came up with something called GoTo.com, a website that not only searched the web based on keywords and phrases, but auctioned its results to the highest bidder. GoTo never became a successful search engine, but its advertising auction software became a gold mine, selling results to sites like America Online, Microsoft, and especially Yahoo . . . so much, in fact, that by 2003, Yahoo acquired the company, by now called Overture, for $1.4 billion.[4]

One of the reasons GoTo/Overture was so appealing to companies like MSN.com (which at one time was its largest client) and Yahoo is that they were e-commerce sites as well as search engines and could therefore follow a search all the way from its origin to the final transaction. Yahoo Direct has now partnered with ACNielsen to provide a service that can perform remarkably sophisticated split testing of creative at all stages of

---

* Edison no longer holds the record for patents by an American. He has been surpassed by Donald Weder, a professional florist of Highland Park, Illinois, whose 1,300-and-counting patents are virtually all related to new and exciting ways to display flowers.

the shopping process. Making the most of this technology, Internet shopping sites will act like a mail-order catalog that can, immediately after its readers spend an extra two minutes on a page, repaginate itself in real time, and display the item those readers are most likely to decide to buy.

Behavioral targeting tools are supposed to measure any number of activities, from purchase histories to creditworthiness, but the one thing they *all* promise to do is measure time. Time spent on every web page. Time from shopping to purchase. Even the time separating the action of placing an item in an online shopping cart to the action of finalizing the order. The promise of behavioral targeting to any business wanting to incorporate stopwatch principles into a marketing plan is therefore huge. The value, however, depends not on its promise but its reality. Luckily, web-based behavioral targeting tools that really work are not only real, but available to businesses of every size.

The behavioral targeting services available to medium-size and large businesses are correspondingly large. SurfAid, a onetime IBM company now owned by CoreMetrics, promises to identify shopping bottlenecks, segment customers by their timed behaviors, even offer valuations of customers over their shopping lifetime. Omniture's SiteCatalyst® and DataWarehouse are designed to map (using their proprietary "ClickMap" software) the flow of customers, their time on site, and entry and exit pages, as well as to highlight the critical shopping moments where visitors make a purchase/nonpurchase decision . . . where they either press the "buy now" key or leave the site.

The costs for using these services are correspondingly robust. Prices for CoreMetrics' products can range as high as $25,000 a month. A standalone package for SiteCatalyst costs more than $15,000, or $1,000/month for a hosted service.

Keynote Research Manager, WebSideStory's HBX, WebFocus, and Fireclick all provide identification of entrance and exit pages, visitor segmentation, and so on. Most will calculate return on investment (ROI) for any online marketing campaign (though, to be sure, ROI remains a far more useful tool for analyzing the profitability of an entire business than a particular marketing effort; it's actually pretty hard to account for either the true costs of a campaign—how does one price twenty years' worth of brand marketing?—or the revenue that can be exclusively associated with one). There's even the *Web Analytics Buyer's Guide* from Sherpa Marketing, an annual publication that evaluates virtually every package on the market, and even cross-tabulates them with nearly 500 of their best-known customers.

Moreover, behavior on the web can—and should—be measured for more than time on site. Typical uses include split tests of particular offers, copy, and terms of payment. Just as stopwatch principles do not accommodate the whole of marketing, web analytics does a great deal more than simply time the search behavior of site visitors.

But even the smallest e-commerce business can use web analytics to measure shopping time and so perform time segment analysis within the reluctant, impatient, recreational, and painstaking quadrants. Economical packages can be purchased off-the-shelf from companies like VisiStat or WebTrends for as little as $15 a month, or as a stand-alone package for only a few hundred dollars. Best of all, the web's largest portal and search engine now offers web analytics, for free. This is not a misprint.

A year before the acquisition of Overture, in 2002, Yahoo had another plan for entering the world of behaviorally targeted web advertising: They bid a little less than $3 billion for Google, the most technologically advanced search engine of all. Even more valuable than search per se was Google's system for automating the auction of keywords in web-based advertising. This keyword auction system granted the best position to ads based on both the highest-price bid *and* on the ad's appeal, measured by the number of times it attracted a searcher. The difference turned out to be critical. Unlike Yahoo+Overture, Google's AdWords service generated money both from selling the ads themselves *and* in selling information about their success to advertisers, ever eager to discover the magic words that produced sales. Ever since Google used the same strategy to acquire the behavior-targeting web analytic software company Urchin in 2006, they have been offering free web analytics, including monthly reports on the number of page views and amount of time spent shopping on a subscribing company's site, tabulated against the size and type of purchase. Google gets to keep the aggregated data (valuable on their own for building the largest possible data universe . . . a happy inversion of the free-webmail-if-you-accept-ads products) and the small-business owner gets to learn how many dollars she is generating from the impatient quadrant. The result has been, literally, revolutionary: As of this writing, Google owns nearly three-quarters of the search-driven advertising business . . . a business that is currently churning $15 billion annually and is predicted to grow by nearly 50 percent a year.[5]

And that is only the beginning. As of this writing, Google has integrated its analytics—its report-writing feature—with its advertising sales arm. Google's AdWords closes the loop on Web-based time segment analysis. Here's how it works:

A potential seller (and given the ability to link up with a gazillion online retail sites, *everyone* can now benefit from an online transaction) can arrange for any word or phrase entered into Google's search function to result in the appearance of a link (a "sponsored link") to the site of the advertiser's choosing. Want your link to be cued by the same phrase as someone else? No problem, since Google auctions off the highest position in its sponsored links page to the highest bidder. Don't want to buy a pig in a poke? Likewise, no problem, since the portal charges only when the link is chosen.

But the real beauty of the web's ability to leverage the principles of stopwatch marketing is apparent to a business with its own web presence, *even if that web presence isn't the site where a final transaction takes place.* This is because AdWords plus web analytics means that any business can receive, in real time, a report that shows precisely how many days, hours, and, yes, minutes your customer spent shopping before making a purchase decision. It can cross-tabulate customers by the amount of time and money they spend; within limits, it can even sort them geographically. The amount of information that can, in theory, be extracted from even a tiny website is literally limitless.

This is something of a mixed blessing.

The *New Yorker* columnist and best-selling author Malcolm Gladwell has famously popularized policy analyst Gregory Treverton's distinction between puzzles and mysteries: the former challenges for which single solutions exist, if only a sufficient amount of information can be found; the latter are fundamentally uncertain problems for which, frequently, too much information exists. The keys to turning data about web traffic from a mystery into a puzzle (to using the tools of web analytics to build a time segment analysis) are:

1. Describing the routes taken by customers
2. Identifying the forks, wrong turns, and dead ends along that route
3. Timing the route

If every keystroke of every visitor to a website is essentially equivalent to a footprint, then assembling thousands (sometimes millions) of such prints into a trail that can be followed—and, more important, aggregated and studied—requires that the ground on which those prints impress themselves be cleaned of confusing undergrowth, and then viewed at the correct angle. Most important, every square inch of the ground needs to be distinct from every other. In order to prepare the ground so that it collects and preserves footprints, every page on your website needs to be indexed, and each index tagged.*

Even knowing where those millions of footprints fit onto a map gets you only halfway home. Making sense of them is done by structuring reports, and, once again, a wide array is available. The most important go under a variety of names, but virtually every web analytic package can report on:

1. Number of travelers along a particular path (Google calls this "Defined Funnel Navigation")
2. The most popular paths ("Reverse Goal Path")
3. The percentage of travelers who enter and exit with *and* without completing a transaction ("Entrance-and-Exit Ratio")
4. The number of times a particular piece of ground is stepped on ("Page Views")

But, critically, each of these measures can be plotted along another axis, the axis of time (Google's report metric is known by the refreshingly simple title, "Average Time"). Dozens of behaviors can be tracked by the amount of time users spend, including the number of seconds (or minutes) spent on each page, the amount of time spent per viewing minute, even—via a "keyword position report"—how different word choices correlate with the amount of online shopping time.

By plotting the Exit Percentage, Page Views, Unique Visitors, and Average Time, as well as any number of other choice statistics, the quality of site searches shows up in the highest of high relief. If a particular purchase is associated with a low Average Time, combined with a high number of Unique Visitors, it is almost certain to suggest occupancy in

---

* When needs appear, solutions can't be far behind. Google's version—its own "enterprise search solution"—is called "Google Mini" but many other providers offer a similar service, usually free, that will index each page on a commercial website.

the impatient quadrant; while a low number of Unique Visitors indicates the reluctant quadrant.

(A word of caution: No simple rule can substitute for judgment. A relatively large number of Page Views combined with a low percentage of Unique Visitors can suggest painstaking shopping . . . or a page that is so poorly designed that it takes a visitor a long time to navigate from it. Similarly, a decrease in the amount of time spent online can indicate loss of interest, or simply a faster Internet connection; in the third quarter of 2004, visitors spent nearly 10 percent less time in average online shopping time than they did a year earlier . . . but nearly twice as many actually bought something. The obvious conclusion is that the decline in viewing time was a direct consequence of the increase in the availability of broadband connections.[6])

Different marketers will use this information differently. As we've seen (and as we will come back to in chapter 10) sometimes the best strategy for a business in a category that derives the bulk of its income from impatient shoppers is to stake out some real estate in the recreational quadrant (see: Whole Foods Market). Sometimes the most successful tactic is to design a product that uses its appearance to sell itself during the minutes that impatient shoppers are willing to spend (see: Goodyear). Both of them would be almost certain to improve performance by reducing the amount of time required for activities that are peripheral to shopping; firms have doubled the percentage of shoppers proceeding to a purchase by automatically filling out the forms that are the necessary evil of online shopping, the equivalent of a supermarket that bags your groceries . . . and a highly underrated touchpoint. Regional businesses will care greatly about tracking *where* customers are when they log on— information that Google and other vendors call "geolocation" reports. Senior executives consume different reports than product managers.

And, of course, different businesses put web analytics to work in different ways. Consider a recreational business like Neopets, an online community for kids owned, since June of 2005, by the division of Viacom that also includes Nickelodeon. Neopets' business model resembles that of both traditional broadcast and premium cable television, generating advertising revenue and subscription fees, and therefore has two objectives that are not always coordinated: attracting the largest number of participants to its free tier, and convincing a large number of them to pay for a premium version of the community. (Premium users can engage in more, and more interesting, activities than can nonpaying visitors, but in order to do either, both need to create unique identities that can play kid-friendly-and-parent-calming games on the site.) Converting the highest possible percentage of the 30 million owners of the virtual pets that gambol around the site into income producers is therefore key to the site's business success . . . and with more than five *billion* page views every month, a lot of data is being generated to figure out how to target the right ones. Because all visitors sign on using their Neopet Names, they also leave a unique record of the time they spend on the site, where they spend it, and the route they take to signing on to more expensive services. The more time users spend on the Neopets site, the more recreation they use . . . and the more profitable the recreational quadrant looks.

In a classically impatient category like fast food, CKE Restaurants, which owns the Carl's Jr., Hardee's, and Green Burrito brands, has used web analytics to time the success of their attempt to make the site a recreational experience, offering movie trailers, music videos, and, most famously, a video of a water-soaked Paris Hilton washing a car while eating a Carl's Jr. burger. Measuring the time and route taken from viewing Ms. Hilton to viewing the Carl's Jr. store locator page is an exemplar of using stopwatch marketing principles to test the viability of the strategy. The country's largest independent tire dealer, Discount Tire, can measure how many minutes, or even seconds, visitors spend on their site before finding a retail location, and knows, in real time, just how impatient those visitors are by marking the time between entrance to the site and arrival at *their* store locator page.

RE/MAX, a giant in the painstaking quadrant, is a real estate sales franchisor with nearly 6,000 offices and 114,000 sales reps. They measure the time it takes for visitors to travel from their first online search to a bricks-and-mortar Realtor®. Decker's, a manufacturer and importer of footwear brands like Teva and Ugg, segments their customers using Google Analytics to make certain each time-based segment achieves the corporate ROI goal of $5 in sales for every $1 invested in search-based advertising.

Using these systems (and lest you think that we are in the pay of Google, or, more fortunately for us, are shareholders in the company, other search engines and portals are racing to offer similar services) you can, quite literally, show how many dollars are generated by shoppers who began searching a week before decision, and how many by shoppers who spent ten minutes. These systems are available to you whether you are a marketing manager in a large company, a marketing consultant seeking to impress clients with your analytic capabilities, or a sole proprietor whose every marketing dollar is, literally, being funded by your own MasterCard. A properly designed time segment analysis permits you to draw a map that shows, over time, the precise locations of the touchpoints that move a web shopper from one level to another. It even allows you to test the messages—the touchpoints—that work best.

The Shopping Continuum

The shopping experience, we have suggested throughout this book, can be broken down into time segments. The time segments we have in mind are defined by a traditional marketing continuum of Awareness through Trial through Loyalty, depicted in Figure 8-1. This continuum is sometimes condensed by, for instance, combining Trial, Purchase, and Usage into one single consumer decision. However, for our purposes we tend to break the continuum down into measurable segments. One of the key messages of this book, after all, is the imperative to be disciplined in such analysis and the attendant quantification of costs and paybacks. The measurement and budget alignment of these time segments are the subjects of chapters 7 and 9.

Few businesses, of course, can rely entirely on the Internet for marketing communication; but one of the key insights to the use of systems like AdWords and ClickTracks is that the stopwatch consumers use while shopping *on* the web turns out to be entirely projectable to the stopwatch they use when shopping *off* the web. That is, people who are thinking about any purchase, from a kitchen renovation to a bouquet of anniversary flowers, are likely to start their shopping the same number of days before making a buying decision whether they start online or offline. Thus, though every business needs to plant touchpoints at dozens of places that don't have .com as part of their addresses, and you need traditional media planning to tell you where, web analytics can tell you *when* they will have the most impact.

Recognizing the need to do something about the continuing fragmentation of media, media salespeople have been hard at work the past few years pitching the case for "integrated marketing." Based on research into

SHOPPING BEHAVIOR TIME SEGMENTS: Detailed Continuum

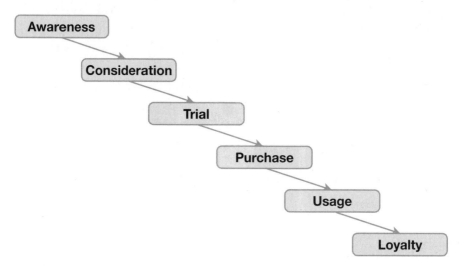

Figure 8-1

INTEGRATED MARKETING OVERVIEW:

As Presented to Marketing Professionals by a "New Media" Firm

The "New" Media Day

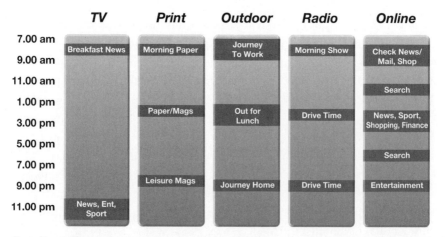

Source: Forrester Research, as shown in "Influencing customers online: From purchase decisions to branding and consideration," PowerPoint presentation by Nichole Peterson of MSN to the Southern California Automotive Executive Summit 2004.

Figure 8-2

consumer media habits, the demonstration of integrated marketing's power is being used effectively by web-based companies to pitch web advertising in its own right, as shown in Figure 8-2. This "New Media Day" graphic was part of a pitch to the auto industry by MSN (aka, MSN.com), in its ongoing efforts to secure web advertising. In a tribute to the continuing ubiquity of search, the reader should know that if you Google (as of this writing, February 2007) "awareness consideration," the entire PowerPoint presentation by MSN to the Southern California Automotive Executive Summit 2004 is the eleventh—yes, eleventh—item on the list!

In any event, let us return to the traditional shopping behavior continuum of time segments as shown in Figure 8-1. Faced with this dynamic, marketers have traditionally used "The Marketing Mix," generally capitalized exactly like that. Unable to pinpoint the true payback of their

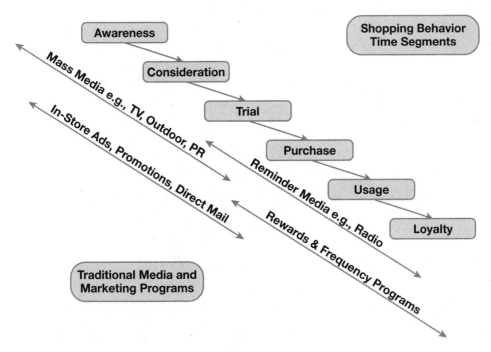

Figure 8-3

spending, marketers have used graphics similar to those shown in Figure 8-3.

Marketers often show this dynamic exactly as we've shown it here, depicting—in presentations to their own bosses—exactly how inexact a science this can be. Note the arrows on the sides of each Media and Marketing Program, suggesting (should we say admitting?) that there is overlap and that the actual impact on any step in the consumer's shopping behavior is necessarily imprecise. Generally, of course, marketers do apply discipline and science after the fact—measuring, for instance, after the expenditure of TV dollars, the impact on Awareness. In fact, they often track this with great diligence, in order to answer the question they get from their superiors: "Did we get anything for all that money we spent on TV last year?"

Now, however, let's look at how much more precise and actionable information is available when marketers use web analytics. In Figure 8-4, we compare the shopping behavior time segments to only one page of measures available from only one of the suppliers of web analytics software and services, in this case, Fireclick.

SHOPPING BEHAVIOR TIME SEGMENTS:

Overlay with Web Analytics Capabilities

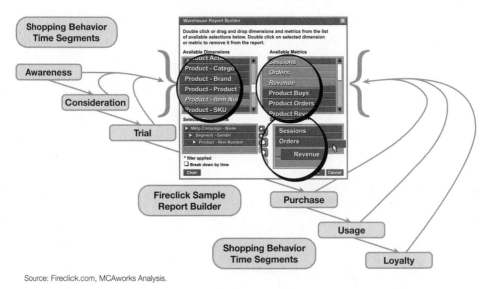

Source: Fireclick.com, MCAworks Analysis.

Figure 8-4

Figure 8-4 shows the measurability of marketing efforts on the web at only the summary level. The beauty—and curse—of the web in this regard is that there is an enormous amount of information available for analysis and action by astute marketers attuned to the ticking stopwatches of their customers. For instance, as shown in Figure 8-5, web analytics suppliers such as Fireclick can provide a report that shows the impact, essentially, of each square inch of the web page.

PERFORMANCE MEASURES THROUGHOUT THE WEB COMMERCE EXPERIENCE:

Fireclick "Site Explorer"

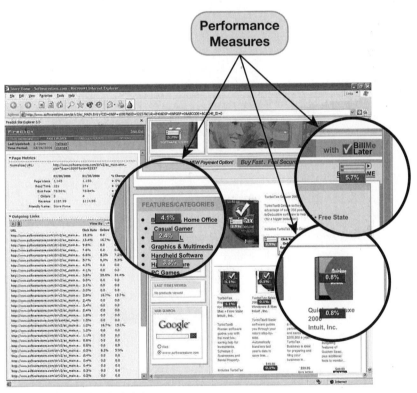

Source: Fireclick.com, MCAworks Analysis.

Figure 8-5

Web Analytics: Costs versus Benefits

Knowing *what* works, and even *when* it works, is only part of the story, as any marketing manager who has ever had to work within a budget knows.

You know that evaluating the benefits of stopwatch marketing means calculating the costs as well. The next step in the process of discovery is economic analysis: identifying the costs of each touchpoint, and comparing alternatives.

After you have measured and tracked each touchpoint's payback, it is important that you cross-reference them against consumer segments. You can then develop and execute programs targeted at the highest-potential consumers. You can do this using traditional segmentation schemes (demographic, geographic, etc.) or newer segmentation approaches made possible by the advent of the web (those using the Mozilla Firefox browser to view your page, those using a mobile device, those who clicked through from another site, etc.). WebSideStory, now part of Visual Sciences LLC, another of the major web analytics suppliers, has a product called "HBX Active Segmentation" specifically designed and marketed to address this.

The foregoing, however, refers to traditional or web-based segmentation schemes. The information you developed this way, while important, is only part of the story. The true marriage of web analytics and stopwatch marketing occurs when you segment according to position in the matrix and track the behavior of quadrant-identified segments through their clicks and purchases on your (your company's) web page. For example, assume you have identified the members of the impatient quadrant as having the greatest potential, as the target affording the highest margin and greatest revenue-production. Armed with the ability to track these impatients through their online shopping behavior, you can then optimize the web experience for all impatients, driving to greater repeat purchase and, ultimately, loyalty.

If there is one consistent bit of advice we offer, it is the importance of measurement to successfully applying stopwatch marketing. And there is simply no better measurement tool than the web. Especially for a small business, it doesn't really require the most sophisticated of the tools discussed above. A stat no one should forgo is "source conversion"—an indicator of the website visited immediately prior to entering your website. Similarly, every marketer can learn an immense amount from quick-and-dirty measurement statistics like the "bounce rate" (one-page visits—or one-minute visits—divided by total visits). When graphed over time, the bounce rate reveals whether visitors are spending more (bounce rate generally declining) or less (bounce rate generally increasing) time shopping . . . and reducing one-page visits automatically improves performance.

The key measurements you should focus on relate to *direction* or *trends:* Is your site and are your marketing tactics increasing or decreasing program efficiency, customer loyalty, and company revenue? Consistent tracking over time is far more important than the precision of a measurement you use. In web analytics as in many other things, the perfect is the enemy of the good, and it is far better to spend a year measuring shopping activities that are imperfectly associated with buying than to spend that same year figuring out what is the absolutely best activity to track. Better to use an imprecise proxy for shopping time and measure whether it is increasing or decreasing for a year than to spend that year finding a better one; better to use an hourglass every day for a year than to wait nine months until you can afford a digital chronometer.

One final, but crucial, point. To make all this work, marketers do need to assign someone, or a team, probably full-time, to executing these analyses, testing alternatives, and revising (in real time) the actual web shopping experience of their target customer base. This may sound like an increase in overhead, but we are convinced it is worth it. Think about it this way: Instead of an army of brand managers spending hours on inexact media plans, meeting with ad agencies, sitting behind the mirror at focus groups, and so on, marketing managers can be actively managing commerce, driving the ROI from a given customer segment by affecting the actual message that customer receives, when he or she receives it, how it is received, and the like, and tracking/driving those customers through a disciplined, stopwatch-informed process of page views, clickthroughs, and so on, all the way to end purchase and loyalty.

• • •

Discovery, of course, is only the first act of the drama; activating the principles of stopwatch marketing—including building a constituency within your business organization that will support the findings established during discovery—is the subject of our next chapter.

Chapter Nine

Distribution: Allocating Your Marketing Resources

 The preceding chapters have been largely concerned with showing how consumer shopping-and-searching behavior can be measured by the amount of time it occupies, and in identifying how those behaviors cluster into discrete segments. In these final two chapters, we move from the descriptive and diagnostic to the prescriptive: how to budget for and apply the theory and constructs of stopwatch marketing. In any business, most notably yours, of course, applying these stopwatch marketing principles will be limited by the resources available, otherwise known as *the budget*. Allocating those resources to the tasks that are most productive is the key responsibility you face as a manager. And, lest we forget to remind you of the obvious, allocating stopwatch marketing resources requires more of you than simply living within a marketing budget; it means more than merely distributing that budget to the most effective channels. In applying the principles of stopwatch marketing to your particular budget, you'll allocate resources not just *where* they have the greatest impact, but *when*.

Fundamental Principles

In turning our attention to the allocation of resources according to stopwatch marketing principles, therefore, two concepts are fundamental:

1. Stopwatch leverage: the ability, in any given time segment, to modify behavior by exploiting a specific touchpoint or set of touchpoints in your favor; that is, the ability to use superior insight (gained via the Discovery

process) at a specific touchpoint to increase preference for and/or close the sale on your product.

2. Alignment of payback: the ability to achieve leverage at an affordable price; that is, to generate a positive ROI from informed marketing action directed at a specific touchpoint.

In a perfect world, you would complete this allocation by creating a dynamic and quantitative model, composed of factors developed using the market research techniques described in chapter 7, such as:

1. Percentage of stopwatch leverage
2. Percentage of dollars/customers/transactions
3. Cost per touchpoint
4. Persuasion power of available marketing tactics aimed at this touchpoint

But, before we get too deeply into development of quantitative models, let's review. Recall the basic construct of stopwatch marketing: In a consumer's stopwatch, as the second hand moves, it is counting down to the final moment of purchase decision. Furthermore, as the second hand moves along this figurative clock face, it passes discrete time segments (Awareness, Consideration, Trial, etc.) within which are consumer/supplier touchpoints—points at which marketing efforts have an impact. This chapter, then, is about allocating scarce marketing resources so that they align with the touchpoints with the most leverage and the highest impact.

One of the more powerful graphic tools we use in our consulting practice is what we (in our more informal meetings) call a Countdown Budget. And the countdown metaphor is an apt one. Despite our distaste for the ways in which military metaphors are used in businesses—it is our experience that executives who think that "business is warfare" have no clue about war—developing your marketing budget according to stopwatch marketing principles requires that the budget overtly recognize the critical touchpoints. The budget can, literally, be organized in a manner intended to recall the planning that precedes a military operation. Thus, the minute when a buyer hands a credit card to a seller is M-Minute, the hour H-Hour, the day D-Day, and the touchpoints that are placed along the timeline are marked D − 365 (or more), D − 30, and D − 7. (In our defense, recall that this bit of linguistic sleight-of-hand is not intended to be used as it usually is . . . as a motivational tool to pump up employees for the Arbor-Day-Sales-Campaign, or the Launch-of-the-Bigger-and-Better-Widget. It is, emphatically, not an opportunity for a sales executive to make a "band of brothers" speech to the, ahem, troops. It is about *consumer* behavior, after all.)

The Countdown Budget

This approach is, nonetheless, a useful "get started" budgeting tool for anyone trying to implement stopwatch principles. Here's an example of how it works: the research described in chapter 7 should have given you a good idea of the total amount of time the consumer spends from initial awareness, through consideration of the purchase, and so on, through full-blown loyalty; that is, the size of their stopwatches. As noted, marketers have for some time used a generic continuum of time segments to describe this:

Awareness

Consideration

Trial

Initial Purchase

Usage

Loyalty

To allocate resources according to stopwatch marketing principles you'll need to align the share of working marketing budget with the share of stopwatch leverage. So, if 30 percent of the stopwatch leverage for your product is to be found in the Trial time segment, then 30 percent of the working budget should be allocated to trial-generating vehicles.

At each "time segment"—and this is critical—the action we want a consumer to take (moving on to the next segment) defines the marketing objective: If the consumer's activity on D − 365 is simply becoming aware of a need, the marketing objective for that time segment, *on that day/at that point in the stopwatch,* is to "stimulate awareness." If, on D − 30, the time segment activity is to consider alternatives, then the marketing objective *on that day/at that point in the stopwatch* is to assure inclusion in the consideration set.

Now, a marketing objective such as stimulate awareness can be achieved via a wide variety of potential touchpoints—marketing activities that we, as marketers, can take advantage of. To stimulate awareness, the potential touchpoints include traditional media advertising, sponsorships, visible retail distribution or locations, publicity, and so on. Further along, to achieve the objective of stimulating trial (i.e., targeting the time segment of "Trial"), the potential touchpoints include sampling, couponing, and discounting, to mention a few.*

We recommend that you begin the process of developing the marketing budget every year by creating a chart like this:

A	B	C
Countdown	Time Segment / Marketing Objective	Potential Touchpoint
D – 365	Awareness	TV advertising Radio ads Outdoor ads Sports sponsorships Publicity
D – 30	Consideration	Media advertising Direct mail AdWords / Internet
D – 10	Trial	Sampling Couponing Discounting AdWords / Internet
D-Day	Initial Purchase	In-store promotion Discounting events AdWords / Internet
D + 1	Usage	Reminder advertising After-sale follow-up
D + 10 . . .	Loyalty	Loyalty / points programs Pantry loading

In this allocation discipline, the specific contents of Column A will have been revealed in the research defined in chapter 7. Identifying your target customer and his or her quadrant-specific attitudes and behaviors is what

---

* Please note, although emphasizing couponing and sampling would appear to give a consumer products bias to this discussion, the concept is the same in all categories: "sampling" to Gillette consists of mailing out millions of new razors, while to a car dealer it consists of the traditional "test drive," and to a retail store, it involves browsing, trying it on for size, or, literally, tasting (in a wine shop or an ice cream shop, for example).

the Discovery process is expressly designed to accomplish. Likewise, the specifics within Column C will vary decidedly from industry to industry, depending on industry practice, history, and, most important, consumer habits and behaviors (revealed in the market research) for your product and your quadrant. The contents of Column B should generally remain the same from brand to brand (or job to job) although there may be some industry-specific alternative language.

We are not done yet. At this point we have identified the quadrants, the stopwatch (Column A, above), the marketing objective at each critical time segment along the stopwatch (Column B), and the potential touch-points or marketing activities (Column C) for each. We don't have an unlimited budget to allocate across all these, so we need to add a couple of columns:

A	B	C	D	E	F = D/E
Countdown	Time Segment / Marketing Objective	Potential Touchpoint	Percentage of Stopwatch Leverage	Percentage of Budget Allocation	Payback Ratio
D – 365	Awareness	TV advertising Radio ads Outdoor ads Sports sponsorships Publicity			
D – 30	Consideration	Media advertising Direct mail AdWords / Internet			
D – 10	Trial	Sampling Couponing Discounting AdWords / Internet			
D-Day	Initial Purchase	In-store promotion Discounting events AdWords / Internet			
D + 1	Usage	Reminder advertising After-sale follow-up			
D + 10 . . .	Loyalty	Loyalty / points programs Pantry loading			

Column D can also be filled out with the results of the research outlined in chapter 7 and further informed by previous media/marketing research and industry knowledge. Recall that some of the stopwatch questions (3 through 6) on pages 132–133 were specifically intended to provide insight into stopwatch leverage—the ability to positively affect consumer behavior at a given time segment. We also are aware that you are likely to be in possession of considerable industry knowledge and previous research into the effectiveness of marketing activities. This column, D, should be filled in with percentages of total. Stopwatch leverage, cumulatively, sums to one hundred.

The logic of the table should be clear now: If our research and experience indicate that 30 percent of the stopwatch leverage occurs at the "Trial" step, and the trial step occurs on the stopwatch at $D - 10$, we should allocate 30 percent of our working marketing budget to trial vehicles, targeted (as much as possible) to engage the consumer ten days before his or her expected purchase.

So, you can fill in Column E with the percentage allocation of your working marketing budget. In the preceding example (30 percent of the decision is influenced at the trial stage), if you are spending only 10 percent of your budget on trial vehicles (the touchpoints in Column B), then your spending is misallocated. Put bluntly, you are spending only one-third as much of your budget against this part of the stopwatch as you should. Column F, then, provides a simple way to track this potential misallocation. If F is equal to D (percentage of stopwatch leverage) divided by E (percentage of marketing budget), then anytime $F > 1$ you are spending too little on that point in the stopwatch and, conversely, if $F < 1$, you are spending too much.

An Example

Let's look at a specific example. Assume TV advertising consumes 60 percent of your total marketing budget for a particular product or service. However, let us further assume that your research indicates that a sizable portion—30 percent—of the stopwatch leverage for that product occurs at the Trial stage. This might be true, for instance, of automobile marketing where billions are spent on mass media and much less is spent (by the manufacturers) on enhancing the experience in the dealership. In this case, your initial allocation table might look like this:

A	B	C	D	E	F = D/E
Countdown	Time Segment / Marketing Objective	Potential Touchpoint	Percentage of Stopwatch Leverage	Percentage of Budget Allocation	Payback Ratio
D – 365	Awareness	TV advertising Radio ads Outdoor ads Sports sponsorships Publicity	15	60	0.25
D – 30	Consideration	Media advertising Direct mail AdWords / Internet	30	10	3.00
D – 10	Trial	Sampling Couponing Discounting AdWords / Internet	30	15	2.00
D-Day	Initial Purchase	In-store promotion Discounting events Adwords / Internet	15	10	1.50
D + 1	Usage	Reminder advertising After-sale follow-up	5	5	1.00
D + 10 . . .	Loyalty	Loyalty / points programs Pantry loading	5	0	N/A

The obvious misalignment of resources is clearly identified in Column F—Payback Ratio—above: You are spending 60 percent of every dollar on a touchpoint that accounts for only 15 percent of the purchase decision, a ratio of .25. It is precisely this kind of analysis that has marketers shifting increasing amounts of their budgets away from mass media and into much more targeted vehicles (touchpoints) like direct mail and Internet advertising. In our experience, however, this evolving change in allocating budget is done with insufficient discipline and precision—today's marketers simply know in their gut what Mr. Wanamaker said so long ago: "Half the money I spend on advertising is wasted; the trouble is, I don't know which half."

Stopwatch marketing is a way to quantify this gut feeling. First, this is done by defining the target consumer, his or her stopwatch, and the quadrant in which this type of purchase lives. Next, we identify the points along the stopwatch allocated across specific measurements of time, in this case, days (Column A) and the appropriate Marketing Objective for each (Column B). Next we populate Column D with the research-informed percentage of stopwatch leverage for each, allowing us to compare the proportion of working marketing spending (Column E) with that proportion of stopwatch leverage. In the above example, assuming you hope to more efficiently allocate your marketing budget, you could say, with a straight face, "Look, our spending is out of whack by a factor of *three* with regard to Consideration and Trial, and by a factor of *four* on mass media! Let's change this."

Now for a more detailed example. Recall that a primary purpose of the market research is to customize Columns A, B, and C for your particular situation—that's what placement in the four quadrants is all about. Column C, then, can and should be further customized by marketing departments, ad agencies, or PR firms—even, it is true, consultants—as informed by the research, quadrant placement, and the customized contents of Columns A and B.

Let's assume the following:

1. The product we are selling is automobiles—we are a manufacturer and we are focused for the moment on a specific brand.
2. Our research has indicated relevant and precise definitions of our time segments. These definitions are:
   A. Awareness of our brand
   B. Consultation on the Internet, selection of three (+/−1) good dealers to visit

      C. Visits to three dealers

      D. Test-driving our brand

      E. Purchase

3. 75 percent of our target market normally is "Aware."

4. 40 percent of those Aware move to the next step, "Consult Internet, consider various dealers." Therefore, absent any new and different marketing at this point, 30 percent of the target market's stopwatch is still ticking at the "Consult Internet, consider various dealers" time segment (40% × 75% = 30%).

5. Continuing:

      A. 50 percent of those who consider dealers actually visit three dealers.

      B. 70 percent of those who visit actually test-drive our brand.

      C. 30 percent of those who test-drive actually purchase our brand (they are visiting three dealerships).

So, with no change in marketing spending, the math so far looks like this:

Target Consumer	A	B	C = A X B
	Percentage at This Time Segment	Percentage of This Time Segment Moving On	Percentage of Total Universe "Still Ticking"
Universe	100.00	75	75.00
Aware of brand	75.00	40	30.00
Consult Internet, consider various dealers	30.00	50	15.00
Visit three dealers	15.00	70	10.50
Test-drive brand	10.50	30	3.15
Purchase	3.15		

Now, assume our research and previous experience tells us that:

1. More mass media on awareness advertising barely moves the needle—we can increase awareness from 75 percent to 77 percent.

2. Targeted direct marketing can increase the percent of Awares who move on to the "Consult Internet, consider various dealers" from 40 percent to 45 percent.

3. Improving the dealer experience overall, marketing against that strategy, and gaining a reputation for doing so (the Lexus strategy) can increase the percentage of those who consider and move on to a dealer visit from 50 percent to 75 percent.

4. Of those who visit, the percentage that moves on to a test drive is hard to affect—they've already taken the time to visit the dealership. Say we can improve it from 70 percent to 75 percent.

5. Finally, discounting, dealer training, improved test-drive experiences, and so forth can move the percentage of those who test-drive and move on to purchase from 30 percent to 40 percent.

So, the analysis so far is:

Target Consumer	A	B	C = A X B	D	E = B + D	F = E X A	
	Percentage at This Time Segment	Percentage of This Time Segment Moving On	Percentage of Total Universe "Still Ticking"	Impact of Marketing Activity on This Time Segment	Percentage of This Time Segment Moving On After Marketing Impact	Percentage of Universe Still Ticking If Marketing Applied	Comment
Universe	100.00	75	75.00	+2	77	77.00	Very difficult to increase awareness
Aware of brand	75.00	40	30.00	+5	45	33.75	Target marketing at those already aware
Consult Internet, consider various dealers	30.00	50	15.00	+25	75	22.50	Improve dealer experience, gain reputation for doing so, market this aggressively

Target Consumer	A	B	C = A X B	D	E = B + D	F = E X A	
Visit three dealers	15.00	70	10.50	+5	75	11.25	Difficult to increase proportion who test—already 70%
Test-drive brand	10.50	30	3.15	+10	40	4.20	Increase at-dealer discounts, incentives
Purchase	3.15						

The remaining analysis consists of calculating the relative share of stopwatch leverage:

Target Consumer	A	B	C = A X B	D	E = B + D	F = E X A	G = F - C	H Index to sum of G
	Percentage at This Time Segment	Percentage of This Time Segment Moving On	Percentage of Total Universe "Still Ticking"	Impact of Marketing Activity on This Time Segment	Percentage of This Time Segment Moving On After Marketing Impact	Percentage of Universe Still Ticking If Marketing Applied	Stopwatch Leverage	Percentage of Stopwatch Leverage
Universe	100.00	75	75.00	+2	77	77.00	2.00	13
Aware of brand	75.00	40	30.00	+5	45	33.75	3.75	25
Consult Internet, consider various dealers	30.00	50	15.00	+25	75	22.50	7.50	50
Visit three dealers	15.00	70	10.50	+5	75	11.25	.75	5
Test-drive brand	10.50	30	3.15	+10	40	4.20	1.05	7

Target Consumer	A	B	C = A X B	D	E = B + D	F = E X A	G = F - C	H Index to sum of G
Purchase	3.15							
Total							15.05	100

Armed with this stopwatch leverage analysis, you are now prepared to do the budget allocation as outlined earlier in this chapter. For example, if we again assume that our auto manufacturer's initial budget calls for 60 percent of spending to be allocated to awareness-building efforts such as mass media, your initial allocation might look like this:

A	B	C	D	E	F = D/E
Countdown	Time Segment / Marketing Objective	Potential Touchpoint	Percentage of Stopwatch Leverage (from Column H in preceding analysis)	Percentage of Budget Allocation (illustrative)	Payback Ratio
D – 365	Aware of brand	TV advertising Radio ads Outdoor ads Sports sponsorships Publicity	13	60	0.22
D – 30	Consult Internet, consider various dealers	Targeted direct mail AdWords / Internet Media advertising	25	10	2.50
D – 10	Visit three dealers	Dealer training Enhanced dealer experience Local & co-op ads AdWords / Internet	50	15	3.33

A	B	C	D	E	F = D/E
D – 10	Test-drive our brand	Dealer training Enhanced dealer experience	5	10	.50
D-Day	Purchase	In-store promotion Discounting events AdWords / Internet	7	5	1.40

Don't forget that such an initial budget decision—allocating 60 percent to awareness building—might be appropriate, but just as easily might not. This is because so many businesses fail to engage in zero-based budgeting, the process by which every dollar (rather than every incremental dollar) of a marketing budget has to be justified during every budget period. Usually, this is a predictable consequence of the organizational dynamic: Since every marketing activity in a typical business requires staff to execute it, *all* activities engender constituencies who are devoted to their perpetuation. The executive who has responsibility for television advertising is typically not only convinced that the TV budget is sacrosanct, she is frequently pretty convincing as well. So are the executives devoted to dealer incentives, promotions, and merchandising. Since every marketing department fights like hell to at least maintain its call on corporate resources, any new activity—which, again, by definition, has no existing constituency—tends to be starved.

This is why we recommend that marketers exert sufficient discipline to construct tables such as those above, populate them with the relevant information and findings, and strive, as heroically as possible, to achieve allocation perfection—that is, deliver a result where Column F is completely filled with numbers extremely close to 1.00. We recognize that not all marketers have the time and budget to complete the extensive research outlined in chapter 7. The Discovery Wines example of a shoestring budget can achieve important and instructive results. In any event, whether you have a large research budget, a tiny research budget, or no budget at all, we do recommend following the discipline outlined above. Even if you live in a "no research budget" world, you still have years of industry experience and gut feel with which to populate the table and enough experience with mathematics to calculate Column F. Even in such a constrained environment, the simple act of going through this discipline and forcing yourself to think through the allocation of stopwatch leverage—forced by the tyranny of 100 percent—will lead you to both fresh insights and a rethinking of your marketing budget allocation.

Practical Considerations

Finally, some practical considerations: We do understand that achieving perfection, defined as a one-to-one alignment between percent of budget and percent of stopwatch leverage, is impossible. Column F will never be filled with numbers vanishingly close to 1.00. TV advertising is very expensive, for instance, and, in many categories (such as autos), share of voice is very important. History, industry practice, and inertia may make shifting big portions of marketing budget impractical. It is also true that the inventory of available "new media" is small—for big marketers, it may be literally impossible to shift funds entirely as indicated by the analysis. Demands for continued "spending as usual" may also be received from dealers, wholesalers, and so on, depending on the industry. All of that said, however, we stand by the following:

First, you need *some* disciplined approach to reallocating your budgets in light of such megatrends as time poverty, advent of the Internet, fragmented media, and other changes in the shopping environment that even Paco Underhill hasn't identified yet. If nothing else, budgets *always* need to be reallocated in the face of competitive pressure, such as the launch of a rival product. Second, if you continue to spend as you always have, you are ignoring not only those megatrends and competitive inroads, but, more important, the key insight of this book: Consumers are subject to the tyranny of their own internal stopwatches. And third, utilizing the stopwatch marketing principles and the allocation approach outlined in this chapter will, at a minimum, provide a real discipline to at least begin the process of reallocating marketing spending in a way that will be more productive.

An ROI Approach

On the next few pages, we outline—at a very theoretical level—an even more quantitative, financial ROI/portfolio-driven approach to budget allocation. You may feel free to skip these few pages and move on to the conclusion at the end of the chapter if any of these statements are true for you:

1. "I have no market research budget, but lots of experience and gut feel. I'm ready to apply the disciplines of stopwatch marketing as outlined above."
2. "I could probably put together a small market research budget, and can probably execute something like the Discovery Wines approach to get me more information than merely gut feel."
3. "Even though I control a sizable market research budget to populate the quadrants and the allocation budget outlined in this chapter, I don't like math much, and ROI calculations work on me like Ambien."

If, however, you are like some of our clients who have both big budgets and a very disciplined, financially-driven, ROI approach to all spending, the following is for you.

Assume, for a moment, that a purchase decision occurs once a threshold of stopwatch leverage is reached . . . when, for purposes of metaphor preservation, the second hand on a consumer's shopping stopwatch reaches vertical. At each identifiable moment on the stopwatch, a simple calculation can, theoretically, be performed:

$$(TSL * LTV) / TC = ROSMI$$

Where:

> TSL = Touchpoint Stopwatch Leverage
> LTV = Lifetime Value of the target consumer
> TC = Touchpoint Cost
> ROSMI = Return on Stopwatch Marketing Investment

To make this fairly traditional ROI model work, one simply needs to quantify in dollar terms the value of successfully influencing purchase at each point: Touchpoint Stopwatch Leverage (TSL) expressed in percentage terms. Put simply, if a given point on the consumer's stopwatch accounts for 30 percent of the stopwatch leverage and the lifetime value of the purchase is $500 and the cost of success in marketing at that touch-point is $135, the ROSMI is 11 percent: (30% × $500) / $135 = 1.11. For those not familiar with the notion of Lifetime Value, here are some examples. A customer, on average, buys replacement tires costing $500, but never buys again because he starts changing cars faster than replacing tires: Lifetime Value = $500. A Whole Foods customer spends $150 per month and continues for seven years until moving to a remote retirement location: Lifetime Value = $150 × 12 × 7 = $12,600. This $12,600 should, of course, be discounted back to a Present Value, but we are getting too far into finance for a marketing book.

All right, not so simple, at least not without a few definitions. What we call *cumulative leverage* is defined as the reciprocal of the time remaining on the stopwatch, expressed as the square root of the percentage of the total time from the moment when the countdown began; thus, for a shopping process that takes two years—as, for example, the choice of a college—the cumulative leverage, at the point in time thirty days before decision, is $1 - \sqrt{(1/24)}$, or approximately 80 percent. At the point in time one *week* before, it is $1/\sqrt{(1/104)}$, or approximately 90 percent. And one *day* before is 96 perccent, or virtual certainty.

What this means, in turn, is that the *Touchpoint Stopwatch Leverage*, or TSL, is the amount of a decision that can, potentially, be influenced during any particular time period. A full 10 percent of a college recruiter's stopwatch leverage occurs during the period from three weeks before an applicant's decision to one week before, but 6 percent is found in the following six days.

However, the cumulative leverage for a two-hour-long search—looking for a new lock for a gym locker—gets to 80 percent only five minutes before the final decision is made, and to 90 percent 1.2 minutes before. Thus, depending on the quadrant in which the majority of your purchasers resides—as revealed by your analysis—widely varying amounts of stopwatch leverage can occur at specific points in time. Roughly the same quantum of behavior that occurs during three weeks of an aspiring collegian's search happens during three minutes of shopping for Master Lock's latest and greatest padlock.

Back to definitions. The *Touchpoint Cost*, or TC, of any marketing effort—of any touchpoint placed in the path of a stopwatch shopper—is self-explanatory. Dividing the TC cost by the *Lifetime Value* (LTV) of a customer* gives the *Return on Stopwatch Marketing Investment,* or ROSMI . . . the real payback for any marketing effort.

Needless to say, execution of all this requires disciplined thinking and management in a financial/portfolio sense. In a perfect world, you would spend on each touchpoint until the diminishing returns drive marginal payback, or ROSMI, to zero.

Three rather important characteristics conspire to make the world in which we live decidedly imperfect:

1. Budgets that are fixed in the short term (one year . . . sometimes less)
2. Job insecurity
3. Your competition, uncontrollable and unpredictable

We would be surprised, therefore, if every reader of this book promptly went "all the way to bright," expending millions in consumer research and justifying each and every penny spent based on ROSMI.

Recommendations

We do believe, however, that you should embrace the overall stopwatch marketing concept, spend where you perceive leverage to positively affect the target consumer's time segment decisions, build success stories to take to your boss, and hold out some dollars for research, testing, experimentation, and so on because it will be necessary to constantly refine the spending allocation as you learn more and more about the dynamics of the consumer's stopwatch. We recommend, at minimum:

1. Recognizing the tyranny of the consumer's internal stopwatch
2. Beginning the process of researching the stopwatch dynamic— presumably with the focus group approach we outlined in chapter 7
3. Outlining a potential countdown and defining the target consumer's time segments

---

* Too many books and online sites to name show how to calculate the lifetime value of a customer.

4. Assessing the level of alignment between current budget and the findings of Steps 1–3, above

5. Reprioritizing your spending based on that assessment of your spending against your target consumer's key time segments

In short, spend where you perceive the most leverage to lengthen the consumers' stopwatches, moving a greater proportion of those consumers further along in the purchase process.

This is where the next chapter will take stopwatch marketing as well: out of the research department and into the marketplace.

Chapter Ten

Activation: Creating, Refining, and Executing Your Stopwatch Strategy

 Some physicians are superb diagnosticians: They can identify the nature of a problem from the simplest description of its symptoms. With experience, a good diagnosis leads to a prognosis, a prediction of the condition's likely consequences. But the best diagnoses and prognoses are pretty unsatisfying unless they are accompanied by a recommendation for treatment.

So, too, with the world of commerce. If you've read this far, we feel safe in guessing that you agree that stopwatch marketing principles offer a powerful set of analytic tools to describe and predict consumer behavior. And, if that were all it offered, perhaps it would be enough. But none of our clients think that's enough, and neither should you. It's all very well to know the rate at which your customers' stopwatches are ticking, but unless you can slow them down when you want, you're in the position of a pre-penicillin doctor treating scarlet fever: You can tell your patients how long they're going to suffer, but can't do anything to change the disease's timetable.

Doing something about the timetable is the subject of this chapter: activation, or using the analyses of the preceding chapters to take action in the marketplace. In our consulting assignments, we generally break the development of marketing plans into three parts, one following the other: creating the plan, refining it, and executing it.

Creating comes first. In our scheme, the creation process consists largely of matching findings with their implications. This is a necessary step for everyone from our smallest clients to those who occupy slots in the Fortune 500 . . . even for a business as small as Discovery Wines.

Creating at Discovery Wines

Let's return to the quadrant analysis for Discovery Wines we performed back in chapter 7 (see Figure 10-1).

The initial finding was that the stopwatches used by the vast majority of the wine shop's customers—more than eight out of ten—are ticking away at a rapid clip; 82 percent of the customers that walk through

THE DISCOVERY WINES SHOPPING MATRIX

Higher Importance / Risk

Impatient

22% of respondents
25% of revenue
Average transaction: $27.70
Average # of bottles: 1.8
Average price per bottle: $15.40

Painstaking

7% of respondents
10% of revenue
Average transaction: $34.00
Average # of bottles: 1.6
Average price per bottle: $21.30

Less Time ← → **More Time**

Reluctant

60% of respondents
46% of revenue
Average transaction: $18.40
Average # of bottles: 1.4
Average price per bottle: $13.10

Recreational

11% of respondents
19% of revenue
Average transaction: $44.60
Average # of bottles: 3.3
Average price per bottle: $13.50

Lower Importance / Risk

CAVEAT: Some calculations within the quadrants of the matrix are based on extremely small sample sizes. These should be viewed as qualitative in nature.

Base: With receipt and all time/risk variables (113).

Figure 10-1

Discovery Wines' doors are shopping in either the impatient or reluctant quadrants.

All of this indicates that the appropriate marketing strategies will, in one sense, echo those typically associated with retail stores. Long-term awareness and image building in anticipation of "the big day" à la automobile brands is clearly *not* indicated. On the contrary, this shopping behavior—this small and rapidly ticking stopwatch—demands a strategy focusing on convenience: being open at the right hours (every hour that is affordable; twenty-four a day if possible) and in the right place (on the daily travel path of as many customers as possible; in New York, that means near a subway stop, on a safe and frequently traveled sidewalk). In fact, since one finding is that because the store's largest set of customers— the reluctants—not only want *fast* (nearly half spend less than five minutes inside the store) but spend well below the average transaction of $24.30, the indicated action is to tell them that they can get in and out in less than five minutes . . . and for less than $20.

As noted earlier, one approach would be to play directly to the reluctant and/or impatient behavior pattern by encouraging multiple purchases during a given visit. Recommending a second bottle to be consumed at an unplanned later date, used for a gift occasion as yet unknown, and the like is clearly indicated. "Buy a second bottle to give to someone you care about" is a strategy that would leverage the short stopwatch (reluctant and impatient) by eliminating the need for a second trip under (presumably extreme) time pressure at some unspecified date. It would also eliminate an opportunity for "switching out" at the later date.

Another clear finding is that the shopping that occurs within the recreational quadrant generates far more dollars per visit (more bottles and more dollars) than shopping anywhere else. As a result, transforming a reluctant visitor into a recreational one holds out the promise of increased sales *and* margin, which would seem to argue for a strategy of stimulating reasons for reluctants to become recreationals, such as in-store events, special programs, and regular tastings.

As the example of Whole Foods Market shows so eloquently, converting reluctant or impatient shopping behavior into recreational is not only possible, but potentially extremely profitable. It is also, however, enormously difficult, dependent on a radical re-creation of an entire shopping category. Absent such a world-shaking idea, our recommended strategy for a client with a matrix such as the one enjoyed by Discovery Wines is the more practical strategy of turning reluctants into impatients . . . though impatients of a particular sort. Since wine bought as a gift represents a more profitable sale than wine bought for personal consumption, increasing impatient gift buying is a real profit driver in this category. Point-of-purchase reminders—for special offers like the "Gift of the Month," for example—can work to turn low-margin reluctant shopping into relatively higher-margin impatient shopping.

Another finding: reluctants outnumber impatients three to one but impatients outspend reluctants by three to two. The indicated action here is to pursue the impatient market by aggressively marketing and expanding a home delivery program, tied in with an ongoing web/e-mail program. Messaging in the e-mail and community program should overtly address the importance/risk issue.

And another: Overwhelmingly, the store's sales are made to customers who made the decision to buy wine—any wine—within two hours of making the actual purchase. Anytime we encounter a stopwatch that ticks down to zero so quickly, we also expect to find significant loyalty challenges; a customer who needs to complete a transaction within hours of even considering it can always be tempted to try a new supplier. The indicated action for this particular finding is to build barriers to impulse switching by this majority of current customers with programs that reward loyalty with incentives, rewards, quantity discounts that encourage pantry loading, and home delivery tied in with regular communication by both e-mail and traditional delivery.

Sometimes, separate findings suggest the same actions. Three-quarters of current customers plan to drink the wine at home with or without a significant other. The action indicated by this particular finding is to expand the store's home delivery program, and to market it as aggressively as possible, tying it in to the same ongoing web/e-mail program intended to ensure loyalty, thus keeping those customers happy and—therefore—unlikely to shift to a competitor. Some of our recommendations for content to be used by Discovery in its regular communications include:

1. The "Need a wine for dinner tonight?" program—a list of food and featured wine pairings;
2. The "Buy a Week's Worth of Wine, Personalized for You" discount, in which a Discovery Wines employee could fill a mixed case to accommodate either a plan of Monday = Sushi, Tuesday = Pasta; or a more generalized

list of customer eating preferences in order to make sure that the customer will always have an appropriate wine available . . . with the added benefit that the store automatically receives a reminder of when the mixed case has likely run out.

A related, and distinctive, finding of the research is that 80 percent became aware because they "saw the store." The only other significant source was "word of mouth," at 18 percent. Based solely on this one finding, we recommended a half-dozen "dos and don'ts":

1. Do make sure the area around and in front of the store is clean, well-lighted, and inviting.
2. Do make sure that the name, phone number, and website address are all visible in as wide an area as possible, for example, from across the street.
3. Do make sure that the displays in the window and the parts of the store that are visible from the street are inviting.
4. Don't spend much on awareness-building efforts such as broadcast advertising.
5. Don't spend more money on Yellow Pages advertising.
6. Do spend time, effort, and money "hugging" your loyal customers and building barriers that keep them from even trying other shops . . . and motivating them to spread the word about Discovery Wines to neighbors and friends.

The simple research program we coordinated with Discovery Wines reveals literally dozens of such findings that reinforce the impulse nature, generally, and the impatient + reluctant nature, specifically, of the current customer base. It also reveals the opportunities available in the other quadrants. Recall that these quadrants were *not* defined by how much money the respondents spent, either on a single bottle or on the entire transaction. The amount spent is a *result or finding* of the research. That is, painstakings and recreationals were defined by how much time they spent in the store. They spent more time and they spent more money. The importance of this cannot be emphasized enough. Marketing strategies for Discovery Wines should strive to encourage and stimulate more time spent in the shop without violating the *option* to get in and out fast. In our terms, every effort must be given to slowing down the ticking of the stopwatch, to make the diameter of the watch much bigger, to get customers to spend—and enjoy spending—more time in the store. When wine buyers spend more time (whether planning or in store) they spend more money. For nearly every customer (82 percent are reluctant or impatient), Discovery Wines has the opportunity to create a loyal customer (on average they buy on 6+ subsequent occasions) by leveraging the "fast" imperative and/or to increase the cash register ring by two and a half times by leveraging the "fun" imperative, turning the customer into a recreational shopper.

Overall, the direction should be clear. The majority of current customers are impatient or reluctant, and have a short stopwatch, with few time segments. Our key marketing objectives should be to lengthen the stopwatch and increase the number of touchpoints, by doing the following:

1. Create a community via web/e-mail, exploiting the capabilities discussed in the chapter on web analytics, utilizing "learn more about wine" (which 60 percent of respondents suggested they found appealing) as the hook.

2. Exploit the desire to "learn more about wine" to drive more staff/ customer interaction, and use the store's computer kiosks to get customers to *spend more time in the store.*

3. Create more and more "fun" activities in the form of events that do so without violating the "fast" imperative, such as book readings; food tastings; cooking classes tied in with; TV monitors in discreet areas displaying sports, stock market reports, and news; even a cappuccino bar. Anything that gets customers to spend more time in the store is a good idea. It doesn't even matter whether the activities have anything to do with wine, so long as they serve the needs of potential buyers instead of attracting nonbuyers or aren't so entertaining that they attract nonbuyers.

4. Create barriers to switching by incorporating loyalty programs tied in with the community.

5. Execute (as much as the law allows) home delivery, quantity discounts, and pantry-loading programs.

Discovery Wines' action plans can be viewed from the perspective of time segment analysis, as well as touchpoints. Efforts aimed at the *Awareness time segment,* with the possible exception of strong word of mouth, will have little payback. The stopwatch for the category is just too short; a reasonable inference is that all shoppers in Manhattan have a similar behavior pattern: they know about the wine shop nearest their home or office and make the decision to purchase on the same day, indeed within two hours of actual purchase.

However, programs targeted at the *Consideration time segment* are very important in a unique sense—we are not interested so much in stimulating Consideration as in *blocking* consideration of other shops, since the bulk of the customers are impulse-driven reluctants and impatients. The pantry-loading, home delivery, and community-building recommendations are all, in part, aimed at dominating the Consideration time segment, albeit in a defensive way. Better, perhaps, to rename this time segment "Preemption" and use it to keep the stopwatch from stopping while it is near a competitor's cash register.

The *Trial time segment* is where Discovery Wines can build its business for the future, by attracting more recreationals and painstakings via events, promotions, and ongoing education—a needs gap clearly identified in the research.

Because discounts and other quick hit efforts are unlikely to be productive in the liquor business, even where they are legal, the *Purchase time segment* is actually the least highly leveraged of all. The stopwatch is so short, with only two hours from decision to buy wine to actual purchase, that the risk of a consumer leaving to go to another shop once already in the store is vanishingly small.

On the other hand, the *Usage and Loyalty time segment* offers great promise. While, appropriately enough, the risk of losing a potential customer once he or she enters the store is small, the risk of losing their next purchase is very high, and for the same reason: if the customer enters a competitive store, he or she is likely to buy there. We can suggest three initiatives. First, we recommend specific loyalty-inducing incentives for the staff, including sales commissions and other rewards that *increase* when they have a measurable impact for repeat customers' purchases. Second, we propose the creation of customer preference databases, each one specific to the salesperson who maintains them.* Third,

---

* Credit where credit is due: In the 1960s and 1970s, when everyone was busy benchmarking Neiman Marcus to understand how they made and kept such loyal customers, one of

we recommend renaming the "blocking" activity to be something like "Maintaining inventory in the home." Since the bulk of the customers are reluctants and impatients, the goal of the store must be to pantry-load, build community, and effectively deliver direct to home. Under ideal circumstances, the end result of such activities within the Usage and Loyalty time segment has the potential to entirely eliminate the need or desire to enter the store, *except* for an entertaining or educational event . . . and, more important, completely eliminate the impulse to enter any other wine store.

Before we turn our attention to creating, refining, and executing stopwatch marketing action plans at some companies with considerably larger budgets than Discovery Wines, we should remind ourselves of a key consideration: Small-budget wine shops must deal with the reality that they can never meet a customer they *don't* emphasize. Hence, our recommendations to focus on customers in both the impatient and reluctant quadrants, to protect that franchise while building for the future among the recreationals.

Creating at a Big-Budget Firm

For larger firms, however, we recommend, almost without exception, focus, focus, focus: Determine where the biggest/highest potential consumers lie and focus on growing them.

What this means, in practice, is that for a brand like Lexus, the stopwatches that matter are located in the painstaking quadrant; for Whole Foods Market, they are in the recreational quadrant, Goodyear's in the impatient, and so on.

Consider Lexus, and its position in the huge, but hugely competitive, automobile market. The most obvious finding (though frequently the least well understood) from analyzing the stopwatches used by Lexus shoppers is that awareness is not a problem. With the $11 billion spent every year on automobile advertising—more than a quarter of all U.S. advertising, after twenty years of 14 percent annual growth—everyone in

---

the distinguishing features of their marketing was the "salesman's book" of customers' needs, preferences, previous purchases, birthdays, grandchildren, and so on. All in an era when computers were larger than some of their branch stores.

the target knows all the important brand names; in fact, in a 2005 study of automotive advertising, Booz Allen Hamilton consultants Evan Hirsh and Mark Schweitzer used a variety of metrics—the number of models supported and launched; market share—to calculate that a significant number of automobile manufacturers had exceeded a budgetary "saturation point" . . . the threshold below which a given brand is undermarketing itself and beyond which it is overspending.[1] Not Lexus, however. As we have seen, the company has acted on this finding by reallocating marketing resources from the Awareness segments on the shopping continuum to the touchpoints surrounding dealer experience and after-sale loyalty . . . in stopwatch marketing terms, from D − 365 to D + 10 and more. (Reinforcing these actions is the unrelated finding that painstaking shoppers believe the dealer experience at competitive auto brands to be so wretched, verging on abusive, for which the indicated action is to shift money from dealer incentives—the traditional Detroit approach—to enhancing the dealer experience.)

Similarly, another key research finding is that two-thirds of auto shoppers spend significant time online prior to making a purchase . . . or, indeed, even deciding *whether* to make a purchase. The indicated action here would be a further reallocation, this time *within* the D − 365 segment of the stopwatch, but from awareness building to brand-building online. And since a related finding is that painstaking shoppers not only spend lots of time online, but have lots of time, generally, to invest in this portion of the shopping experience, Lexus acted to create the best possible and most engaging website, including such efforts as the industry's best "design-your-own" program. In fact, the painstaking stopwatch ticks for such a long time (yet another finding) and shoppers in the quadrant can be reached at such a correspondingly huge number of touchpoints, one of the most clearly indicated actions is an ongoing one: shifting assets from awareness building into multiple touchpoints within time segments closer to purchase, and measuring which have the most stopwatch leverage over time. In the painstaking quadrant, multiple touchpoint opportunities exist and multiple touchpoints must therefore be addressed. Among the mistakes Detroit has made over the years is to spend far too large a proportion of the marketing budget on awareness building and dealer incentives, far too little on brand-building and enhancing the experience of customers at retail.

Enhancing the retail experience, of course, is at the heart of the strategy of our iconic recreational success story, Whole Foods Market. Perhaps the most basic finding of Whole Foods—one not unique to the natural foods super-retailer—is that the more time customers spend in a store, the more money they spend . . . and on higher-margin goods. The obvious goal for any ambitious supermarket is to increase customers' time-in-store.

But since the choice of a supermarket is made with enormously higher frequency than the choice of an automobile (or even a wine shop), managing the stopwatch in this category is correspondingly complicated. One of the complications is the finding that while powerful touchpoints exist within all the category's time segments, from awareness to loyalty, by far the most promising strategy, applying stopwatch marketing principles, calls for leveraging the time spent on the purchase itself. This means that the most powerfully indicated action is shifting virtually all available resources to the Usage segment on the Countdown Budget. In a category in which customers regard a weekly trip to a supermarket as a cost—a desert to be crossed—it actually isn't really difficult to divert them with a sign that says "this way to the oasis." Put another way, the Trial segment is always affordable. But to get customers to return time and again, it must be an oasis, not a mirage, and that means Usage and Loyalty.

Long before John Mackey put his findings to work—in all likelihood, before he had anything as formal as findings—he had identified his target customer for Whole Foods Market: affluent, educated, and socially aware. As noted earlier, his proxy for the complex and sophisticated store location algorithms that better-funded retailers have was to simply locate near colleges, leveraging both the demographic and psychographic profiles of those living in college communities. The more affluent the potential consumer, the more time they are willing to spend on entertainment. The more educated they are, the higher the premium—in time *and* money— those potential customers would be willing to spend on socially responsible goods: the sort with labels that guarantee natural/organic components and the absence of ingredients that sound like they came out of a chemistry set.

But one clearly actionable finding about those consumers is that even the most dedicated natural shopper finds reading those labels a tedious exercise. The indicated action is at the center of Whole Foods' strategic advantage: the halolike endorsement they grant products by the simple act of displaying them. This doesn't merely reduce the dreariest part of shopping to a minimum (freeing shoppers to spend their time sampling the food, instead of analyzing it) but improves the retailer's margins. Because Whole Foods provides suppliers not only with distribution but with a seal of approval, they enjoy better terms in dealing with those suppliers . . . and it translates into an even larger premium on house-branded merchandise, with even higher margins to Whole Foods, who look more and more like the Quakers who came to the New World to do good, and ended up doing very well indeed.

The Creating phase took a different path with Master Lock, the epitome of success in stopwatch marketing's impatient quadrant. Here, the key finding was the overwhelming importance of the Consideration time segment. Because locks are purchased either as replacements for other locks or to lock up something recently acquired, customers are buying security, not locks per se. And, having already spent time as recreational, or even painstaking shoppers for backpacks, boats, or bicycles, Master Lock's target customers have already used up all the ticks on their respective stopwatches before starting to search for protection. The indicated budgetary action is to allocate assets into this (very brief) Consideration time segment, all of whose touchpoints are found at the point of sale.

But the indicated *marketing* action, once faced with the finding of the paramount importance of Consideration in this commodity-like impatient category, is to own those few ticks of the stopwatch at the point of sale in a way that limits the ability of the shopper to find competitors. Master Lock's master stroke was using marketing dollars to put its point-of-sale materials not exclusively in the hardware section (where all the other locks can be found) but as close as possible to the product needing security: bike locks in sporting goods, trailer locks in the auto section. Knowing how precious a few seconds of shopping time are to the impatient lock purchaser led Master Lock to its uniquely successful merchandising strategy.

In fact, the company's related finding—that the lack of any dominant competitor meant that they could build awareness on the cheap—led to another action explicitly designed to dominate the last few ticks of the shopper's stopwatch. Shifting a modest level of resources from the Trial and Loyalty segments to Awareness (keeping the bulk of marketing resources in Consideration touchpoints), the company invested in some of the shortest television spots in advertising history. The most famous was the company's 1998 one-second commercial, which worked in part because the image of a rifle bullet unable to destroy a Master Lock had been driven into the consciousness of consumers for more than thirty years.

Faced with a position in the reluctant quadrant, Microsoft (in their marketing of both operating systems and the Office suite) was dealing with two related findings. The first was the simplest definition of placement within the reluctant quadrant: people just don't really want to shop for these things. The second finding was the fact that people weren't really shopping for operating systems and word processing software; they were, at minimum, shopping for computers. Moreover, they quite possibly weren't shopping for computers per se, but for ways to get things done—work, word processing, playing games, sending and receiving e-mails, and so on. Microsoft's brilliantly effective solution, then, was to eliminate shopping altogether—to bundle and license their operating system and Office software so that the end consumer's shopping time was literally reduced to zero. In the words with which we described this effort in chapter 5, Microsoft worked hard to minimize switching costs "in" and maximize switching costs "out." Among the terrific strategies pursued by Microsoft to make this happen was the notion of giving free (yes, free) copies of Word with the purchase of a *PC World* magazine subscription (low switch-in costs) while making the transportation to Lotus programs of graphics and features from Word and Excel nearly impossible (high switch-out costs).

Referring back to Figure 5-1, you will note that the movement of "PC Operating Systems" to "Microsoft Windows" is northward (higher margins, more touchpoints—as one would expect, branded marketers try to increase margins) but also westward (quicker/smaller stopwatch). This is one of the few cases of this solution that we have witnessed (or described in this book). In most cases, we recommend *expanding* the stopwatch, lengthening the time the customer spends considering and shopping for our product. Microsoft, in the reluctant quadrant, strikingly turned this logic on its head, recognizing, in effect, that if customers are reluctant to shop for their product, why make them shop for it? Conversely—and equally brilliantly—this strategy made it necessary for someone who did, indeed, want to shop for an operating system or office productivity suite to have an unusually big/slow stopwatch—shopping for non-Windows/non-Microsoft product requires a lot of time, effort, consideration, weighing of pros ("people will think I'm cool if I use Mac or Linux") and cons ("my stuff may not be compatible with that of my clients, I'll have trouble getting good customer support, etc."). In effect, Microsoft has been saying for years to its consumers, "You're reluctant. Good. Stay reluctant. But stay with us."

As Microsoft, in its efforts to pursue growth, now applies its "Embrace, extend, and extinguish" strategy to other areas, they should continue to be a fascinating study. They are—or will be—competing in clearly different quadrants, namely recreational and painstaking, in attempting to dominate, for example, the gaming category in the future.

Refining

Creation of a stopwatch marketing strategy is a necessary start, but scarcely sufficient for what must be the ongoing process of applying stopwatch marketing principles. Because painstaking shopping is notable for the number of potential touchpoints, one overall recommendation is to test all of them regularly. In truth, however, this is appropriate advice for any stopwatch marketer; when we meet with clients, this is what we call Refining.

In brief, what Refining adds up to is a four-step process:

1. Execute annual follow-up versions of the market research recommended in chapter 7 (if budget permits, at precisely the same level of investment, but if not, at the level that is the highest that the company can afford) to track how consumer behavior is changing.
2. Plan and pursue at least three annual experiments. By experiments we mean a split test of some fundamental activity, with a clear segregation of control groups and experimental groups. Each experiment should compare either a new technology with an existing one (interactive vs. static point-of-sale displays, for example) or a new media opportunity against an established one.
3. Plot the impacts at each time segment with *both* comprehensive research follow-ups and experiments. This means that you should put in place quantifiable tracking mechanisms (more on this below).
4. Develop a revised stopwatch leverage matrix every budget/planning season. If your company budgets quarterly, you need to complete a new matrix quarterly.

Refining should, we would argue, be taken literally—we fervently recommend that you should always be experimenting. Every budget should set aside some monies for testing of new approaches to enhance market performance. In general, we recommend constantly testing ways to lengthen the customer's stopwatch—to extend the amount of time a customer will spend considering and shopping for our product or service until the critical event—turning that shopping behavior into a buying moment. Constant testing is, of course, not only good business, it's good career insurance: when the CEO sees a competitor doing something and calls you in for a performance evaluation, you need to be able to say, "We already researched/tested that a year before they did . . . it doesn't pay back."

Executing

The execution of a stopwatch marketing plan is, of course, the reason for the exercise, and if preceded by the appropriate level of analysis, resource allocation, creation, and refinement, ought to be the least controversial step of all. In the real world, however, executing is generally one of the hardest steps to complete, precisely because it is the step where an organization is forced to put more than research dollars at risk. While careers can be made by trying to alter the competitive landscape, they can be unmade even more quickly by lousy execution.

It is because of the natural tendency of organizations to resist that sort of risk/reward decision that we recommend that our clients do nothing less than reorganize their entire marketing departments, as well as their budgets, around time segments and stopwatch leverage. Traditional marketing organizations tend to organize themselves around categories of expenditure, rather than categories of consumer experience: a department responsible for national advertising, one for dealer incentives, and so on. For more than a little time, unfortunately, marketers will have to carry two sets of books. Budgets and continuous tracking mechanisms for very traditional metrics such as market share, ad awareness, brand preference, brand imagery, and the like will need to be maintained. This tracking must occur for at least two reasons: First, these traditional measures are the measures that every marketer—and her bosses—has grown up with. The question "What happened to our share last quarter?" is, and will remain, quite familiar to any marketing person who has been on the payroll for more than six months. More important, these traditional metrics remain very good measures of performance. Nothing we have said in this book should be construed as a recommendation to completely junk, over the short term, such traditional measures in favor of stopwatch-focused measures. Quite the contrary, much of what we are recommending is intended very specifically to more intelligently, efficiently, and profitably drive market share, brand preference, and so on. Business performance remains, after all, the ultimate performance metric.

However, we are suggesting that the more important set of performance metrics—the second set of books, if you will—should be stopwatch marketing focused: minutes spent on our site, participation in our after-sale programs, frequency of visit, level of enjoyment of the shopping experience. For a more precise example, consider the Goodyear Assurance with TripleTred example. Much of Goodyear's initial marketing of that breakthrough product was intended to make TripleTred an "ask for" subbrand. In stopwatch marketing terms, the company strove to expand and lengthen the consumer's stopwatch at the Awareness and Consideration time segments, driving the replacement tire consumer to make his decision *in advance* of visiting the dealer and *asking for* TripleTred once this consumer is actually at the dealership; that is, shortening or eliminating the stopwatch once the consumer has entered the dealership. Thus, some of the measures we would have recommended to Goodyear include traditional ones such as "brand preference" and "ad awareness" (which should be increasing due to the efforts of the marketing campaign), traditional ones such as "time spent in dealership" (which should be *decreasing*), combined with stopwatch-focused measures such as "time spent comparing alternative brands," "willingness to spend time to make the right decision," "importance of the purchase," "risk of making a bad decision," "level of knowledge/understanding of the category/technology," "brand asked for upon entering dealership," "willingness to change decision upon meeting with the dealer/sales rep."

The stopwatch marketing version of "best practices" demands not only a budget and a tracking mechanism but also a Director of Marketing for each time segment, skilled in the specific marketing activities that are relevant to the time segment. A wise stopwatch marketer, operating in the auto business, for example, will have a Director of Awareness, Director of Internet Marketing, Director of Dealer Superiority, Director of Dealer Experience Enhancement, Director of Test-Drive Enhancement, and so on. The specifics will differ across companies and industries, but the principle—

organizing around and budgeting for the important time segments—will remain the critical imperative.

Our own experience argues that only such a stopwatch marketing organization can fully implement budgets according to stopwatch marketing principles. Building on the allocation approach developed in chapter 9, you should restate the working marketing budget to allocate across time segments, not media vehicles. It is far less important to know how much is spent on TV versus the Internet than it is to know how much is spent on Awareness versus Retail Experience.

Finally, you should consider rethinking the reporting and tracking functions around stopwatch marketing principles. It is axiomatic, in every business, that one *cannot* manage what one *does not* measure, and—as outlined in chapter 9—the analysis of both expense and consumer reaction to those expenses must be done across time segments, not traditional reporting headings. If there is a theme to the entire subject of stopwatch marketing, it is that what matters most about touchpoints is not what they cost, but when they are encountered . . . and measuring the timing of those encounters is both the first and the last stage of every stopwatch marketing plan.

• • •

In this concluding chapter, we have recommended that you develop budgets and quantitative tracking metrics for both the traditional measures of marketing success and entirely new ones that will be revealed as critical to your specific situation in pursuing stopwatch marketing principles. The carrying of "two sets of books," for at least the short term, may seem redundant but any marketer who has been around for a long time will recall that he or she has already done this before. In the consumer packaged goods industry, for instance, accounting was done originally by *factory*, long before it was done by *product*. That is, the company knew that "Plant #6" was profitable but didn't know whether the product, detergent, say, or coffee, produced at three other plants in addition to #6 was profitable. Eventually, accounting for products morphed into accounting by *brand*, itself a wrenching and difficult mind-set change. Next, talented consumer marketers understood that they needed to determine profits and performance among *consumer segments across brands and products*, another wrenching change. By the late 1980s, the growth in power among retailers required yet another major change—profitability by *customer* (i.e., retailer or wholesaler) was a necessary measure. We are not exaggerating here: One of our clients at the time, a big, sophisticated, well-known and well-resourced consumer products company, was well aware of their profitability by factory, by geography, by product, by brand, and by consumer segment. They could tell us in great detail whether their investment in marketing to teenagers was paying back in deeply sophisticated financial planning/Net Present Value terms. They also, at that time, had no idea whether their sales to Wal-Mart (20 percent of their business) were profitable or not. Rejiggering their management information systems and reorganizing their sales and marketing efforts to achieve greater customer intimacy were huge, difficult, but eventually rewarding tasks. Readers old enough to have studied business books from the 1980s and 1990s will recall that many best-selling such books from that era were about exactly that: customer intimacy. The recommendations included putting whole customer teams (not just salespeople but IT, marketing, customer service, logistics, etc., personnel) in Bentonville rather than at corporate headquarters. Shocking as this may seem today, it was a shocking recommendation then.

Marketers have largely solved their problems of understanding and targeting the right segments and have undertaken at great expense to better integrate their operations and offerings with those of powerful customers such as Wal-Mart. We are recommending here no less than another such significant recasting of their thinking and strategy. As consumers deal with huge amounts of readily available information while continuing to (knowingly or unknowingly) shrink their shopping stopwatches and speed up the ticking, marketers must, of necessity, understand, track, and market against the important time segments, turning shopping behavior into buying moments. Doing so will require budgeting for and organizing around those time segments.

This book began with two different families: the Blues and the Greens, each making travel plans. The metaphorical—though very real—stopwatches that stood watch over Mr. Green and Ms. Blue ticked to completely different rhythms. You will, by now, recognize these as the tempo of a painstaking stopwatch in one house, and an impatient one in the other. As described, the description of their actions should seem not only intuitively correct, but—ten chapters later—confirmed by examples drawn from the consumers of the products and services of America's largest and most successful manufacturers and retailers . . . and from a business as small as a corner wine shop.

Unsaid, back in our chapter 1 visit, was whether the hotels, airlines, and car rental companies being investigated by Mr. Green and Ms. Blue were themselves using stopwatch marketing techniques—budgeting, web analytics, allocation, and measurement—to place the most effective touchpoints in their customer's path. Readers are free to speculate on which travel businesses are using these principles, and which are not.

We certainly hope that you recognize stopwatch marketing as a powerful concept. The tools, analytic constructs, and principles outlined in this book (and further brought to life on our website, www.stopwatch marketing.com) can be put into action at your organization, large or small, to improve your understanding of your product or service, the customers you should target, and *how, why, and when they decide to buy.* More important, we hope you agree that knowing all this can improve your results.

And, we hope that the question of whether these principles offer businesses using them a significant, even a decisive, competitive advantage has been answered once and for all. And that answering that question was worth your time.

Appendix A

Further Reading

It is a rare client who has ever called marketing consultants humble. Anyone interested in introducing a consultant to the virtues of humility should consider inviting one to write a book. After spending so many months in the company of books written by others, we are tempted to direct readers to head directly to the best business library within driving distance, sit down in front of the *A*s, and continue reading until they reach the *Z*s, since almost every work might contain at least one nugget that will prove more valuable than the time needed to find it.

However, some nuggets are closer to the surface than others, and some books deserve special mention. The ones we have dog-eared the most during the writing of *Stopwatch Marketing* are:

Advertising Management, 4th edition, by David A. Aaker, Rajeev Batra, and John G. Myers

Competitive Advantage by Michael Porter

Diffusion of Innovations, 5th edition, by Everett Rogers

The Google Story: Inside the Hottest Business, Media, and Technology Success of Our Time by David Vise and Mark Malseed

Lexus: The Relentless Pursuit by Chester Dowson

The Long Tail: Why the Future of Business Is Selling Less of More by Chris Anderson

Marketing Channels, 7th edition, by Anne Coughlan, Erin Anderson, Louis W. Stern, and Adel el-Ansary

Marketing Communications: Engagement Strategies and Practice by Chris Fill

Marketing Management: Analysis, Planning, Implementation, and Control, 7th edition, by Philip Kotler

Marketing to the New Natural Consumer: Consumer Trends Forming the Wellness Category by Harvey Hartman

Marketing Research: Methodological Foundations by Gilbert A. Churchill and Dawn Iacobucci

The Online Advertising Playbook: Proven Strategies and Tested Tactics from the Advertising

Research Foundation by Joe Plummer, Steve Rappaport, Taddy Hall, and Robert Barocci

A Piece of the Action: How the Middle Class Joined the Money Class by Joseph Nocera

The Search: How Google and Its Rivals Rewrote the Rules of Business and Transformed Our Culture by John Battelle

Trading Up: Why Consumers Want New Luxury Goods—and How Companies Create Them by Michael J. Silverstein and Neil Fiske

Treasure Hunt: Inside the Mind of the New Consumer by Michael J. Silverstein with John Butman

University Economics by Armen Alchian and William Allen

The Wal-Mart Effect: How the World's Most Powerful Company Really Works, and How It's Transforming the American Economy by Charles Fishman

Why We Buy: The Science of Shopping by Paco Underhill

In addition, a number of websites have proved well worth bookmarking:

The web analytic firm Fireclick stores a huge amount of illustrative information at www.fireclick.com.

Google Analytics can be visited at www.google.com/analytics.

The URL for The Institute of Behavioral Finance is www.psychologyandmarkets.org/research/research_main.html.

Appendix B

Discovery Wines Stopwatch Marketing Research

FINAL REPORT

February 2007

This Appendix provides the detailed results of the Discovery Wines Survey, undertaken to provide a real-world example of the Discovery process, critical to understanding the stopwatches of your customers and the quadrants(s) in which their consumption takes place. Quoting from the text of the book: We offer here an example of how a small business might go about gathering the information necessary to determine its shopping quadrants. It remains our firm conviction, borne out, we hope, by the findings below, that even single-location, small businesses can better understand their customer base, revisit their marketing strategies, and revitalize their business by applying stopwatch marketing principles.

In the summer of 2006, we approached the owners of an upscale Manhattan wine shop (fortuitously named "Discovery Wines") to cooperate in proving this hypothesis. Like the proprietors of nearly every small business, the owners at Discovery Wines were interested not only in increasing revenues and profits, but also in understanding the usefulness of various marketing innovations in which they had heavily invested. These included informational computer kiosks in the store, daily tastings, home delivery, and so on (all described in more detail later). The owner and key managers told us directly that they had made these investments in the hope of creating a truly differentiated consumer experience but really had little idea of their value. The leaders at Discovery Wines were fascinated with the idea that they could take advantage of the tools generally thought to be available only to Fortune 1000 companies.

Methodology

- Customers at Discovery Wines were given a one-page questionnaire to complete while their transactions were completed. The questionnaire included sixteen questions. The general topics included:
  - Purchase occasion and timing of purchase decision
  - Source of awareness of the Discovery Wines store
  - In-store experience
  - Importance of the choice of wine; expected usage occasion
  - Interest/expertise in wine
- The goal was to attach each customer's transaction receipt to his or her questionnaire in order to capture the following information:
  - Date
  - Time of day
  - Name of wine(s) purchased
  - Dollar amount of transaction
- This survey began in mid-June 2006. This final report is based on a total of 221 completed questionnaires.
- A caveat: Findings presented in this report should be considered directional or in some cases qualitative in nature.
  - Due to the difficulty of collecting questionnaires during peak shopping hours, the data may underrepresent the more "typical" Discovery Wines customers.
  - 52 percent of questionnaires (115 of 221) included a receipt with transaction information.

Summary of Key Findings

Overall, Discovery Wines' customers in this survey can be characterized as follows:

- Most **became aware of the store simply by seeing it** and seem to **shop there on a regular basis** (66 percent have shopped there six or more times). Only 14 percent were new customers.
- For the most part, they consider themselves "**moderately knowledgeable**" about wines and are **interested in learning more** about wine.
- Respondents were typically **purchasing wine to consume at home**, that same day or the next day. Despite fieldwork being conducted over the holiday season, gift purchases were reported at very low levels.

- When it came to their choice of wine, half of these respondents were **helped by a store employee.**
- The Discovery Wines customer's stopwatch appears to be quite short:
  - Over 50 percent decided to buy wine **within the past <u>hour</u>;** only 19 percent decided more than a day before. This is consistent with the low level of reported gift (planned) buying. Since most customers are buying wine to drink at home that day, the timing of the decision to buy wine would **suggest they are in the neighborhood.** Reinforcing this hypothesis is the fact that the **decision to shop at Discovery Wines occurs almost simultaneously** with the decision to buy wine.
  - Once in the store, the Stopwatch continues running quickly, with respondents averaging **nine minutes** on their purchase decision. About **half spent five minutes or less.** Weekend

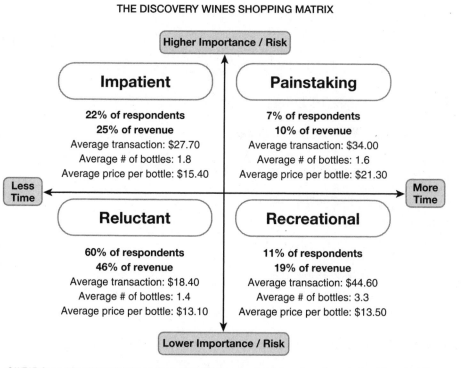

THE DISCOVERY WINES SHOPPING MATRIX

Higher Importance / Risk

Impatient

22% of respondents
25% of revenue
Average transaction: $27.70
Average # of bottles: 1.8
Average price per bottle: $15.40

Painstaking

7% of respondents
10% of revenue
Average transaction: $34.00
Average # of bottles: 1.6
Average price per bottle: $21.30

Less Time ← → **More Time**

Reluctant

60% of respondents
46% of revenue
Average transaction: $18.40
Average # of bottles: 1.4
Average price per bottle: $13.10

Recreational

11% of respondents
19% of revenue
Average transaction: $44.60
Average # of bottles: 3.3
Average price per bottle: $13.50

Lower Importance / Risk

CAVEAT: Some calculations within the quadrants of the matrix are based on extremely small sample sizes. These should be viewed as qualitative in nature.

Base: With receipt and all time/risk variables (113).

Figure B-1

customers spend more time in the store, but represent a minority of customers.

Using the time investment and risk factors reported by respondents in the survey, we can array Discovery Wines' customers and revenue on the Stopwatch matrix in Figure B-1 on the previous page.

As demonstrated by the Stopwatch matrix:

- The majority of customers are found in Quadrant III (lower time investment/lower risk). They represent 60 percent of customers but only 46 percent of revenue. They **spend less;** they buy fewer bottles and tend to buy lower-priced bottles.
- The smallest percentage of customers are found in Quadrant I (more time investment/higher risk). While just 7 percent of total customers, these customers tend to **buy the highest-priced wines.**
- Customers in Quadrant IV (more time investment/lower risk) are not a sizable segment but are important because they **buy more wine** than other customers. While they represent only 11 percent of customers, they account for 19 percent of revenue . . . not because they buy expensive wines but because they buy roughly double the number of bottles of other customers.
- Overall, **higher risk seems to drive higher-priced** bottles of wine.

Detailed Findings

The detailed findings that follow are organized into five sections:

A. Respondent Characteristics
B. Stopwatch Factors
C. Stopwatch Marketing Matrix
D. Miscellaneous Subgroups
E. Logistic Regression

A. Respondent Characteristics

The current clientele is a loyal one, with two-thirds of the respondents claiming to have shopped six or more times. This loyal base first became aware of the store simply by seeing it—an important reality in a pedestrian-based location. On an overall basis, the shopper's stopwatch cannot be expected to tick for very long—at most a day or two: Nearly all respondents expected the wine to be consumed the same day as purchase and only one in five decided to actually shop for wine more than a day before visiting the store. The majority of respondents were purchasing wine to be consumed at home, either alone or with a significant other.

AWARENESS OF OR PREVIOUS EXPERIENCE AT DISCOVERY WINES

The vast majority of these customers first became aware of the store by simply seeing it. Two out of three have stopped there six or more times. (See Figure B-2.)

SOURCE OF AWARENESS AND NUMBER OF TIMES SHOPPED

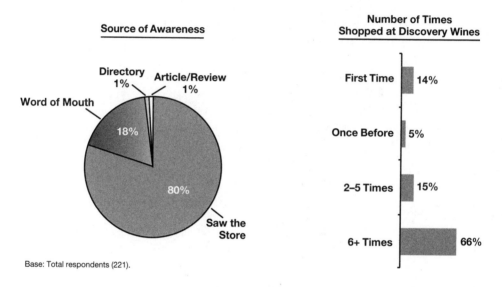

Base: Total respondents (221).

Figure B-2

EXPERTISE AND INTEREST IN WINE

Few respondents claim to be wine experts, though the majority consider themselves "moderately knowledgeable" and "very interested" in learning more about wine. One in four admits to being a novice when it comes to wine. (See Figure B-3.)

PURCHASE OCCASION

The majority of respondents were purchasing wine to be consumed at home, either alone or with a significant other. Gift giving (other than for taking to a party) was reported at relatively low levels. (See Figure B-4.)

CONSUMPTION OCCASION

Nearly all respondents expected the wine to be consumed the same day or the next day. A slight majority (63 percent) expected the wine to be consumed with a meal. (See Figure B-5.)

EXPERTISE AND INTEREST

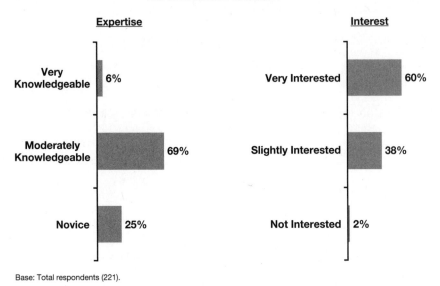

Expertise   **Interest**

Very Knowledgeable — 6%   Very Interested — 60%

Moderately Knowledgeable — 69%   Slightly Interested — 38%

Novice — 25%   Not Interested — 2%

Base: Total respondents (221).

Figure B-3

PURCHASE OCCASION

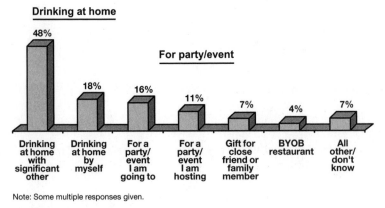

Drinking at home

For party/event

48% — Drinking at home with significant other

18% — Drinking at home by myself

16% — For a party/event I am going to

11% — For a party/event I am hosting

7% — Gift for close friend or family member

4% — BYOB restaurant

7% — All other/don't know

Note: Some multiple responses given.

Base: Total respondents (221).

Figure B-4

ASSISTANCE IN STORE

One in two respondents were helped with their selections by a Discovery Wines employee, and one in three reported using a computer kiosk. (See Figure B-6.)

CONSUMPTION OCCASION

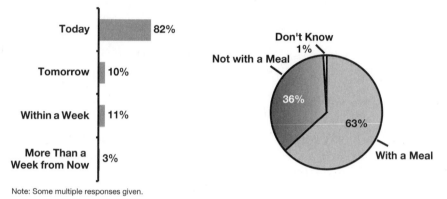

Note: Some multiple responses given.

Base: Total respondents (221).

Figure B-5

ASSISTANCE IN STORE

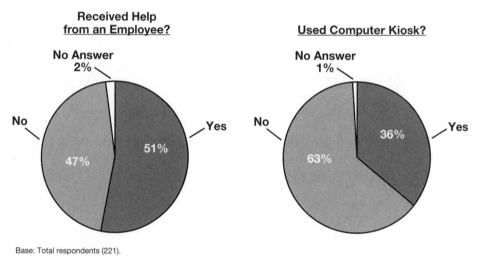

Base: Total respondents (221).

Figure B-6

B. Stopwatch Factors

Over 50 percent decided to buy wine within the past hour; only 19 percent decided more than a day before. How quickly is the stopwatch ticking once the customer is actually in the store? *Very* fast. On average, respondents spent nine minutes on their purchase decision. About half spent five minutes or less, while only 22 percent spent more than ten minutes. The store and staff have less than ten minutes to create and satisfy a customer while turning him or her into a loyal one, as well. **On average, respondents spent about twenty-four dollars in the store, or roughly fourteen dollars per bottle.**

TIMING OF DECISION TO BUY WINE

Over 50 percent decided to buy wine within the past hour; only 19 percent decided more than a day before. The decision to shop at Discovery Wines seems to occur almost simultaneously with the decision to buy wine (consistent with the fact that the vast majority of respondents are regular customers). (See Figure B-7.)

TIME SPENT ON WINE SELECTION

On average, respondents spent nine minutes on their purchase decision. About

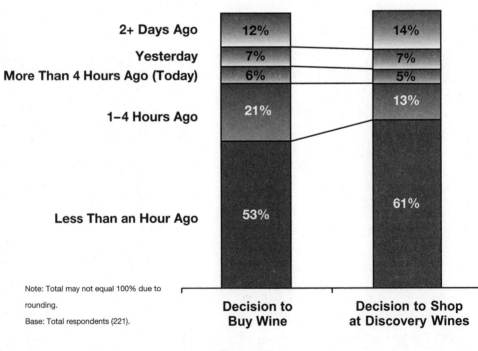

Figure B-7

half spent five minutes or less, while only 22 percent spent more than ten minutes. (See Figure B-8.)

TIME SPENT ON WINE SELECTION

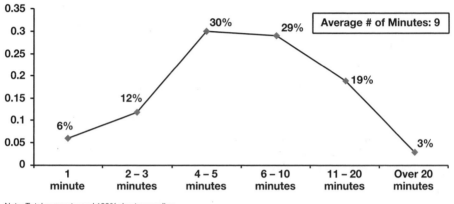

Note: Total may not equal 100% due to rounding.

Base: Total respondents (221).

Figure B-8

IMPORTANCE OF WINE SELECTION

While only a few considered the choice of wine to be *un*important, there is a fairly wide range of importance reported by Discovery Wines shoppers. Just under 20 percent rated the importance of their selection as a "9" or "10," but the average rating was 6.2. (See Figure B-9.)

IMPORTANCE OF WINE SELECTION

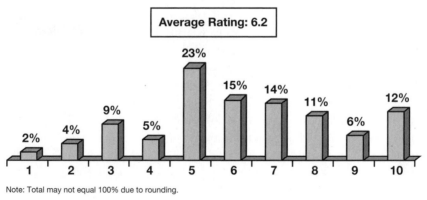

Note: Total may not equal 100% due to rounding.

Base: Total respondents (221).

Figure B-9

SPENDING

On average, respondents spent about $24 in the store, or roughly $14 per bottle. For most respondents this was typical spending, though a few reported spending more than usual. (See Figure B-10.)

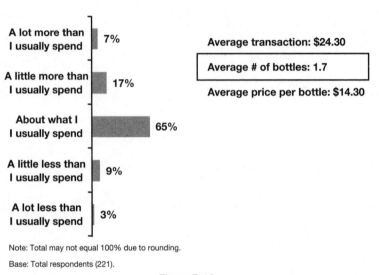

SPENDING PER SHOPPING OCCASION

A lot more than I usually spend — 7%

A little more than I usually spend — 17%

About what I usually spend — 65%

A little less than I usually spend — 9%

A lot less than I usually spend — 3%

Average transaction: $24.30

Average # of bottles: 1.7

Average price per bottle: $14.30

Note: Total may not equal 100% due to rounding.

Base: Total respondents (221).

Figure B-10

C. The Stopwatch Marketing Matrix

To specifically address the issue of locating the quadrant for each shopper, we needed to define the horizontal axis (diameter/speed of stopwatch). We asked directly of the customer, "When did you *first* think about purchasing wine today?" and "How long did you spend in the store before making a purchase decision?" and "Once you decided to buy wine, how long ago did you decide to purchase at Discovery Wines?" For the answers to these specific questions, see Figures B-7 and B-8. For the vertical axis (Margin/Touchpoints) we needed a good, quick proxy that could be captured in one or two questions; this is, after all, a one-shop retailer, not a billion-dollar manufacturer with a million-dollar research budget. So, we went with the customer-defined risk profile for this purchase. The specific question we asked was, "On a scale of 1 to 10, how important would you say your choice of wine is for this occasion? '10' means extremely important (for example, wine for a very special occasion or a wine that will make the right impression)." (Answers are in Figure B-9.)

When these answers are compared to the actual amount spent, the resulting matrix is shown in Figure B-11.

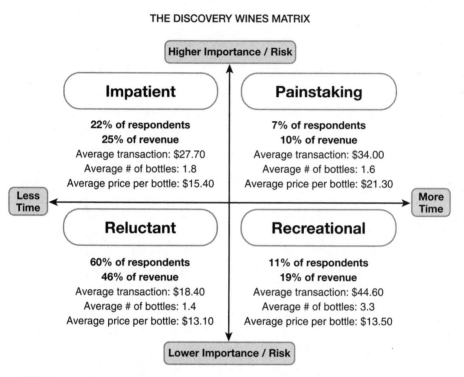

THE DISCOVERY WINES MATRIX

Higher Importance / Risk

Impatient

22% of respondents
25% of revenue
Average transaction: $27.70
Average # of bottles: 1.8
Average price per bottle: $15.40

Painstaking

7% of respondents
10% of revenue
Average transaction: $34.00
Average # of bottles: 1.6
Average price per bottle: $21.30

Less Time ←→ More Time

Reluctant

60% of respondents
46% of revenue
Average transaction: $18.40
Average # of bottles: 1.4
Average price per bottle: $13.10

Recreational

11% of respondents
19% of revenue
Average transaction: $44.60
Average # of bottles: 3.3
Average price per bottle: $13.50

Lower Importance / Risk

CAVEAT: Some calculations within the quadrants of the matrix are based on extremely small sample sizes. These should be viewed as qualitative in nature.

Base: With receipt and all time/risk variables (113).

Figure B-11

DEFINITIONS USED FOR TIME INVESTMENT, ON THE HORIZONTAL AXIS

- **More Time:** Decided to buy wine more than an hour ago *and* spent at least six minutes deciding what to buy
- **Less Time:** Decided to buy wine within the past hour *or* spent five minutes or less deciding what to buy

DEFINITIONS USED FOR RISK, ON THE VERTICAL AXIS

- **More Risk:** Rated the importance of their wine selection as "7" or higher on a ten-point scale
- **Less Risk:** Rated the importance of their wine selection as "6" or lower on a ten-point scale

Key Observations from the Stopwatch Marketing Matrix

As demonstrated in Figure B-11, the majority of customers are found in Quadrant III/Reluctant (lower time investment/lower risk). They represent 60 percent of customers but only 46 percent of revenue. They spend less; they buy fewer bottles and tend to buy lower-priced bottles.

The smallest percentage of customers is found in Quadrant I/Painstaking (more time investment/higher risk). While just 7 percent of total customers, these customers tend to buy the highest-priced wines.

Customers in Quadrant IV/Recreational (more time investment/lower risk) are not a sizable segment but are important because they buy more wine than other customers. While they represent only 11 percent of customers, they account for 19 percent of revenue . . . not because they buy expensive wines but because they buy roughly double the number of bottles of other customers.

A Closer Look at Subgroups

To better understand the dynamics of the matrix, the following subgroups were analyzed:

TIMING OF DECISION TO BUY WINE

- Decided to buy wine within the past hour versus an hour or more in advance

TIME SPENT ON WINE SELECTION

- Spent five minutes or less making their wine selection
- Spent six to ten minutes
- Spent eleven minutes or more

IMPORTANCE OF THE WINE SELECTION

- High-importance rating (8–10)
- Average-importance rating (6–7)
- Low-importance rating (rating 1–5)

TIMING OF DECISION TO BUY WINE

Respondents who plan to buy wine more than an hour in advance consider it more important. They spend more time and money in the shop, likely because they buy slightly more bottles (often for a party). They are also more likely to get help from an employee and buy a wine they have not purchased before.

	Within Hour	1 + Hours Ago
Base: Total Respondents	(118)	(103)
	%	%
Occasion		
Drinking at home	71	57
For a party	17	34
Gift	6	11
Time spent on wine selection (minutes)	8.1	9.7
In-store Assistance		
Helped by store employee	47	55
Used kiosk	37	35
First time purchased this wine	57	68
Importance of Wine Selection (average rating)	5.9	6.5
Bottom three rating (1–3)	21	8
Spending		
Spent "more than usual"	19	28
Average transaction	$20.50	$29.60
Average number of bottles	1.5	2
Average price per bottle	$13.60	$14.80

TIME SPENT ON WINE SELECTION

Respondents who spend the most time on their selection are more likely to plan their wine shopping further in advance and less likely to drink the wine the same day. They do *not* take more time because their purchase is more important or because they are novices, but perhaps because they are more likely (three times) to be a new customer at Discovery Wines. They are more likely to get help from an employee and buy a wine they have not purchased before. They also tend to *buy slightly more expensive bottles.*

	5 Minutes Or Less	6–10 Minutes	11+ Minutes
Base: Total Respondents	(107) %	(63) %	(49) %
Decision to Buy Wine			
Within past hour	56	59	41
Yesterday or longer	16	17	29
In-store Assistance			
Helped by store employee	36	54	80
Used kiosk	26	49	41
First time purchased this wine	55	60	82
Importance of wine selection (average rating)	5.8	6.6	6.5
Expect wine to be consumed same day	89	87	65
First time at Discovery Wines	10	10	29
Spending			
Spent "more than usual"	13	30	37
Average transaction	$20.40	$26.30	$37.70
Average number of bottles purchased	1.4	2	2.1
Average price per bottle	$14.57	$13.15	$17.95
Wine novice	24	27	25

IMPORTANCE OF WINE SELECTION

Respondents who place less importance on their wine purchase are more likely to be drinking it at home themselves and virtually never buying a gift. They spend less *time and money,* and are less likely to be helped by an employee. Of note, the more important the wine, the less likely respondents are to buy a new wine.

	High (Rated 8–10)	Avg (Rated 6–7)	Low (Rated 1–5)
Base: Total Respondents	(64) %	(62) %	(92) %
Occasion			
Drinking at home	61	60	70
For a party	28	24	23
Gift	14	11	1

	High (Rated 8–10)	Avg (Rated 6–7)	Low (Rated 1–5)
Time spent on wine selection (minutes)	9.9	9.7	7.7
In-store Assistance			
Helped by store employee	56	52	47
Used kiosk	34	32	39
First time purchased this wine	52	66	67
Expect wine to be consumed with a meal	56	61	70
Spending			
Average transaction	$29.20	$26.20	$19.00
Average number of bottles purchased	1.8	1.6	1.7
Average price per bottle	$16.22	$16.38	$11.18

D. Miscellaneous Subgroups

One of the key themes of *Stopwatch Marketing* is that you should *always* be gathering data to refine your knowledge of your target customers, how they fit into the matrix construct, and the ticking of their stopwatches. All of the above and the following were developed from a one-page questionnaire and a few hundred responses. The findings below, which we've called Miscellaneous Subgroups, demonstrate the power of even a little research. Armed with the database developed in such research, you can query this database in great detail. For example, you might want to know everything there is to know about shoppers who used the kiosk or those who bought for a party. Whether or not their stopwatch is the issue of the day, the data in the research may still provide important information with which to run your business. For instance, as shown below, those who used the kiosk do, indeed, spend more than those who don't. And, those who are buying for a party spend less than those who are buying for a gift.

The following subgroups were also analyzed:

PURCHASE OCCASION

- Purchased wine to drink at home (alone or with significant other)
- For a party (taking to or hosting)
- A gift

IN-STORE ASSISTANCE

- Helped by an employee (vs. those who were not)
- Used a kiosk (vs. those who did not)

WINE KNOWLEDGE

- Consider themselves moderately or very knowledgeable about wine versus novices

WEEKDAYS

- Shopped Monday through Thursday versus Friday/Saturday

PURCHASE OCCASION

The dynamics of a purchase for home appear very different than one for a gift. Of note, gift buyers in this study seem much less likely to be frequent customers of the store.

	Home	Party	Gift*
Base: Total Respondents	(143) %	(55) %	(18) %
Timing of Decision to Buy Wine			
Less than one hour ago	59	36	39
Yesterday or longer	11	33	46
Time spent on wine selection (minutes)	8	8	13
In-store Assistance			
Helped by store employee	47	51	61
Used kiosk	39	29	50
Importance of Wine Selection (average rating)	6	6.3	7.9
Spending			
Spent "more than usual"	20	18	56
Average transaction	$25.90	$21.30	$33.00
Expect wine to be consumed same day	83	84	44
Expect wine to be consumed with a meal	69	53	39

*Caution: Small base size.

	Home	Party	Gift*
Times Shopped Discovery Wines			
First time	10	16	22
6+ times	76	75	39

*Caution: Small base size.

IN-STORE ASSISTANCE

When customers are helped by employees, *they spend more time and money in the store*. Though they do not consider their selection more important, they tend to buy slightly higher-priced wines. They are also more likely to be a new customer.

	Helped by Employee		Used Kiosk	
	Yes	No	Yes	No
Base: Total	(112)	(104)	(80)	(140)
Respondents	%	%	%	%
Occasion				
Drinking at home	60	72	70	61
For a party	25	23	20	28
Gift	10	6	11	6
Importance of wine selection (average rating)	6.4	6.0	6.0	6.3
Time spent on wine selection (minutes)	11	6	10	8
First time at Discovery Wines	21	5	10	16
First time purchased this wine	71	55	66	61
Spending				
Spent "more than usual"	37	9	23	24
Average transaction	$27.50	$21.50	$25.90	$23.40
Average number of bottles purchased	1.6	1.7	1.6	1.7
Average price per bottle	$17.18	$12.60	$16.18	$13.76

WINE KNOWLEDGE

Less knowledgeable customers are more likely to be helped by an employee and buy a wine they have not purchased before. Though they do not necessarily spend less than their more knowledgeable counterparts, they do not consider their purchase as important. They have shopped at Discovery Wines less often and express less interest in learning more about wine.

	Knowledgeable	Novice
Base: Total Respondents	(166)	(55)
In-store Assistance		
Helped by store employee	48	58
Used kiosk	38	31
Importance of Wine Selection (average rating)	6.4	5.5
Spending		
Average transaction	$24.50	$23.60
First time purchased this wine	58	73
Times Shopped Discovery Wines		
First time	12	20
Six-plus times	71	51
Very interested in learning more about wine	66	44

WEEKDAY VERSUS WEEKEND CUSTOMERS

Weekday customers appear to *spend less time shopping* and are more likely to be buying a wine to have with a meal than weekend customers. They buy slightly fewer bottles at a slightly *lower price*.

	Weekday	Weekend*
Base: With receipt	(92)	(23)
	%	%
Time spent on wine selection (minutes)	6.9	9.3
Importance of wine selection (average rating)	6.3	6.4
Expect wine to be consumed with a meal	67	48
Spending		
Average transaction	$22.30	$32.10
Average number of bottles purchased	1.6	2
Average price per bottle	$13.93	$16.05

*Caution: Small base size.

E. Logistic Regression Results

We pursued one additional analysis to determine the criticality of time on spending at Discovery Wines. That is, we were interested in determining which answers to the questions displayed an impact on the amount spent in the store. To do this, we ran a logistic regression. With an r-squared statistic of 0.30, we were able to get a correct classification rate of 73 percent. This means that, given our survey questions, we can predict with 73 percent accuracy whether or not a customer would be a high spender or a low spender. The following are some key findings of interest:

- If the wine is likely to be consumed *tomorrow,* there is a 73 percent chance that the consumer is a high spender (> $18).
- The *longer ago* the consumer made the decision to buy at Discovery Wines, the *less likely* they are to be a high spender.
- The greater the perceived "importance" (risk), *the more likely* the consumer is to be a high spender.
- Someone indicating that she is "very knowledgeable" about wine is *less likely* to be a high spender.
- Someone for whom this is his first purchase of this particular wine is *more likely* to be a high spender.
- The inputs to the model—shown in the table on page 228—ranked in terms of their impact on someone being a high spender:
  - If Exp(B) = 1 (or close to 1) then the variable is not helpful in determining spending level. Exp(B) > 1 indicates that the variable has a positive effect on being a high spender, while Exp(B) < 1 indicates that the variable has a negative effect on being a high spender. For example, someone who indicates that they are "very knowledgeable" about wine actually has a lower probability of being a high spender.
  - The probability column shows the likelihood that someone is a high spender given that she exhibits the characteristic of the predictive variable. Someone who indicates that he is likely to consume his wine tomorrow has a 73 percent chance of being a high spender (given the other parameters of the model and holding all else constant).
  - The sig. column indicates the statistical significance level of a predictor in the model. The top item has a sig = 0.187, which means it is significant at the 81.3% confidence level.
  - "Change in probability" is simply the probability column minus the total sample average probability of being a high spender (24.9 percent).

	B	S.E.	Wald	Sig.	Exp(B)	Probability	Change in Probability
q12_2 When likely consumed: Tomorrow	2.119	1.606	1.740	0.187	8.322	0.734	0.485
q2_8 Occasion: Something else	1.593	1.260	1.598	0.206	4.919	0.620	0.371
q12_3 When likely consumed: Within a week	1.240	1.855	0.447	0.504	3.454	0.534	0.285
q10 Is this the first time you have purchased this particular wine?	1.221	0.560	4.748	0.029	3.390	0.529	0.280
q15_3 Expertise in wine: Very knowledgeable	-2.799	1.784	2.463	0.117	0.061	0.020	-0.229
q2_2 Occasion: Drinking it at home with my significant other	0.984	0.825	1.424	0.233	2.676	0.470	0.221
q2_5 Occasion: It is for a party/event I'm going to	0.801	0.935	0.733	0.392	2.227	0.425	0.176
q2_1 Occasion: Drinking it at home by myself	0.696	0.826	0.711	0.399	2.006	0.399	0.150
q2_6 Occasion: It is a gift for a close friend or family member	0.576	1.341	0.185	0.667	1.779	0.371	0.122
q9 Do you expect this wine to be consumed with a meal?	0.403	0.548	0.540	0.462	1.496	0.331	0.082
q5_1 First heard: Word of mouth	-0.496	1.575	0.099	0.753	0.609	0.168	-0.081
q14_2 Price: Less (net)	-0.447	0.889	0.253	0.615	0.640	0.175	-0.074
q14_1 Price: More (net)	0.352	0.668	0.278	0.598	1.422	0.320	0.071
q8 Did you use one of our computer kiosks?	0.323	0.490	0.436	0.509	1.382	0.314	0.065

	B	S.E.	Wald	Sig.	Exp(B)	Probability	Change in Probability
q12_4 When likely consumed: More than a week from now	0.306	2.549	0.014	0.904	1.359	0.311	0.062
q12_1 When likely consumed: Today/ tonight	-0.242	1.802	0.018	0.893	0.785	0.206	-0.043
q5_3 First heard: Saw the store	0.210	1.586	0.018	0.895	1.234	0.290	0.041
q7 Did a Discovery Wines employee help you with your purchase decision?	-0.181	0.513	0.125	0.724	0.834	0.217	-0.032
q11 On a scale from 1 to 10, how important would you say your choice of wine is for this occasion?	0.163	0.111	2.131	0.144	1.177	0.281	0.032
m13 Times previously shopped at Discovery	0.118	0.105	1.262	0.261	1.125	0.272	0.023
q2_4 Occasion: It is for a party/event I'm hosting	-0.082	0.929	0.008	0.930	0.921	0.234	-0.015
r16_3 Learning more: Very interested	0.035	0.504	0.005	0.945	1.035	0.256	0.007
q6 How long did you spend in the store before making a purchase decision? (min.)	0.029	0.058	0.257	0.612	1.030	0.255	0.006
m4 Hours since decided to buy at Discovery Wines	-0.017	0.011	2.281	0.131	0.983	0.246	-0.003
m3 Hours since decided to buy wine	-0.002	0.014	0.015	0.903	0.998	0.249	0.000
Constant	-3.765	2.575	2.139	0.144	0.023		

Dependent Measure = High ($18+) versus Low ($6–17) Spending

R-Squared = 0.30

Hit Rate = 73%

Acknowledgments

Our first thanks must go, of course, to our partners at MCAworks, John Hawkins, Sean Folan, Dana Langham, and Matt Freeman, who provided not only their powerful insights into modern marketing theory and practice, but perhaps more important, displayed great patience while we completed this book. John's insight into the rapidly growing world of web analytics was particularly helpful in completing that portion. Sean helped us to brainstorm innovative "out of the box" companies and case studies to consider. And Matt continued to be our wise mentor, providing limitless counsel and criticism.

We will certainly be forever indebted to Bill Rosen, who accepted our offer to buy him lunch a couple of years ago, presumably unaware that we would rope him into three years of assisting with the development and writing of this book. Through Bill, we were able to make contact with the best agent in the business of business books, Jim Levine, and the great editing, publishing, and publicity team at Portfolio—Adrian Zackheim, Adrienne Schultz, Will Weiser, Allison Sweet, and Jillian Gray. We would be quite remiss if we did not thank Francesca Belanger at Portfolio and Beth Tondreau of BTD for making certain that this book is at least as visually appealing as it is (we hope) intellectually stimulating. All of them displayed great confidence in us in the early days and great professionalism as we moved toward the publication date. We will long remember when we reviewed Adrian's contract offer and were speechlessly wondering how to respond—Bill remarked, "We have an offer from our preferred publisher; the one we hoped would listen to us. That cannot be a bad thing!" *Stopwatch Marketing* is our first book and it has been quite an enlightening experience to discover how much a first effort can benefit from good editing. Adrienne has been of great assistance in guiding this book into its final form. Through Bill we also developed rewarding relationships with Russell Hicks, our topflight illustrator, who continues to amaze us with his quick turnaround times, and our brilliant publicist, Mark Fortier, who continues to amaze with his ideas, strategies, and contacts.

For the many chapters on researching and quantifying the principles of *Stopwatch Marketing*, we were blessed with the assistance of three fine market researchers—Michael Piacentini, Bob Ference, and Kathy Bonnist. All three of them have, on one occasion or another, helped us provide our clients with superb market research direction, execution, and results. Kathy was her usual creative, disciplined, and tireless self in driving us to a professional completion of the

Discovery Wines research effort. Speaking of Discovery Wines, we are indeed grateful to Scott Morris, who agreed to let us set up the research effort at the shop and the managers there (Scott Reiner and Mike Foulk) who did the grunt work of collecting questionnaires. We hope the results are of some help in their marketing efforts. We have certainly enjoyed the wine.

A special thanks goes out to Andy Traicoff of Goodyear Tire & Rubber, for his courtesy in reviewing the Goodyear Assurance sections, providing his insights and recollections from our work together in launching that superior product, and, not incidentally, securing approval for us to discuss the effort in *Stopwatch Marketing*. Likewise, we'd like to thank Mie Kanai of Hakuhodo and our shared client, Sean Sumitomo of Kagome, a truly great Japanese company that is just starting to build a sizable presence in the United States, for their support, encouragement, and advice on the sections of the book dealing with natural foods and retailing. Three additional consulting colleagues proved that friendship can occasionally trump commercialism by providing, uncompensated, much useful advice in their areas of substantial expertise: Les Dinkin of Novantas, with regard to retail banking; Tom Weigman of AirCell, with regard to the wireless telephony market; and Harvey Hartman of The Hartman Group, with regard to natural foods.

As the book has moved forward, Laura Kellerman and Sara Dinkin of MCAworks have found themselves called upon to contribute many hours' worth of assistance, generally in response to cryptic e-mails from us—at all hours of the day and night.

There are, of course, a number of friends and clients with whom we have worked and from whom we have learned much over the past several years. Among these are Eddie Nishi of Kagome, Laura Lang of Digitas, Mark Frissora of Hertz, John Schwab of Pactiv, Kevin Bowen of the Cambridge Group, Larry Flanagan of MasterCard, Al Giazzon of Targus, Mylle Mangum of IBT, Jan Dziewior of Cardinal Health, John Haugh of Mars, Roy Hutchinson of Bank Millennium, Ken Hicks of JCPenney, Joe Plummer of The Advertising Research Foundation, and Gary Lancina of RedBox. We often leave their offices and remark, "They need to join our firm so we can continue the creative collaboration!"

Finally, in a nod to our misspent youth, each of us would like to thank our families and recognize some mentors from our past. Joseph Goldsten and Lawrence Lamont, John Rosen's first B-school professors at Washington & Lee University, had the foresight to convince John to change majors and pursue marketing rather than accounting. For this, if nothing else, John will be forever grateful. AnnaMaria Turano is forever indebted to the University of Chicago—and specifically the New Product and Strategy Laboratory (under the direction of Jonathan Frenzen)—for giving her initial real-world experience in both marketing and consulting. And, finally, AnnaMaria would like to thank John for helping her "check off" one of her New Year's resolutions.

Notes

Chapter One

1. DDB Life Style Study (2000), Patrick O'Halloran et al., quoted in Accenture's *Insight Marketing* (August 2001).
2. Ibid.
3. Ibid.
4. Pew Internet Survey, April 2006.
5. George J. Stigler, "The Economics of Information," *Journal of Political Economy* 5 (1961): 69.
6. Michael Porter, *Competitive Advantage* (New York: Free Press, 1985). Porter explicitly points out that the buyer's value chain includes "not only financial costs, but also time. . . ."
7. Porter, *Competitive Advantage.*

Chapter Two

1. Kristy E. Reynolds, Jaishankar Ganesh, and Michael Luckett, "Traditional malls vs. factory outlets," *Journal of Business Research* 55 (2002): 687–96.

Chapter Three

1. Scott Schosnick, "Pistons Hamilton 'Heads Up' Tire Ad," *Detroit News* (February 1, 2005).
2. L. Chappell, "Bridgestone Waxes as Firestone Wanes," *Advertising Age* 5958, (November 2001).
3. V. K. Reddy et al., "When Marketing Efforts Go Flat," *Marketing Management* 13, #3 (May 2004).
4. David Bennett, "Goodyear Tire and Rubber: Working to Bounce Back," *Crain's Cleveland Business* (May 16, 2005).
5. Lloyd Stoyer, "Competing Against an 800-Pound Gorilla," *Modern Tire Dealer* (December 2000).

6. Goodyear conference call, 2005.

7. "Goodyear Makes Primo Tire Push: Hitchcock Fleming at Wheel of $50 Million Ad Campaign," *Crain's Cleveland Business* (April 26, 2004).

8. *Modern Tire Dealer*'s 2004 Performance Tire and Custom Wheel Survey.

9. *Modern Tire Dealer* (November 2004).

10. Ibid.

11. Charles Fishman, "The Wal-Mart You Don't Know," *Fast Company* (December 2003).

12. Gabriella Lojacono and Gianfranco Zaccai, "The Evolution of the Design-Inspired Enterprise," *MIT Sloan Management Review* 45, no. 3 (Spring 2004): 75–79.

13. Gianfranco Zaccai, "Design Strategy and Strategic Design at Master Lock," *Design Management Journal* 31, no. 18 (Winter 2002): 18–25.

14. Ibid.

15. The Yellow Pages Association research, quoted in *Contractor Magazine* (June 2005).

16. Gerald L. Lohse, "Consumer Eye Movement Patterns on Yellow Page Advertising," *Journal of Advertising* 26, no. 1 (Spring 1997): 1–13.

Chapter Four

1. David Yoffie and Barbara J. Mack, "Apple Computer 2005" Harvard Business School Case Study, January 6, 2005.

2. Rob Enderle, NPR interview, March 1, 2006.

3. Shaw Wu, analyst at American Technology Research.

4. Steve Jobs, MacWorld keynote address, January 9, 2007.

5. Steve Lohr, "Apple, A Success at Stores, Bets Big on Fifth Avenue," *New York Times* (May 19, 2006) (quoting Forrester Research).

6. "The Impact of the Internet on the Financial Services Industry" (paper submitted to the 2003 FMA Annual Conference, Denver, CO).

7. Ibid.

8. Chris Copeland and Greg Rogers, "The Multi Channel Impact on Shopping Behavior." Available at http://www.shoplocallc.com/white_papers.html.

9. Seth Stevenson, "Money Toons," *Slate* (December 5, 2005).

Chapter Five

1. Redacted public version of *USA v. Microsoft*.

2. Pamela Parker, "Inside Microsoft's Marketing Machine," *Forbes.com*.

3. Interview with Bill Gates. *Washington Post* (March 9, 1998).

4. Shostek Group.
5. Anja Lambrecht and Bernd Skiera, "Paying Too Much and Being Happy About It: Causes and Consequences of Tariff Choice-Biases," Stanford Business School Symposium (March 2, 2004).
6. Tim Harford, "Confusion Pricing," *Slate* (April 15, 2006).
7. Eugenio J. Miravete, "Choosing the Wrong Calling Plan: Ignorance and Learning" (paper presented at the CEPR Conference, Lisbon, July 2000).
8. Larry Platt, "Vernon the Barbarian," *Philadelphia Magazine* (August 2001).
9. Commerce 2005 Annual Report.
10. Platt, "Vernon the Barbarian."
11. Ibid.
12. Ibid.
13. Commerce 2003 Annual Report.

Chapter Six

1. Rebecca Mead, *One Perfect Day* (New York: Penguin Press, 2007).
2. Penelope Green, "There's Money in the Mattress," *New York Times* (July 12, 2007).
3. Green, "There's Money in the Mattress."
4. Mark Rechtin, "Lexus Checks into the Four Seasons for Ideas," *Advertising Age* (June 6, 2005).
5. Dan Thisdell, "Lexus Target Is 'Informed' Premium Buyers," *Automotive Week* (July 25, 2005).
6. Mike Kilander, "The Internet, Consumer Data, and Selling Cars," *Edmunds. com* (August 2004).
7. Lillie Guyer, "Lexus Leads Automakers in Interactive Marketing," *AutoWeek* (February 13, 2006).
8. Alex Miller, "Cross-Media Case Study: Defining IS," *OMMA* (April 2006).
9. Hester Stuart-Menteth, Simon Arbuthnot, and Hugh Wilson, "Multi-Channel Experience: Evidence from Lexus," *Interactive Marketing* 6, no. 4 (April–June 2005).
10. U.S. Department of Education, National Center for Education Statistics, Youth Survey and Parent Survey of the 1999 National Household Education Surveys Program.
11. Erin Strout, "Breaking Through the Noise of a Crowded Field," *Chronicle of Higher Education* (May 19, 2006).
12. Noel-Levitz 2005 Study of Recruitment Costs.
13. Peter Bryant and Kevin Crockett, "The Admissions Office Goes Scientific," *Planning for Higher Education* 22, no. 1 (1993): 1–8.

14. "Marketing Institutions and Recruiting New Students: What Works Best?" *Chronicle of Higher Education* (April 30, 2004).

15. Ibid.

16. Ibid.

17. Strout, "Breaking Through the Noise."

Chapter Seven

1. NYCvisit.com.

Chapter Eight

1. Adam Arvidsson, "On the Prehistory of the 'Panoptic Sort': Mobility in Market Research," *Surveillance and Society* 4, (2004): 18.

2. *Advertising Age* 2006 FactBook. This is a U.S. number only; the worldwide figure is closer to $500 billion annually.

3. Theodore F. D'Amico, "Magazines' Secret Weapon," *Journal of Advertising Research* 39 (1999): 53–60.

4. Fred Vogelstein, "How Yahoo Blew It," *Wired* (February 2006).

5. Ibid.

6. E-Commerce Site Trend Report from *DoubleClick,* Q3 2004, doubleclick.com, November 2004.

Chapter Ten

1. Evan Hirsh and Mark Schweitzer, "The Advertising Saturation Point," *Strategy + Business* (Fall 2005).

Index